THE STRUGGLE FOR DEMOCRACY IN EDUCATION

The Struggle for Democracy in Education extends the insightful arguments Michael W. Apple provided in *Can Education Change Society?* It provides detailed examinations of both local and system-wide struggles around conflicting versions of democracy. Grounded in a key set of ethical and political responsibilities for those who care deeply about education, Apple and his co-authors interrogate conflicting models of democratic education, one interested in the common good and the creation of critical citizens, the other market-oriented and meant to meet a set of more conservative economic needs. Through a series of powerful national and international case studies, this volume explores the contested terrain, combining powerful theory with the "stuff" of schools, political and pedagogical actions, and the lives of individuals. These detailed examinations provide the reader with a more nuanced understanding of how policy, history, and varied actors with varied agendas come together, and the very real people and systems that are impacted by these conflicts. *The Struggle for Democracy in Education* asks us to face and understand these myriad forces and actors—both progressive and retrogressive—and to ask what we can do to ensure that the education that is created is worthy of its name. In the process, the book gives us real examples of critically democratic education and what we can learn from these struggles.

Michael W. Apple is John Bascom Professor of Curriculum and Instruction and Educational Policy Studies at the University of Wisconsin, Madison and Distinguished Professor of Education at Rowan University. He has written extensively on the relationship between culture and power in education and on the limits and possibilities of a socially transformative education. He has been named one of the 50 most significant writers in education in the twentieth century.

THE STRUGGLE FOR DEMOCRACY IN EDUCATION

Lessons from Social Realities

Michael W. Apple

WITH

LUIS ARMANDO GANDIN, SHUNING LIU,
ASSAF MESHULAM, ELENI SCHIRMER

Routledge
Taylor & Francis Group

NEW YORK AND LONDON

First published 2018
by Routledge
711 Third Avenue, New York, NY 10017

and by Routledge
2 Park Square, Milton Park, Abingdon, Oxon, OX14 4RN

Routledge is an imprint of the Taylor & Francis Group, an informa business

Library of Congress Cataloging-in-Publication Data
A catalog record for this book has been requested

ISBN: 978-1-138-71450-2 (hbk)
ISBN: 978-1-138-72115-9 (pbk)
ISBN: 978-1-315-19468-4 (ebk)

Typeset in Bembo
by Deanta Global Publishing Services, Chennai, India
Printed and bound by CPI Group (UK) Ltd, Croydon, CR0 4YY

CONTENTS

ACKNOWLEDGMENTS

We would like to express our gratitude and solidarity to the educators, cultural workers, community members, youth, union activists, social movements, and progressive governments who both in the past and today have worked so hard to create and defend a more critical democracy in education and the larger society. Many are known and even more remain less publicly visible. But their commitment and accomplishments live on.

1

THE STRUGGLE FOR DEMOCRACY IN EDUCATION

Michael W. Apple

Seeing Contradictions

I want to begin this book with a story about the complex realities involved in the struggle for critical democracy in education. For a number of years, my wife Rima and I spent time working with activists, community groups, the ministry of education, critical educators, and others in one of the more progressive states in India. Its high rates of literacy were well known. The left-leaning government was expressly dedicated to improving the economic lives of the population, especially those at the bottom of the class and caste structure, and those who were identified as "tribal" peoples. The respect offered to different religious and cultural traditions was also seen as a model for other areas.

I don't want to minimize these commitments at all; nor do I want to criticize the very evident hard work and sacrifices that went into creating and pushing forward this agenda. Indeed, these commitments and sacrifices were one of the major reasons that we had agreed to work with groups there.

The ministry of education had been influenced by critical pedagogical theories and practices, including the powerful work of Paulo Freire as well as some of my own work. It had also developed connections with groups engaged in movements such as "people's science," which aims to popularize and organically connect science to the lives of ordinary people, and similar local critically oriented educational strategies that were building "counter-hegemonic" educational programs from the ground up as well as from the top down.

There was a very visible commitment to improve the lives of young women and girls, an initiative that was of considerable interest to Rima as well as myself, since Rima is a well-known historian of women's health. We wanted to see how this actually went on. Seeing things close up is crucial to us. We've had too many experiences of rhetorical reforms—including supposedly quite radical policies and programs—that sound so very good when seen from afar, but the words were often very different than the realities.

A primary initiative involved giving much more access to technological skills and knowledge in schools that served poor and marginalized students. It was thought that this emphasis would have benefits not only for poor children but for women as well, since they were doubly marginalized, not only by class and caste but profoundly by gender and by the patriarchal norms that were still so present in their communities.

Communities were consulted about the new programs. Even with the real scarcity of resources in education, the ministry worked hard to ensure that schools in these areas were given large numbers of computers. Time was set aside for their use and integration into the daily activities of the schools. Curricula were prepared that urged teachers to connect these new skills with the everyday experiences of the students and their lives.

Having already written about the worries I had about "technological fixes" for educational inequalities (Apple 2014), I was prepared to be somewhat skeptical about all of this. But Rima and I had learned to trust that the ministry and the activists working with them were serious in their conscious attempts to interrupt the role of education in reproducing social difference. Thus, we went in with an open mind that combined solidarity with the critical and progressive commitments that had been taken seriously before and yet still had some questions about the curriculum and the reliance on technology.

What we saw pushed us even further toward understanding the complex contradictions that can be present in critical education, contradictions that refocused our attention not so much on the curriculum and pedagogy in the school, but on the material realities of gendered specificities in daily life.

The sun beat down as we walked from the car to the school. The temperature was nearly 100 degrees with a humidity nearly as high. There was little respite from the heat inside the school. New computers lined the walls of the classroom. The teachers were hard at work with groups and individual students, most of whom were between the ages of 11–14. While they were clearly conscious that we were there, after a short time normal classroom routines took over.

The students were soon at the computers. At first glance, even with the oppressive heat and humidity, everything looked fine. But after a while watching and then interacting with teachers and students, Rima and I looked at each other and recognized that we both had come to the same realization about what was happening underneath the progressive aspects that were visible. Now the story gets more substantive about contradictions and the politics of intersecting dynamics of power in daily life.

What we had nearly simultaneously come to realize was that almost all of the students working so diligently at the computers were the boys. This was not "planned." It wasn't because the teachers were sexist in the usual sense of that word. It was more complicated than that.

In this school, there were no clean bathrooms for the girls. Boys faced a similar situation, but the boys could go behind the school buildings and urinate, something they regularly did. This was an act that had very different meanings and implications for the girls. To publicly urinate in an "open space" was to risk not only being seen as "dirty" but also to be seen as sexually "available." The dangers associated with this in a climate of male dominance and female subordination— even with a government deeply committed to interrupting this—were not abstract. They were very real and based on all too many experiences.

Because of this, in order to "protect their modesty," many girls did not attend school. The girls who did come to school tried very hard not to drink anything during the school day so that they would not have to urinate. With the heat and humidity so very high, many of the girls had no energy or even fell asleep at their desks.

None of this was planned. The ministry, in association with activists and critical educators, had prioritized a process of schooling that was meant to interrupt dominance and to provide a curriculum and a set of tools that lead to more democratic outcomes for poor and marginalized students, and that was overtly aimed at doing this for girls and young women. Very real economic sacrifices had been made to provide the students with the machinery, the curriculum, and teacher skills to give them experiences that were simply taken for granted by affluent parents and communities. In class terms, this was indeed progressive. Yet students have *gendered bodies*. The politics of bodies, built into the materiality of physical environments, powerfully interrupted the official attempt at interrupting dominance. "Simple" things like bathrooms and the gendered dynamics of schools and daily life contradicted the very well-intentioned class- and caste-based policies of a ministry that was trying so very hard to live out its commitments and to democratize the processes and outcomes of education. Why is there an economic choice between computers and bathrooms?

I begin this book with this story not to make us cynical. Cynicism has no place in the struggle to create an education that is worthy of its name. Rather my aim is to remind us that reality bites back and that we need to be conscious that building a lasting critically democratic education requires us to understand that doing so will at times be filled with tensions and contradictions. The politics of this will be complicated. It will involve a combination of joy and sometimes sorrow. Ignoring all of this won't make it any easier. We are talking about the real lives of teachers, students, communities, and so many other groups of people who have a stake in the future of our societies. As much as we might wish it wasn't the case, we can't hide from the visible and invisible politics, and the conflicts these entail, involved in building and defending an education worthy of the best in us.

Democracy and a Transformative Education

The story with which I began this introductory chapter has serious implications for why we have chosen a key word in the title of this book. The struggle for democracy in education has been and still is exactly that—a *struggle*. It has a long and valued history. This history encompasses multiple movements to transform educational institutions so that their means and ends respond to the lived needs and aspirations of that ongoing experiment of creating critical and knowledgeable citizens. This has rightly required that we take seriously the demands of those who do not benefit from the ways our societies are currently organized—those "marked" by dominant understandings of class, race, gender, sexuality, disability, and so much more (see Apple et al. 2009; Apple and Au 2014). It has also required a constant critical interrogation of who "we" are in the first place. All of this places an ethical and political, as well as educational, set of responsibilities on those who care deeply about the role of education in the larger society, a set of responsibilities that are even more compelling for those of us who are in education itself.

In *Can Education Change Society?* (Apple 2013), I argue for an activist role on the part of educators. In the process, I detail a number of tasks in which critically democratic educators should engage as "public intellectuals." While I'll say much more about this later in this book, among them are: bearing witness to negativity—that is, telling the truth about what is happening in education and the larger society; showing spaces of possibility where critically democratic policies and practices might flourish; and acting as critical secretaries of the actual realities of these possibilities as people build these more progressive policies and practices in the real world.

Can Education Change Society? constructed a set of arguments about the possible roles education might play in social transformation. It also examined the histories of a number of our attempts to answer this difficult question and gave concrete examples now and in the past of educators, community activists, and others striving to build a critically democratic education. There have been and are victories.

However, one of the most important things we must face is the fact that while we need to be optimistic about the possibility of creating lasting transformations, we should not be romantic. Critically democratic educators, progressive movements, and community members are not the only individuals and groups who are acting on this terrain. As I demonstrate at much greater length in *Educating the "Right" Way* (Apple 2006), neoliberals, neoconservatives, authoritarian populist religious movements, and new managerial regimes of authority are also working hard to change education so that it meets their own needs.

In essence, there is an ongoing contest over different versions of democracy. "Thick" understandings of democracy that seek to provide full collective participation in the search for the common good and the creation of critical citizens are up against "thin," market-oriented versions of consumer choice, possessive individualism, and an education that is valued largely as a tool for meeting a set of limited economic needs as defined by the powerful. This has important implications for those of us who are committed to more robust forms of democracy and for an education that is richer in its visions of what education is for.

Because of this, we need to better understand what actually happens when these different ideas about democracy confront each other in schools and communities. This requires us to be honest that this is a time when rightist ideological visions, assumptions, and commitments are powerfully present, are well funded, and increasingly have become core parts of the prevailing common sense in so many nations of the world. In a social context such as this, certain questions become even more essential. Can thicker forms of critically democratic education remain true to their values and principles? Can they last? What does the reality of this "democracy" look like? What forces are at work to challenge it? What compromises have been made? And what can we learn from these conflicts and compromises?

In answering these questions, we don't want to simply offer slogans. While it pains me to say this, all too much of the existing literature in critical education and "critical pedagogy" has been overly rhetorical. It is almost as if the realities of actual schools and actual policies might serve as a threat to theoretical purity. Powerful theory is important of course. But it is most influential when it is organically connected to the "stuff" of schools, political and pedagogical actions, and the lives of individuals and groups trying to deal with the ways in which a socially critical democracy is contested. And it is best when it is connected as well to the victories and sometimes losses that accompany these actions.

This is where *The Struggle for Democracy in Education* enters and makes an important contribution. It is a collective project, the product of a good deal of discussion among all of the co-authors. In many ways, it is a sequel to my earlier books *Educating the "Right" Way* and *Can Education Change Society?* It provides detailed examinations of both local and system-wide struggles over thicker versus thinner versions of democracy. It is both national and international, thereby giving the reader a much better sense of how differences in government policies and traditions, histories of political mobilizations, and varied actors and movements have major impacts on who wins and who loses in these conflicts. Who the actors are makes a huge difference here. On the one hand they include: social movements from below; teacher unions; activist educators and community members; student activists; progressive governments; and school board members who are willing to support more robust and responsive educational policies and practices. But, on the other hand, they also include: middle-class parents who change the nature and realities of progressive reforms by looking for an advantage for their own children both in the United States and elsewhere; well-organized and well-funded rightist groups and foundations; corporate pressure groups; anti-union activists; and managerial types within governments and school administration whose commitments involve supporting what have been called "audit cultures," efficiency, and cost saving above all else. All of these actors will be visible here.

Thus, this is quite a complicated situation, one with multiple actors and multiple agendas. But ignoring complexity will not help us create and defend a critically democratic education. As the detailed analyses that make up the majority of the chapters in this book indicate, there are crucial lessons to be learned—and crucial battles to be fought. *The Struggle for Democracy in Education* asks us to face these forces and actors, both progressive and retrogressive, and to ask what we can do to ensure that the education that is created is worthy of its name.

The State and Official Knowledge

In many of the analyses we detail here, the focus will be on movements and critical educators and community members. But one of the elements that we also need to stress is the government (what we will call the "state") at local, regional, and national levels. In most nations, much of education is a state function, and government agencies and policies at multiple levels play a major role. Theories about the role of the state in social and cultural life are varied and often complicated. Although they are very important, many of these theories are also more than a little abstract (see, e.g., Stewart 2001; Jessop 2002). However, one of the most important insights about the state is that it is often an arena of intense conflict over the politics and policies of distribution, recognition, and representation (Fraser 1997). Thus, it is a site where competing visions of class, gender, race, "ability," and other relations of dominance and subordination, and over policies that would defend or change these relations, contest each other (Apple et al. 2003). As anyone who is paying attention to the current politics inside and outside of education can see, these contests are not always battles among equal forces. And, given unequal power and resources, it is more usual that dominant groups emerge from these contests with more victories than losses. Yet dominant groups are often forced to compromise, to give something to oppressed groups, in order to maintain control. At times, they actually lose. Such losses may only emerge after years of contestation. But they are real nevertheless, as are the spaces these contests and partial losses open for further progress over time. This will be part of what we will document here.

One of the most important insights in the more general approaches to understanding what the state does is that states often rely on *negative selection*. That is, keeping things out is just as important as letting things in. This speaks to the power of dominant groups in the creation of what is best called an "epistemological fog" (Davis 2006). Making certain that the public, and even dominant groups themselves, don't know or see something is crucial to the maintenance of existing power relations. To make critical understandings of these relations and their histories visible is to be subject to demands. When dominant groups are pressured to provide space for these oppositional understandings and knowledge, they will do so in a manner in which the resulting compromise doesn't threaten their overall control of the space of conflict (see Fraser 1997). Sometimes this is successful, but not always.

This often involves struggles over something else that is visible in the stories we tell here. The very content of what is taught in school is also a site of struggles that as we shall show plays an important role in how democracy is actually lived in schools, in whose vision of democracy is sponsored, and in how movements from below sometimes get formed to oppose dominance. There again will be compromises and losses; but also, sometimes very real victories (Apple 2014). [Historically, then, the actual stuff of the curriculum has been important both in maintaining an epistemological fog, but also in providing an arena for successful mobilizations and gains.]   *Significant   !*

This is not only of historical significance. The battles over official knowledge have not subsided. In many ways they have intensified. Examples of this abound. In Arizona, conservative activists have mandated that Ethnic Studies courses be eliminated from the school curriculum because they can supposedly "create racial tension." Well known and widely respected fiction and non-fiction books, many of which are award-winning, have been removed from classrooms. Teachers have been put under threat. And a climate of fear and resistance has been created. In Texas, there has been pressure on and from the state textbook commission to not approve textbooks that even mention climate change as settled fact, that give legitimacy to evolution, that have positive things to say about labor unions—the list goes on and on. Indeed, one text even noted that enslaved people were basically "guest workers" who came to the United States for employment purposes.

This kind of material can be deeply distressing. But, at the same time, there is a rich history of movements to challenge these ideologically and ethically problematic positions. It helps to ground ourselves in this history of "counter-hegemonic" education so that we can remember the traditions (the plural is significant) that we stand upon. Here I must draw upon some of the examples I documented in *Can Education Change Society?*

Counter-hegemonic education included many kinds of institutional and ideological forms and orientations, all of them aimed at a politics of interruption. A number of anarchist schools were built throughout the country (Avrich 1980). Socialist Sunday Schools, Workers Schools, and other kinds of radical children's schools sprang up in such diverse places as Minneapolis, Cleveland, Harlem and other areas of New York City, Philadelphia, Boston, Chicago, Milwaukee, Baltimore, Rochester, Newark, and elsewhere (Teitelbaum 2009, pp. 320–1; see also Teitelbaum 1993). These schools, and especially the Socialist Sunday Schools, overtly challenged dominant forms of knowledge and ideology.

In his cogent description and analysis of these schools and of the people who built and worked in them, Teitelbaum (1993, 2009) points to both possibilities and limitations in their curricular and pedagogic emphases. Their educational practices often embodied what was then considered socially responsive education:

project-based methods, community projects, group work, connecting the curriculum to the socio-economic and cultural worlds outside the school and to what we might now call the "funds of knowledge" that the children bring with them. It was an education consciously aimed at social transformation, with a curriculum that challenged what was usually counted as "official knowledge" and which replaced it with knowledge that was grounded in a more accurate understanding of the world so that students and teachers could talk back to that world.

The influences of these kinds of transformative interests were not limited to individual teacher's efforts or to counter-hegemonic institutions such as Socialist Sunday Schools, however. They were also prominently displayed in official curriculum documents and materials, often in surprising places. For example, both before and during the 1940s, even in the officially segregated schools of parts of the South, the official Course of Study for the elementary schools of Virginia included some striking statements about the kinds of understandings that both black and white students were to get. After two years of study by thousands of teachers, and then a five-week-long series of meetings and conferences in which the state superintendent and other central administrative staff, professors at local and national institutions, and representatives of both "Negro" and white administrators and teachers of the segregated schools of that state participated, a Course of Study was agreed upon that had emphases that even today would be considered more than a little radical (Virginia State Board of Education 1943).

For example, under the goal of "The Understanding That the Masses of Men Struggle Constantly to Gain Freedom from Domination by the Few," among the sub-goals that were stressed were the following:

> Individuals and powerful minorities have always sought to control and subjugate the masses.
>
> Many of the significant movements of history have been caused by man's efforts to throw off the yoke of oppression and slavery.
>
> The present social order is not fixed and permanent. Man continues to modify it in his search for justice and freedom.

Under other overarching goals, there are other statements that speak clearly to an understanding that their society needed to be reconstructed in important ways, with schools playing a key role in this reconstruction:

> The perpetuation of democratic government is dependent on the universal education of the people governed.
>
> Minorities, organized for advancing all types of selfish interests, attempt to control the government, but those with the greatest financial resources have the advantage.

It then goes on to include other powerful goals that the schools should have in creating critical citizens who have a more fundamental understanding of the world in which they live and of the relations of dominance that organize and disorganize it. Among these are:

> The minority of wealth derived from business and industry has succeeded the landed aristocracy.
>
> Powerful minorities secure control of the government in their special interests by subsidizing political parties, investing in propaganda, and by controlling the officials of the school, church and press.

These goals for students in elementary schools were sometimes placed side by side, with more conservative moral, intellectual, and economic agendas such as capitalism being seen as largely a major wealth creator, being punctual, supporting the traditional family, speaking of "men" as the model of human experience, and so on. Still, after reading these more critical goals, one is left nearly breathless in their scope. Their impulses sound as if they could have come directly from the pens of educators who would have found much to their liking in the perspectives advocated so well in the work of Howard Zinn (2015) and in such very important journals as *Rethinking Schools*.

The fact that the above material is indeed an *official* course of study, discussed and mediated by the interests of people in an existing apartheid system in the South, is more than a little interesting. The state itself had become a site of conflict and compromise, signifying once again the importance of pushing against the usual policies that might come from the state (Apple 2012; Apple et al. 2003). Constant organized pressure on government policies and on taken for granted ideological assumptions can, and in this case clearly did, make a real difference. Many of these compromises provided space for radical understandings of the nature of inequality, of the relationship between the economy and government, and of the importance of collective struggle in transforming one's society (see also Eagles 2017).

The fact that black students would be taught powerfully critical perspectives in an officially recognized way is a recognition of the growing influence of the continuing protests and insurgent movements in the state and civil society against a set of structures that were deeply oppressive. Thus, there were victories here that should not go unnoticed. Official knowledge was radically transformed. Voices and perspectives from below were included. And the school was among the central institutions for learning how to speak back against a number of key forms of dominance.

This history continues to this very day, with an expanded focus on movements involving race, sexuality, "ability," immigration, and so much more. Once again, the journal *Rethinking Schools*, among others, has become an important site both for describing these movements and for documenting workable educational policies and practices that respond to the needs of oppressed and marginalized students and communities (see also Apple and Beane 2007; Ashby and Bruno 2016; Emdin 2010; Stovall 2017; Watson et al. 2012; Laes 2017; Kallio 2015; Knoester 2012; Nichols 2002; Uetricht 2014; Verma 2017). We will highlight the importance of conflicts over the curriculum and their role in progressive victories later on in this book as well.

The authors of this book believe that we need more case studies of conflicts and movements both now and in the past. However, one of the concerns that we have about case studies is that they often do not adequately illuminate the connection between the specifics of the case and the larger issues surrounding the politics of official knowledge and the surrounding economic, political, and cultural dynamics that form the context in which these cases live. Our response in this book is to situate each of the chapters into the context of the historical and current status of the ongoing struggles over democracy and its various meanings and tensions. These struggles and tensions may have certain similarities across each of the stories we tell, yet in important ways they will also be different. Strong states differ from weak states. The national and international histories of social movements are different. The growing influence of "dark money" and of rightist influences (MacLean 2017; Mayer 2016; Schirmer and Apple 2016; Anderson and Montoro Donchik 2016) is specific to certain nations but not others. Racializing dynamics and their histories, while almost always present in many nations even when they are not visible, will play different roles. Thus, the dynamics of differential power inside and outside of education will be varied. This is a crucial point. Interrupting these dynamics will require more than slogans. It will require that we think about histories and contexts and that we remember not to reduce everything to one cause in an oversimplified way (Apple 2013).

This has required us to walk a fine line. We have tried to recognize complexity and the existence and intersections of multiple dynamics, while at the same time *not* minimizing the power of certain dynamics such as class. Indeed, issues surrounding class relations and class conversion strategies (Bourdieu 1984; Wright 1989; Eder 1993; see also Isenberg 2016) will be visible throughout this book. Thus, the ways in which neoliberal agendas open spaces for more powerful class actors to carve out spheres of influence will be present. Race as well will be a central element in a number of the stories we tell, as it must be for historical and very contemporary reasons (e.g., Baptist 2014; Berrey 2015; Haley 2016; Rothstein 2017; Mills 1997; Omi and Winant 2014; Gillborn 2008; Dixson et al. 2016; Eakin 2017; Roth-Gordon 2017). The idea of a robust democracy and the struggle to keep it alive as a thick process of full collective participation will be on display—at the same time as there is constant economic and ideological pressure to minimize its influence and to change its very meaning into consumer choice.

This last point has major consequences for our analysis. Its power is most visible in the current and growing neoliberal emphasis on democracy in education embodied in voucher plans, in placing schools and teachers on a competitive market, and in turning schools into centers for profit generation. There is little empirical support for such policies and the dangers very often heavily outweigh the gains (the literature here is vast, but see for example Apple 2006; Lubienski and Lubienski 2014; Ball 2012, 2007, 2003; Burch 2009; Welner 2008). We don't want to simply rehearse the data again here, but in coming to grips with why this very thin vision of democracy has become ever more powerful, we need to be honest about what happens as this becomes our common sense.

Let us openly name one of the major structural reasons for the growth and maintenance of a particular kind of understanding of the socio-cultural world and our place in it. While many educators may feel more than a little uncomfortable employing the word "capitalism," its basic logics do indeed need naming. Capitalism in the form of neoliberalism acts as a set of too often taken for granted classed, raced, and gendered structures that reorganize our societies in truly pervasive ways (Harvey 2007; Leys 2003; Lynch et al. 2012; Root 2007). This makes the prospects of creating the egalitarian conditions for thick democracy and human flourishing difficult. Thus, any serious egalitarian project needs to take account of the power of the "ordinary" nature of these relations and how even the best of reforms can get incorporated under the umbrella of prevailing logics and actions (Wright 2010, p. 34). This is perhaps best seen, for example, in the ways in which the processes and logics of commodification and profit exert immense pressure on how people understand how democratization should go on and just as importantly what democracy itself actually *means*. These processes and logics deeply embody the manner in which dominant economic forces, relations, ideologies, and identities channel our justifiable efforts to search for more democratic structures and the ways such structures are understood and built—and not built.

Let us take the processes of commodification. We know that commodification corrodes community. It devalues moral norms of solidarity, reciprocity, mutual concern, and mutual caring (Wright 2010, p. 79; see also Lynch et al. 2009). Furthermore, marketization stimulates identities and motivations that are antithetical to community by cultivating "dispositions that sharply contradict the kinds of motivations needed for strong community" (Wright 2010, p. 80). As Lynch et al. (2009) document, the norms and identities associated with possessive individualism and "audit cultures" replace historically vital norms of care, love, and solidarity. The effects are profound in the attacks on labor, on teacher unions, on minoritized people, on the paid and unpaid lives of women, on the public institutions that have been sources of support and mobilization, and indeed on the entire public sphere (see Lipman 2011; Anyon 2014; Fabricant and Fine 2012; Baker et al. 2004).

I am not automatically assuming that one should take an absolutist rejection stance on markets of any kind (Wright 2010, p. 262). But we need to have a widespread and genuinely honest discussion and debate, one in which everyone can and should participate, over whether markets can be used as a primary mechanism for social justice. The position that I take is that given the risks and the evidence in education of the negative effects of markets and commodification (see Apple 2006), we should have a truly skeptical stance about any proposals that rely on such structures and processes under the claim of "democratization." Given a choice between thick and thin, we should strive to choose thick whenever possible—and collectively and individually struggle to change the conditions that make such a choice difficult.

Where We Stand

The analyses included in this book are not only grounded in a negative appraisal of the thin understanding of democracy and of commodifying logics and process, they are also grounded in a particular set of positive principles. As a group, we the authors are guided by a broad set of moral and political commitments, by what has been called "radical democratic egalitarianism" (Wright 2010). As I have argued elsewhere (Apple 2013), this rests on a conviction that "robust egalitarianism" is necessary for a flourishing and fulfilling personal and social life. Because of this, it is guided by a critical impulse, one that seeks to challenge the social, economic, and cultural policies and practices that generate inequalities in the material and social conditions of people's lives, and that limit the possibility of such flourishing. It seeks to remove the barriers that limit "individual freedom and collectively empowered democracy" and to illuminate the possible paths to building more responsive policies and practices (Wright 2010, p. 33; see also Williams 1989; Solnit 2016).

This set of commitments has its roots in the tradition of "radical democracy" and involves the free and equal participation of all people in the constitution of their lives. Although electoral politics will play a significant role in our discussion of how the Right colonizes electoral spaces at a local level and of the importance of still engaging in such electoral politics, our emphasis goes well beyond the act of voting in elections for someone to represent us in the formal mechanisms of government. Rather, it extends to all spheres of social life—paid and unpaid workplaces, educational and cultural institutions, community groups, religious and spiritual organizations, social mobilizations, homes and elsewhere. Dahlberg details the conditions of this in the following way:

> Developing radical democracy from a culture of limited political participation requires not just winning and instituting legal protections (such as freedom of speech), but the formation of a politically active citizenry that comes into being through successful political activism, where citizens see their engagements as contributing to their own and societies' self-constitution (in contrast to a discouraged and passive citizenry).
>
> *(Dahlberg (Feb 26 2013, p. 3)*

As John Dewey and so many others recognized, schools have been and are places where such democratic "self-constitution" can be learned and practiced—or unfortunately made invisible and more difficult to live out (see, e.g., Dewey 1997; Apple and Beane 2007; Hess and McAvoy 2015; Arnot and Dillabough 2000; Hannan 1985; Delpit 2012; Ladson-Billings 2009; Freire 1971). The multiple traditions of working for a more thickly democratic education are vast and we forget them at our risk. They help us keep alive recognition of the "shoulders on which we stand" and of the individuals and groups of people who have sacrificed so much to keep the vision of a critically democratic school alive.

These traditions have a close resemblance to the socially critical movements involved in deliberative democracy as both a theory and a set of institutions and practices, and we consciously connect to this. As Cohen and Fung put it: "The ambitious aim of a deliberative democracy, in short, is to shift from bargaining, interest aggregation, and power to the common reason of equal citizens as a dominant force in democratic life" (Cohen and Fung 2004, p. 24). one for defining democracy.

Once again, this is not simply a rhetorical claim. We know that such participatory–deliberative arrangements contribute to political equality by increasing the role of popular mobilization and deliberation around issues that are crucial to people's daily lives (Cohen and Fung 2004 p. 30; see also Wright 2010, pp. 155-167). Furthermore, we also know that there is a good deal to be gained though the value of self-government. Participatory-deliberative institutions foster self-government by subjecting the policies and actions of agencies that affect people's lives "to a rule of common reason." When a government's policy or decision "is judged in collective deliberation to be unreasonable or unwise, they change it. When that policy turns out to be reasonable upon reflection, its justification is made publicly manifest" (Cohen and Fung 2004, p. 31).

Making such deliberative practices systemic is not and will not be easy. Thus, one of the major challenges we face is to extend the scope of radical democracy to all of the institutions that are central to our daily lives. Can such participatory democratic forms be mobilized to go beyond the local to help democratize substantive deliberations of such pressing areas as war and peace, economic inequalities, the restructuring of health care, a more responsive education system that actually interrupts the reproduction of racial trajectories, and so much more? In answering this, Cohen and Fung suggest the following:

> One way to address these larger questions is to connect the disciplined, practical, participatory deliberations about solving particular problems—say, efforts to reduce asthma rates in a low-income community—to the wider public sphere of debate and opinion formation—about the costs of health care, access to it, and the importance of health relative to other basic goods. Participants in direct deliberations are informed by the dispersed discussions in the informal public sphere, and those more focused deliberations in turn invest public discussion with a practicality it might otherwise lack. The ambitious hope is that citizens who participate in constructing solutions to concrete problems in local public life may in turn engage more deeply

in informal deliberation in the wider public sphere and in formal political institutions as well.

(Cohen and Fung, 2004, p. 32)

Cohen and Fung's points are significant. Even though we shall document a number of the gains, worries, and contradictory tensions associated with establishing and defending thicker forms of democracy in education, we need to keep in mind that difficult does not mean impossible. For this very reason, as you will see shortly, we place our chapters in this book in a particular order. These ongoing movements to institutionalize strong forms of participatory and deliberative action will be made most visible in our last case. This is a detailed analysis of a specific case of robust thick democracy in education and in state policies and practices in general, one that is both local and so much more. But we also want to stress that we should be aware again about the need to be careful not to romanticize these models of deliberative and participatory forms. They can be rather utopian. They can assume that "rational" models of public deliberation can and will lead to non-conflictual "solutions." Conflicts cannot be wished away and at times there will be no "talking solution" to deep-seated differences (Apple 2004). In addition, the dominant vision of "rationality" may be limited and may have its basis in an ahistorical view of the public sphere that itself has always been subject to race, gender, and class distinctions (see, e.g., Fraser 1989; Mouffe 2000; Mills 1997; Lynch et al. 2009. For a specifically educational discussion of this, see also Gottesman 2016).

For this very reason, that final case in Chapter 5 provides an instance not of abstract "rationality," but of a jointly constructed project of "collective reasoning" built also by and through social mobilizations that were aimed specifically at valorizing knowledge from below. It is an instance of thick democratic forms that act not to reproduce an epistemological fog, but are part of an ongoing project of demanding epistemological and political/educational respect. It also required not simply deliberation but a long and steady effort of mobilizing against the forces and structures that made inequalities and oppressions inside and outside of education both visible and unacceptable.

This entire book of course represents a complicated set of projects. One of its aims is to assist in the creation of new possibilities and new institutions. But often this also requires defending and democratizing existing institutions in the process of transforming them to support a new network of thick democratic practices across institutions and sites (Murray 2014). We aim to give robust examples of both of these aims.

Real School and Real Struggles

So far the focus of this introductory chapter has been on the general outlines of what guides our discussions. It is now time to "get real," to closely examine a number of the realities in which the conflicts over the meaning of democracy and its practices in schools and communities play out. The central chapters of this book, Chapters 2 through 5, constitute the core examples of how the politics of democracy in its various forms works out under current conditions. Democracy in education is seen as a contested terrain. In general, this is a contest in which neoliberal, neoconservative, authoritarian populist, and new managerial forces and movements (what can be called "conservative modernization") engage in well-resourced attempts to shift our common sense understandings of democracy toward thin consumer choice variants and dominant curricular and pedagogic forms. Opposing this are groups and movements that have as their aim the transformation of our institutions and knowledge forms so that they embody a collective and more fully participatory egalitarian democracy.

The book has a recursive character. It begins at the most local of all levels, in a school and in classrooms, with the classed and raced struggles to form an education that is socially and culturally critical. It then goes up a level to the politics of school boards and their decisions that have very real effects on schools, classrooms, and teachers. It next moves to the national level and how schools and parents in a very different socio-political context interact with national policies in creative ways that may seem "democratic," but unfortunately not in a way that interrupts neoliberalism. Finally, all of these levels come together in an example of robust democracy where the local school and community interact with the state in creating financial, pedagogical, and curricular policies and practices that challenge dominance.

More specifically, Chapter 2 starts us out by looking inside a school that is expressly committed to something all of us involved in this book are deeply committed to—a truly caring educational environment, deeply dedicated teachers, community involvement, culturally responsive teaching and critically oriented curricula, with anti-racist and anti-homophobic sensibilities, and so much more. This is a school that deserves its reputation as an important instance of counter-hegemonic education, one we all support. But in the process of describing what is happening there, the chapter examines the raced and classed contradictions and compromises that have emerged over time. We raise a number of the questions that guide much of this book, including: Can "thick" critically democratic education last? And what is the nature of the compromises that are made to keep it alive?

Chapter 3 takes us outside the classroom to look at the ways in which local democracy works in the mechanisms in school systems that set policies for school finance, curriculum, evaluation, teachers' rights and responsibilities, and so much more. It illuminates the ways in which the elections for school boards have increasingly become highly political. They have become the arenas where well-organized and well-funded rightist groups have sought to make certain that anti-union, neoliberal and neoconservative, and decidedly non-critical policies and practices dominate. The chapter looks specifically at two places, one where conservatives were victorious and one where more progressive positions were successfully defended and a neoliberal and neoconservative-dominated school board was defeated. We will also ask what lessons we can learn from these struggles about defending thicker forms of democracy.

The last two chapters of the central section of this book purposely focus on international examples. They are critical analyses of two very different struggles over democracy. Chapter 4 examines recent educational choice policies in China and how they work both overtly and covertly. It shows how thinner versions of democracy emerge out of the specific historical context of state programs and the political economy of educational finance—and out of demands by upwardly mobile class factions who appropriate these policies for the benefit of their own children. It also takes us inside a school that benefits from such choices to demonstrate both what this means in terms of who goes there and what is taught. The chapter reminds us of what is at stake in these supposedly more "democratic" policies, and how the compromises from which they arise construct a system that privileges those with particular forms of economic, social, and cultural capital. The state plays a central role here, but it cannot totally control the outcomes of its policies as it reproduces an epistemological fog by turning a "blind eye" to some of the very "thin" hidden results of its policies.

While we want to be honest about some of the international results of neoliberal policies such as in China, we also want the final example to focus on a more positive instance of policies and practices that are robustly egalitarian. Thus, the second of these international chapters, Chapter 5, provides a capstone to these analyses, leaving us with an honest picture of (unromantic) hope and possibilities that require continuing struggles if they are to be defended and go forward.

Chapter 5 turns our attention to more progressive outcomes that, like our discussion of the Chinese experience, are also the result of a specific historical context, and national and regional social and political movements. It directs our attention to Brazil, and especially to Porto Alegre in the state of Rio Grande do Sul, where the successful struggles for thicker versions of democracy have played a crucial role in creating much more collective participatory forms. Here too the state was an important actor—but as a *learner*, not only as a leader. Its educational and social policies often evolved from movements from below. They came from demands from oppressed, marginalized, and poor communities that only through full participation could transparency be more than rhetorical. Only in this way could the demand that there must be no "fog" be met.

The final chapter, Chapter 6, asks us to consider the implications of the four central analyses. What can be learned from them? Are there reasons for optimism? What roles should critical educators play in the politics of building and defending thicker forms of democracy inside and outside of education? We point to a number of important lessons and detail a set of continuing individual and collective tasks to be taken up by critically democratic educators.

The chapter concludes by reminding us that one thing is certain: there are no guarantees. The building and expanding of socially critical thick forms of democracy is a long-term project—what Raymond Williams so eloquently called the long revolution (Williams 1961). Answers again will not be easy. But as the long history of critically democratic education demonstrates, there have been and can be victories. It is not simply trite to repeat a phrase that also has a long history in movements for social justice: the struggle continues.

References

Anderson, G. and Montoro Donchik, L. (2016). Privatizing schooling and policy making: The American Legislative Exchange Council and new political and discursive strategies of education governance. *Educational Policy 30(*2): pp. 322–64.

Anyon, J. (2014). *Radical Possibilities* (2nd ed.). New York: Routledge.

Apple, M. W. (2004). *Ideology and Curriculum* (3rd ed.). New York: Routledge.

Apple, M. W. (2006). *Educating the "Right" Way: Markets, Standards, God, and Inequality* (2nd ed.). New York: Routledge.

Apple, M. W. (2012). *Education and Power* (Revised Routledge Classic ed.). New York: Routledge.

Apple, M. W. (2013). *Can Education Change Society?* New York: Routledge.

Apple, M. W. (2014). *Official Knowledge* (3rd ed.). New York: Routledge.

Apple, M. W. and Beane, J. A. (Eds.). (2007). *Democratic Schools: Lessons in Powerful Education* (2nd ed.). Portsmouth, NH: Heinemann.

Apple, M. W. and Au, W. (Eds.). (2014). *Critical Education, Volumes 1–4.* New York: Routledge.

Apple, M. W., Au, W., and Gandin, L. A. (Eds.). (2009). *The Routledge International Handbook of Critical Education*. New York: Routledge.

Apple, M. W., Aasen, P., Cho, M. K., Gandin, L. A., Oliver, A., Sung, Y-K, Tavares, H., and Wong, T-H. (2003). *The State and the Politics of Knowledge*. New York: Routledge.

Arnot, M. and Dillabough, J. (Eds.). (2000). *Challenging Democracy: International Perspectives on Gender, Education and Citizenship*. New York: RoutledgeFalmer.

Ashby, S. and Bruno, R. (2016). *A Fight for the Soul of Public Education*. Ithaca, NY: ILR/Cornell University Press.

Avrich, P. (1980). *The Modern School Movement*. Princeton, NJ: Princeton University Press.

Baker, J., Lynch, K., Cantillion, S., and Watch, J. (2004). *Equality: From Theory to Action*. New York: Palgrave Macmillan.

Ball, S. (2003). *Class Strategies and the Education Market*. New York: RoutledgeFalmer.

Ball, S. (2007). *Education plc*. New York: Routledge.

Ball, S. (2012). *Global Education Inc.* New York: Routledge.

Baptist, E. (2014). *The Half Has Never been Told: Slavery and the Making of American Capitalism*. New York: Basic Books.

Berrey, S. (2015). *The Jim Crow Routine*. Chapel Hill, NC: University of North Carolina Press.

Bourdieu, P. (1984). *Distinction*. Cambridge, MA. Harvard University Press.

Burch, P. (2009). *Hidden Markets*. New York: Routledge.

Cohen, J. and Fung, A. (2004). Radical democracy. *Swiss Journal of Political Science*, pp. 23–34. www.archonfung.net/papers/Cohen_Fung_Debate_SPSR2004.pdf. Accessed 7/1/17.

Dahlberg, L. (2013). Radical democracy in contemporary times. *E-International Relations* (February 26). www.e-ir.info/2013/02/26/radical-democracy-in-contemporary-times. Accessed 5/31/17.

Davis, M. (2006). *Planet of Slums*. New York: Verso.

Delpit, L. (2012). *"Multiplication is for White People": Raising Expectation for Other People's Children*. New York: The New Press.

Dewey, J. (1997). *Democracy and Education*. New York: Free Press.

Dixson. A., Rousseau Anderson, C., and Donnor, J. (Eds.). (2016) *Critical Race Theory in Education* (2nd ed.). New York: Routledge.

Eagles, C. (2017). *Civil Rights Culture Wars*. Chapel Hill, NC: University of North Carolina Press.

Eakin, M. (2017). *Becoming Brazilians*. New York: Cambridge University Press.

Eder, K. (1993). *The New Politics of Class*. London: Sage.

Emdin, C. (2010). *Urban Science Education for the Hip-Hop Generation*. New York: Sense Publishers.

Fabricant, M. and Fine, M. (2012). *Charter Schools and the Corporate Makeover of Public Education*. New York: Teachers College Press.

Fraser, N. (1989). *Unruly Practices*. Minneapolis, MN: University of Minnesota Press.

Fraser, N. (1997). *Justice Interruptus*. New York: Routledge.

Freire, P. (1971). *Pedagogy of the Oppressed*. New York: Herder and Herder.

Gillborn, D. (2008). *Racism and Education*. New York: Routledge.

Gottesman, I. (2016). *The Critical Turn in Education*. New York: Routledge.

Haley, S. (2016). *No Mercy Here*. Chapel Hill, NC: University of North Carolina Press.

Hannan, B. (1985). *Democratic Curriculum*. Sydney: George Allen and Unwin.

Harvey, D. (2007). *A Brief History of Neoliberalism*. New York: Oxford University Press.

Hess, D. and MacAvoy, P. (2015). *The Political Classroom*. New York: Routledge.

Isenberg, N. (2016). *White Trash*. New York: Viking.

Jessop, B. (2002). *The Future of the Capitalist State*. Cambridge: Polity Press.

Kallio, A. (2015). *Navigating (Un)popular Music in the Classroom*. Helsinki: The Sibelius Academy, University of the Arts.

Knoester, M. (Ed.). (2012). *International Struggles for Critical Democratic Education*. New York: Peter Lang.

Ladson-Billings, G. (2009). *The Dreamkeepers: Successful Teachers of African American Children* (2nd ed.). New York: Jossey-Bass.

Laes, T. (2017). *The (Im)possibility of Inclusion*. Helsinki: The Sibelius Academy, University of the Arts.

Leys, C. (2003). *Market-Driven Politics*. New York: Verso.

Lipman, P. (2011). *The New Political Economy of Urban Education*. New York: Routledge.

Lubienski, C. and Lubienski, S. (2014). *The Public School Advantage*. Chicago: University of Chicago Press.

Lynch, K., Baker, J., and Lyons, M. (2009). *Affective Equality: Love, Care and Injustice*. New York: Palgrave Macmillan.

Lynch, K., Grummell, B., and Devine, D. (2012). *New Managerialism in Education*. New York: Palgrave Macmillan.

MacLean, N. (2017). *Democracy in Chains: The Deep History of the Radical Right's Stealth Plan for America*. New York: Viking.

Mayer, J. (2016). *Dark Money: The Hidden History of the Billionaires Behind the Rise of the Radical Right*. New York: Doubleday.

Mills, C. (1997). *The Racial Contract*. Ithaca, NY: Cornell University Press.

Mouffe, C. (2000). *Deliberative Democracy or Agonistic Pluralism*. Vienna: Institute for Advanced Studies.

Murray, D. (2014). Prefiguration or actualization? Radical democracy and counter-institution in the occupy movement. *Berkeley Journal of Sociology* (November 3). http://berkeleyjournal.org/2014/11/prefiguration-or-actualization-radical-democracy-and-counter-institution-in-the-occupy-movement/. Accessed 06/09/17.

Nichols, J. (2002). *Uprising*. New York: Nation Books.

Omi, M. and Winant, H. (2014). *Racial Formation in the United States* (3rd ed.). New York: Routledge.

Root, A. (2007). *Market Citizenship*. London: Sage.

Roth-Gordon, J. (2017). *Race and the Brazilian Body*. Berkeley, CA: University of California Press.

Rothstein, R. (2017). *The Color of Law*. New York: Liveright.

Schirmer, E. and Apple, M. W. (2016). Capital, power, and education: "Dark money" and the politics of common-sense. *Education Review 23*. Available at: http://dx.doi.org/10.14507/er.v23.2145

Solnit, R. (2016). *Hope in the Dark*. New York: Nation Books.

Stewart, A. (2001). *Theories of Power and Domination*. Thousand Oaks, CA: Sage.

Stovall, D. (2017). *Born Out of Struggle: Critical Race Theory, School Creation, and the Politics of Interruption*. Albany, NY: SUNY Press.

Teitelbaum, K. (1993). *Schooling for Good Rebels*. Philadelphia, PA: Temple University Press.

Teitelbaum, K. (2009). Restoring Collective Memory: The Pasts of Critical Education. In *The Routledge International Handbook of Critical Education*. M. W. Apple, W. Au, and L. A. Gandin (Eds.) pp. 312–326. New York: Routledge.

Uetricht, M. (2014). *Strike for America: Chicago Teachers Against Austerity*. New York: Verso.

Verma, R. (2017). *Critical Peace Education and Global Citizenship*. New York: Routledge.

Virginia State Board of Education (1943). Course of study for Virginia Elementary Schools. *Bulletin State Board of Education* 25(10): pp. 506–515.

Watson, N., Roulstone, A., and Thomas, C. (Eds.). (2012). *The Routledge Handbook of Disability Studies*. New York: Routledge.

Welner, K. (2008) *Neo Vouchers*. Lanham, MD: Rowman and Littlefield.

Williams, R. (1961). *The Long Revolution*. London: Chatto and Windus.

Williams, R. (1989). *Resources of Hope*. New York: Verso.

Wright, E. O. (1989). *The Debate on Classes*. New York: Verso.

Wright. E. O. (2010). *Envisioning Real Utopias*. New York: Verso.

Zinn, H. (2015). *A People's History of the United States*. New York: Harper Perennial Modern Classics.

2

THE CONTRADICTIONS OF A CRITICALLY DEMOCRATIC SCHOOL

Assaf Meshulam and Michael W. Apple

Introduction

Public education systems lie at the heart of cultural, political, and economic struggles over consciousness, social identity, and the distribution of social positions (Meshulam and Apple 2010; Wong 2002). Amongst the many players who take part in these struggles are educators, parents, and activists who strive to create and defend an education for a democratic and more socially just society. These efforts, however, are especially difficult today with the unremitting neoliberal assault on public education. Any socially committed educational endeavor in the public system faces ongoing budget constraints and resource cutbacks, inbuilt biases within the state, and the intensifying commodification of education and its attendant alterations in common sense (Apple 2006). Yet in the face of all of these pressures, some counter-hegemonic institutions manage to survive. They do so through a combination of partial victories, what may seem to be necessary compromises, and, at times, partial losses. But they do last.

In this chapter, we examine a public elementary school in the United States that is well known for its attempt at building and then defending a critically democratic and socially transformative education that seeks to challenge existing relations of dominance and subordination across a variety of differences. During its three decades of existence, this school has been particularly distinguished by two flagship programs: its bilingualism (English and Spanish) program and its grounding in critical multiculturalism. The latter, in particular, is organized around an overtly antiracist set of goals. Yet these goals notwithstanding, the school lives in the real world. Its experiences can tell us a good deal about many of the challenges facing critical education today. It can illuminate how schools act as a site of constant struggle and compromise between different, at times contradictory, interests, agents, and ideologies. And at the same time, it can demonstrate some of the powerful forces in the (racial) state and civil society that make educating for social equality and justice difficult to accomplish, even in a school deeply committed to interrupting the reproduction of the unequal structure of class and race relations within its own walls.

This chapter begins by presenting the historical and socio-political contexts to the establishment of the school and background to its bilingual, multicultural, and antiracist agenda. We then consider the challenges to implementing the school's antiracist vision, deriving from neoliberal demands and pressures to which the school is subject. We examine the complex factors and dynamics in the concessions the school has made in response to these challenges, and consider how and why, even in this most antiracist of schools, issues of race and racism persist and cultural, racial, and class inequalities are reproduced.[1]

The Socio-Historical Contexts of Antiracist Schooling

Any substantive understanding of the socio-historical contexts on which we focus here must rest on two interrelated realities about the racial structuring of the United States. First, powerful forms of segregation persist in US society in general and in public schools in particular, which are more segregated than ever (Orfield 2009). Second, race itself and racializing policies and practices, inside and outside education, are primary factors accounting for this segregation in education. Indeed, "[i]ssues of race and racism permeate US culture—through law, language, politics, economics, symbols, art, public policy—and the prevalence of race is not merely in those spaces seen as racially defined spaces" (Ladson-Billings 2004, p. 5). More than half a century after the US Supreme Court's landmark Brown versus Board of Education decision in 1954, in which official segregation was ruled unconstitutional, the public school system continues to be a space in which unequal race relations are by and large reproduced and reinforced.

How this works out, however, is always conjunctural. As Stuart Hall (1996) reminds us, race and racialization—and how the state operates as a racial state— are not always the same, nor do they operate in the same ways in every context (see also Mills 1997). The contexts of this particular city and school clarify why Hall's point is so crucial and requires that we spend time critically examining their racial history.

The city in which the school is located, as well as its public education system, provides a fine example of the complex socio-historical conditions in which schools of this type function. An industrial Midwest port city, it has traditionally drawn immigrants from across the world, and within the United States, who have brought with them cultural and social diversity. By 2008–09, the year in which the school was researched, the city's population was 40% White, 38% Black, 15% Hispanic, 3% Asian, and about 1% Native American (US Census Bureau 2008). Yet despite its strong tradition of social progressiveness and activism, the city also has been notorious for deep-rooted segregation and racial inequality. This gives credence to Mills' (1997) argument that social democracy is based on a racial contract, a contract that can be weakened and even withdrawn when the "other" enters into the geographical and political space. Thus, racism, discrimination, and inequity prevail to this day, suffered most acutely by African Americans but also by the city's Latino/Latina population (Miner 2013).

Two prominent socio-political movements in the city served jointly as the breeding ground and setting for the school and its antiracist, multicultural, bilingual agenda: the battle, since the 1960s, of civil rights activists against segregation in housing and education, on the one hand, and the Spanish-speaking community's demand and struggle for bilingualism in public education, on the other.

Despite the 1968 enactment of a federal open housing law and the passage of a local ordinance essentially making segregated housing illegal, residential segregation in the city continued. Real estate agents, city zoning laws, and lending institutions prevented African Americans from moving into White neighborhoods, while suburbanization led to the abandonment of the inner city to African Americans and other minoritized groups. An intensification of neighborhood segregation was the result, which inevitably produced and exacerbated segregation in the city's schools. Because the city was so segregated geographically, its schools did not integrate following the 1954 Brown ruling. Only in 1976 did a federal court rule that the city's schools were illegally segregated and order their immediate integration, and only in 1979 did the public school board follow this up with a five-year desegregation plan. Nonetheless, when the school first opened in 1988, the city was ranked amongst the top five most racially segregated cities in the United States (Year One 1989). This led to even further mobilizations, especially within the African American community (Miner 2013).

Parallel to the efforts to desegregate neighborhoods and schools, a broad movement around the need for bilingual education in the city's schools emerged within the Latino/Latina community. In 1968, the Bilingual Education Act was passed, allocating federal funding to "encourage local school districts to try approaches incorporating native-language instruction" (History of Bilingual Education 1998, p. 1). This legislation and the city's failure to implement it served as the impetus for protests and walk-outs by Mexican and Puerto Rican parents and students, who demanded the establishment of Spanish–English bilingualism programs in the city's schools.

In addition, a movement emerged to build new high schools in minoritized communities, with a coalition forming between African Americans, Mexican-Americans, and White working-class groups towards this cause. Such joint mobilizations are unusual in many parts of the United States, where inter-ethnic solidarity is often hindered by dominant groups' ideological work using racializing discourses to enhance differences.

At the city and state levels as well as within the affected communities, the anti-segregation movement, bilingualism, and critical visions of multiculturalism gained political momentum during this period. But in spite of its growing strength, this activism did not have a meaningful impact on segregation in the city's public school system or on educational equality within the schools. The system remained unequal, segregated, and seemingly indifferent to the needs and rights of the minoritized populations it served. In the 1986–87 school year, one year before the school opened, the Grade Point Average for Black high school students was 1.46 and for Hispanic students 1.67 out of a possible 4.0. The completion rate for entering ninth graders in the city stood at 46% for Blacks and 49% for Hispanics, as opposed to 62% for Whites (Year One 1989). Against this backdrop of sweeping social and political activism alongside ongoing inequalities and racism in public education, the two-way bilingual (Spanish–English), multicultural school was envisioned: "We started to dream about a school that would provide the highest quality education for our children, Black, White, and Hispanic," explained a community parent and representative (Year One 1989, p. 68).

Understanding Democratic Schools

Before we go on to elaborate on the ways in which community members, parents, and educators worked to realize their vision, we should briefly explain our understanding of democratic schools to see why we take this specific school to be such a good example. As a starting point, the struggles, formation of movements and alliances, and mobilization of parents, community members, and educators of the type we have described are all crucial aspects of democratic schooling, as they are indispensable for building and then sustaining these schools in particular. Second, crucial in our understanding of democratic schools are the democratic nature of their structures and processes, and of their curricula, pedagogy, and evaluation methods, on the one hand, and the diversity of the school body, on the other (see Apple and Beane 2007). These two aspects of democratic schooling are intertwined. A school cannot be democratic, as we conceive it, with one but not the other.

The democratic nature of a school's structure and process relates to who participates in the school's decision-making processes and how. The ability of all school community members—teachers, students, parents—to take part in setting the rules and policies that govern school life is critical. This participation, especially on the part of students, cannot be relegated to mere tokenism and must ensure full and equal voice for all. This is not enough, however, for a school to be democratic in the "thick" sense we espouse and hold the school in this chapter to represent. It is not enough that a school is internally governed by democratic processes and structures while externally selective in terms of the families and educators that have access to it. Well-known private schools, such as Summerhill in the United Kingdom and the Sudbury model adopted in the United States and elsewhere, might meet the first requirement of democratic governance but not the second, namely, diversity and inclusion. Despite their democratic structures and processes, these schools are less thickly democratic than non-sorting public schools that represent and serve the economic and cultural diversity of their communities.

The second critical aspect of democratic schools is the nature and contents of the curricula and pedagogy. Whose culture, history, and identities are present and valued in the school curricula and pedagogy? Is the school producing the "official knowledge" of the dominant culture (Apple 2014)? In terms of the pedagogy, are the "best practices" in the school tailored, as they usually are, to the social and cultural advantage of the middle-class (Ladson-Billings 2014), or do they address a diverse body of students, including the minoritized and marginalized? A democratic school's curricula and pedagogy will be inclusive and diverse in contents and structure, exposing students to a multiplicity of histories, cultures, and identities.

Relatedly, another aspect of democratic schooling goes beyond the walls of the school: namely, the development in students of a critical awareness of their social reality and a recognition of their ability to effect change in the world. This refers to what Freire (1970) calls "conscientization" and Ladson-Billings (1995) calls "sociopolitical consciousness."

As will emerge from the discussion below, both in vision and practice, the school we examine here clearly follows the lines of our view of democratic schooling in all aspects: structure, governance, pedagogy, and curriculum.

Building a Collaborative, Community School

The school first opened its doors in September 1988 as a public pre K-5 elementary school in a working-class neighborhood populated by the communities most impacted by the city-wide discrimination and inequality. The ongoing racial and cultural diversity and integration in this neighborhood, despite a "parade of change" in its demographics over the decades (Tolan 2003), have always been unique in the city. The 2000 census data portray the neighborhood as "one of the city's—and state's—most integrated" neighborhoods, "one of just four in the state with the most equal proportions of black, white, and Hispanic residents" (Tolan 2003, p. viii). This has been vital to both the success in mobilizing the community to fight for the school's establishment and the school's ability to serve and promote diversity. In its first year of operation, 42% of its students were Black, 37% Hispanic, and 21% "Other." Approximately 90% of the students qualified for free lunch (Year One 1989). Twenty years later, in the 2008–09 school year, the diversity remained although the demographics had shifted. The majority was now Latino/Latina (59%)—a critical point in the account of how "race" works that we offer later in this chapter. This was followed by 19% African Americans and 12% White, with the remainder Asian-American and Native-American. Seventy-four percent of the students qualified for free or reduced lunch.

The school, in its previous incarnation, was "slated to be razed" in 1988 and turned into an "Exemplary Teaching Center" by the school district (Year One

1989, p. 68).Valuing the neighborhood's diversity, a small group of teachers, parents, and community activists organized to resist this plan and proposed establishing instead a "two-way bilingual, multicultural, site-based-managed school" (ibid). The path from proposal to opening the school was not without arduous political struggle, in the face of initially strong resistance from the school board and district administrators. But the timing was right. The community activism was supported by the success of two political battles being waged in the city at the time, pushing the school board to eventually back the initiative. The one struggle revolved around allowing site-based management and a whole-language model, two approaches the school board endorsed. A second source of pressure on the board was the growing criticism of its apparent unwillingness to engage in dialogue with African American parents and their demands for an independent school district that would be controlled by the city's African American community. The conjunction of these two struggles led the school board, fighting for its own political legitimacy, to pass the proposal to establish the school.

The school's two-way bilingualism and, in some respects, even more its overtly critical multicultural curricula and pedagogy are what set it apart from many other schools. From the outset, there was a firm conception of the school's mission. As expressed in its "Our School Vision" document, its founders aimed to educate students in Spanish and English "through a program of academic excellence" and to construct a multicultural program founded on an antiracist perspective.A central requirement of the two-way bilingualism model the school adopted is a mixed, optimally balanced, number of native English-speaking and native Spanish-speaking students. On the one hand, this ensures meaningful exposure to diversity for both groups of students. Significantly, however, it also empowers the Spanish-speakers, through peer-learning, to develop multicultural identity and self-esteem (Skutnabb-Kangas and García 1995) and "deep academic proficiency and cognitive understanding through their first language to compete successfully with native speakers of the second language" thereby equalizing the cultural power relations (Baker 2006, p. 270; Thomas and Collier 2002). The need to balance between Spanish-speaking and English-speaking students in the school eventually led to the busing-in of Spanish-speakers from outside the neighborhood, which had a significant impact on the school demographics.

Fundamental to the school's identity and mission is sustaining the organic connection and collaboration with parents, the local community, grassroots movements, and social organizations, which was a driving force in the original activism to open the school. As a founding member explained in an interview, there was "an ideological commitment ... to be accountable to the general population." In line with its site-based management approach, the school is democratically and collaboratively run by educators, parents, and the community.Various bodies and committees composed of parents, staff, and community members decide jointly on most major matters, including funding, staffing, budget allocation, and school curriculum policy.

Moreover, the school has always sought to generate and facilitate parental participation and representation, never an easy task. A teacher explained the loss of momentum: "Once we won the school: A lot of parents said, well, now it's the staff's turn to … take responsibility. It was sort of a natural drop-off of involvement." In order to foster involvement, particularly among African American and Latino/Latina working-class parents, two paid part-time positions were created for parent coordinators from these communities. Yet diversifying parental representation in school governance has remained a challenge. Relative to "many other inner city schools," noted a school administrator, "parent involvement is impressive. But when it comes to decision-making, there's an inequality, a disparity, between middle-class parents of all races, although they tend more to be White."

The school's approach to curriculum development also reflects its collaborative aims and orientation. The original curriculum was "an outgrowth of a dynamic process in which parents, teachers, and community members have come together to build a school that serves the needs of an integrated neighborhood and the city as a whole" (Year One 1989, p. 33). This served as the model for curriculum development at the school. An ongoing organic process, it is central to the multicultural program, which is anchored on dialogue, mutual support, and an integrative approach. It is also, however, what has made the program most vulnerable in the struggle for resources and prioritizing. Although the multicultural and bilingualism programs shared "top billing" in the original vision and agenda, with time, their needs—structural, resources, funding—and notably, objectives, evolved in ways that led to clashes. As we shall see, this was generally at the expense of multiculturalism and antiracism at the school.

Building Multicultural Antiracist Education

A transformative, critical notion of multiculturalism (Banks and Banks 1997; Ladson-Billings 2004; McLaren 1994) has been pivotal in the school's educational agenda from the proposal stage. The founders embraced a broad vision of democratic multicultural education that goes well beyond human relations, embodying a strong commitment to directly challenging differential power and racism. It also overtly focuses on other categories and forms of difference, such as gender inequities and the politics of sexuality (see Ladson-Billings 2003). The aim is teaching students to not only understand what it means to be antiracist, anti-biased, and multicultural, but to put these values into practice: "It's not just lip-service … This vision actually drives the curriculum … And that you are going to take something away from this. Hopefully school doesn't happen in a vacuum," said a teacher.

In interviews, teachers described the school's curriculum as infused with lessons about culture and power and identity and community. This echoes Nieto's (2004) conception of multicultural education as far more than "cultural and linguistic maintenance," where not only "issues of difference" are confronted but also "issues of power and privilege in society. This means challenging racism and other

biases as well as inequitable structures, policies, and practices of schools and, ultimately, of society itself" (2004, xxvii). The school addresses these inequities by, as
a veteran teacher explained: "taking those issues from under the table and putting
them on top of the table to look at and begin to talk about." This enables students
to recognize and contend with their manifestation in their own lives, communities, and cultures, and in those of others. Students learn to acknowledge and confront their biases, preconceptions, and stereotyping, and their origins in sources
other than race and ethnicity. Ultimately, this multicultural approach understands
the school to be "a social system that consists of highly interrelated parts and vari-
ables" and that all of its major components must be substantially impacted to build
an institution that grounds itself in the reality, not only the theory, of educational
equality and antiracism (Banks and Banks 1997, 26).

This antiracist, multicultural understanding underlies all aspects of the school's
curriculum and pedagogy. "Our whole curriculum I think is based around a multicultural, anti-bias, antiracist curriculum. It's kind of integrated and woven into everything that we teach. That's paramount here," stated a teacher. This was reiterated
in multiple interviews with teachers and staff: "It drives what we read, why we read
it." This has required that the experiences of people of color feature prominently,
and the history, literature, art, and music of various groups (not only the food,
holidays, and celebrations, which are often the limits of schools' commitments) are
integrated into the curriculum in different contexts and ways. The school seeks
to thereby impart a transformative, activist message through its curriculum. As
a founding educator expressed: "The ideas and the ideals that they are learning
here will be things that the students will take out into the culture, into the main
predominantly White culture and maybe make some changes." This conception
of multiculturalism lay at the foundation of the school's original vision statement:

> Multicultural anti-racist education is more than just familiarizing our stu-
> dents with a few facts, faces, and foods of various nationalities who live in
> our country. Children should develop an 'ethnic literacy' (Banks 1981) in
> which they understand, analyze and respect their own cultural roots, an
> understanding of the historical nature of racial oppression in our country
> and the advantage of multicultural multilingual society.
>
> *(Year One 1989, 48–49)*

As powerful as this statement is, veteran teachers concede that the sweeping and
lofty principles do not always offer sufficiently concrete guidelines for coherent
and consistent curriculum development. "The statement is a good starting point,
and helps orient new staff and parents" but is not enough to understand "how to
teach multiculturally" (Peterson 1995, 68). Integral to realizing the school's ambitious vision, it was understood, was a dynamic "back and forth" process of curriculum construction and implementation, where teachers said they "learn from
each other … and from the children."

Such an approach depends on both collaboration and teachers' independent initiative and creativity. Early on, there was an explicit decision to make only selective use of textbooks and that imposing ready-made materials on teachers would be "sort of meaningless," as a veteran noted in an interview. This made teachers ultimately responsible for developing their pedagogy and curriculum, with significant freedom and agency in setting their syllabi and teaching materials and methods. At the same time, teachers were to work closely with one another as well as with parents and the community to develop a basic model and retool it over the years.

These two facets of the curriculum development have created a robust culture and practice of dialogue, collaboration, and mentoring at the school, as a matter of ongoing routine. One teacher stated, "Without ongoing conversation, any curriculum becomes moribund." Almost all teachers stressed the mutual support and mentoring amongst the teaching staff, in weekly teachers' meetings or informally "in the lunch room" as indispensable for ensuring consistency and coherence in the curriculum: "[There is] unity within all the staff and they're willing to help each other and come up with ideas together, collaborate together, and I think that's very helpful and unique."

To support teachers, especially newcomers, the original school schedule devoted one full day a week to curriculum planning in each grade level, allowing teachers to meet for team teaching and curriculum development. This was facilitated by scheduling art, music, and gym classes back-to-back to free homeroom teachers to collaborate on planning. Crucial to this, however, was funding for full-time special subject instructors, which was strongly impacted later on by district budget cuts. Other techniques supplemented this to educate teachers regarding the multicultural, antiracist agenda: "For instance, the principal has extra meetings with the teachers. The teachers generally work with another staff person at their level who is a veteran teacher. They are certainly provided with materials. They're encouraged to go to workshops."

Central in the evolution of this approach to curriculum development has been the school's early recognition of the challenge of passing down the founding generation's multicultural, antiracist vision consistently and effectively to "newcomers." A founding member explained:

> If you are a newcomer, you don't know sort of the party line. You think you kind of have an idea of it. But it has all sorts of nuances and it's reflected in different ways. So, we have to really work at making sure that new people are mentored and that we do have staff development, specifically about multiculturalism and antiracism and how the dual-language model works.

To contend with "unnecessary duplications and omissions" in curricula across classes and grade levels (Peterson 1995, p. 68), the generalities and ambiguities had to be fleshed out and clearer guidelines provided. The school set its multicultural program on a continuum (Banks 1981; Miner 1991; Peterson 1995), beginning with teaching the contributions of people of color, moving to non-European cultures, and culminating in a critical thinking phase, where messages from outside—the media, books, textbooks—are critiqued. For coherence in contents and message, four school-wide themes were developed as the overarching framework for teaching multiculturalism at every grade level. These curricular frameworks were aimed at training teachers to better teach transformative multiculturalism and antiracism.

In its binding of multiculturalism to antiracism and its approach to being multicultural education, the school has broken the "either/or" choice between what Fraser (1997) calls the "false antitheses" of "social equality and multiculturalism." It melds equally redistribution and recognition, understanding that neither alone is sufficient (1997, p. 3). But as will be shown, powerful pressures arose that undermined the full realization of these admirable ideals and aspirations. The attempt to develop, convey, and concretize the multicultural, antiracist agenda was only partially successful, hampered by the shift in district (and national) ideology towards neoliberal policies and goals. No less significant, however, was that the school proved not to be immune to the pervasiveness of the unequal structure of race relations in US society. It is to this that we now turn.

What Happened to Race?

What happened to race at this antiracist, multicultural school? What can account for its inability to implement a truly critical approach to multiculturalism and to equalize the racial power structure?

This school, like all public schools, is a site of conflict and tension among different ideologies, interests, and forces. The ascent of the neoliberal agenda in public education impacted budget and resource allocation at the school and forced compromises in its programs and an adjustment of priorities. National policies such as No Child Left Behind (NCLB) and the testing regime it imposed (Apple 2006) were a stream through which neoliberal ideology slowly but steadily flowed into the school. The appeal of the bilingualism program to the mobility strategies necessary in a capitalistic neoliberal market indelibly harmed the antiracist setting and orientation of the school, as it led to a process of commodification of knowledge. But neoliberalism's frontal attack on transformative, "thick" democratic education is only one factor in the erosion of the antiracist program and setting at the school. No less significant, and not unrelated, the experience of this school, in its failure to equalize the education experience across the race spectrum, points at the deep-rootedness of structural racial inequality in the United States and the difficulty of removing it from the educational space (Ladson-Billings 2004; see also Apple 2013).

The undermining of overt antiracism at the school occurred on three interconnected planes. The first is the direct impact of the district-wide implementation of neoliberal educational policies of reductive forms of accountability and fiscal "efficiency." This led to budget and resource cuts and reallocation and to a shift to a regime of testing and standards. Second is the commodification process that the school and its bilingualism program underwent, which led to the latter's prioritization and the subordination of the antiracist, multicultural program. This is closely connected to the third sphere of impact: the reproduction of structural racial inequality at the school in terms of exclusion of African Americans and their unique needs as a community, as well as the general need to equalize the education experience at the school. In all three contexts, the changes were most prominently to the detriment of the African American community's relationship with the school and its representation there.

The frequent city-wide budget cutbacks in public education over the last decade impaired significantly the school's ability to realize its original conceptualization of its multicultural program. Although, in being site-based managed, the school had full discretion over how it allocates its budget, it had little control over the total amount of funding it receives from the district or cuts in that funding. Moreover, the growing need to meet district standards and targets was an added pressure in allocating the funding. Thus, when compromises had to be made, in terms of both resource allocation and choice of resources, tension developed between the needs of the cornerstone goals at the school.

One of the central clashes of priorities emerged in the context of staff cutbacks. Several positions that were vital to sustaining the antiracist program and representation of the African American community were cut early on when fiscal constraints arose. Most notable were the elimination of the parent coordinators and a significant reduction of paraprofessionals and support staff. The school had originally budgeted for two parent coordinators at the school, one African American and the other Latino/Latina, to liaise with the two less-participating groups in the school's governance. With the loss of funding for these positions, a choice was made to eliminate the African American coordinator. The logic behind this decision was clear: as a bilingual school, the bilingual parent liaison was preferred. But this decision exacerbated the general under-participation and under-serving of the African American community at the school and reflects the prioritizing of Latino/Latina representation. Unfortunately, no other liaising framework with African American parents was set up to replace the parent coordinator position. As one teacher noted, this was "a real blow to our school." It also brings to light one of the racializing effects of neoliberal economic decisions. These decisions aggravate racial differences and tensions not only between dominant and marginalized populations but amongst marginalized groups as well.

The second significant development was the loss of most of the school's paraprofessionals and assistants over the years. It also had to give up its full-time special subject teachers, which led to the elimination of the full day devoted each week to grade-level curriculum planning and collaboration. The result was a very real intensification of teachers' work (see Apple 2012). Like so many other teachers in public schools in the United States and elsewhere, teachers described how they were forced to plan their curriculum "outside of the regular school time" as support "dwindled and dwindled and dwindled," in isolation from their peers and those who could guide and train them. The severe impact on curriculum planning time and quality was a central complaint expressed in interviews: "We have virtually no money for professional development. And we're all overworked, as you can tell, in terms of time. That's an ongoing struggle that we face." Moreover, early on, the position of program implementer, who oversaw the task of developing and implementing a coherent and comprehensive curriculum, was also eliminated. This was especially critical in the context of the need to ensure consistency and a "conversation" in the antiracist, multicultural curriculum. This lack of adequate support for teacher mentoring, dialogue, and collaboration combined with new staff lacking the understanding, theoretically and practically, of how to teach critical multiculturalism—"We get new staff in who are trained at the universities who don't really know very much about this" —led to variations and inconsistencies in the multicultural curricula among classes and grade levels (see Bhopal and Preston 2012). The unevenness was recognized early on at the school and emerged in both interviews with teachers and classroom observations. Some teachers expressed and taught an expanded and nuanced, multilayered notion of multiculturalism. A first-grade teacher described how she integrates empowerment and racism and sexism as they connect to the children's lives: "I talk about racism. We talk about sexism. We study women's rights ... because they live that. They know ... So why am I going to pretend that those things are not issues for first-graders?"

Other teachers articulated a narrower understanding, their descriptions focusing on more obvious issues and dimensions of culture. There was no extension of racism to its intersection with other "isms" and little evidence of a complex exploration of social justice, power, and other inequities. As Ladson-Billings (2003, p. 51) notes, "[E]thnoracial distinctions [are] a limited way to talk about multiculturalism and multicultural education." The tension, between an awareness of the multiplicity of ways and forms of oppression and identity and a more limited view, where ethnic and racial differences take center stage, was evident from the teachers' varying descriptions of the multicultural curriculum and program. In interviews, leaders at the school were clearly reflective and critical about the school's multicultural preparation of new staff members and allocation of resources to ensure coherence and continuity of the vision. They indicated an understanding of how current realities prevent them from realizing their aspirations, with one stating frankly, "We don't do a good job at it."

Exacerbating this situation was the introduction of the NCLB testing regime and the focus on standards, test scores, and achievement assessment. In constructing the curriculum, teachers were now expected to follow district guidelines and meet its targets. Many told of the pressures and frustrations of contending with the conflicting requirements and objectives after the implementation of NCLB.

This has hugely impacted the prioritization of time and resources and hindered meaningful pursuit of antiracism and multiculturalism at the school. As expressed in one interview with an educator at the school,

> Many people who come to our school, in terms of teachers—many but not all—know of our beliefs and come because they're attracted to it. However, that's not always the case, and even those who do, their version of social justice or antiracist multiculturalism might be really problematic. Not that mine is perfect, but what we need is conversation. What does that mean in our classroom? What does that mean in our relationship to parents? What does that mean in our relationship to each other? Those things are a challenge in terms of finding time to discuss them because the district is pressuring us to use the time we do have together to talk about test scores.

Class Conversion Strategies at Work

The pressure to conform to the testing, standards, and assessment regime was only one channel through which neoliberalism entered and impacted the school. Less direct was the hegemonization of the school and its bilingual program. The success of the school and the reputation it gained were vital for justifying the district's continued support for its programs. But there was a cost to this: "Especially as the school has become more popular, we have a long waiting list of middle-class people who want to get in, who tend to be English dominant," described a veteran administrator. Attracting and serving White, mostly middle-class families also means that the school has to contend with the demands of their common sense, which is shaped by the material reality they experience and live (see Ball 2003). This is a crucial point. Bilingualism has its own cultural capital in the global capitalist market. For some parents, command of the Spanish language is an advantage with "purchasing power." While some White parents reported sending their children to the school out of full support for the social justice-oriented, antiracist curricula and agenda, others expressed this as a good "consumer choice" in a supermarket of commodities, where bilingual education is a means of improving their children's chances in a competitive globalized market and enhancing their cultural capital, as part of a class conversion strategy (see Apple 2004, 2006; Bourdieu 1984). A middle-class, self-identified White mother explained, "As the world keeps changing more and more, I think that it's important to be bilingual in some way, to be able to function." Her aspiration for her child to be bilingual is not driven by a commitment to transforming society or reducing racial and cultural biases and inequities. Rather, it reflects neoliberal alteration of the common sense around schooling, perceiving it as a "private good" and bilingualism as a means of "upgrading" oneself, of becoming a "well-rounded individual" within the dominant hegemonic perspectives.

This reality is apparent in studies of parental choice of bilingual programs (Meshulam, forthcoming), which could offer a partial explanation for the recent growth in their popularity (see Center for Applied Linguistics 2016) and the emerging trend of White middle-class parental choice of urban schooling (Billingham and Kimelberg 2013; Cucchiara 2013; Posey-Maddox 2014). Moreover, the phenomenon illustrates Reay et al.'s observation of middle-class choice to go "against the grain" in choosing socially mixed schools, as "directed toward 'consuming the desired other' in an act of appropriation" (2007, p. 1054).

To sustain its success, then, the school has had to accommodate middle-class hegemonic common sense and demands, forced to maneuver between its bilingual program and its critical multicultural program. This has been an additional factor in its prioritization of bilingualism over the needs and objectives of antiracist, multicultural, equalized education: namely, access, recognition, and representation for cultural and social minoritized groups. In supporting and endorsing bilingualism—making it easier to "teach," on the one hand, and a desired commodity, on the other—the school district's neoliberal agenda and the legitimation needs of the local state have created a context in which subordinating antiracist multicultural aspects of the school's life seems a necessary and unavoidable compromise. Thus, when choices have had to be made between ensuring the duality of the bilingual program and transforming race relations, the former has won out on most fronts.

The Absent Presence of "Race"

This leads to the third, overarching element of the challenges faced by the school in realizing transformative multiculturalism: its partially unsuccessful prevention of the reproduction of the structures of racial inequality dominating US society and education. This has manifested most prominently in African American representation in school governance and staffing and the blurring of the group identity of the African American students.

Not only have attempts to diversify and strengthen parental participation in the school fallen short from the perspective of the African American community, as we saw earlier, but at the time the study was conducted, the school's professional staff was completely devoid of even one African American.[2] One teacher sharply criticized the conspicuous absence of African American teachers at the school as inbuilt racism: "I don't think that the African American population is well served. There's one African American assistant. Nobody else. How can that be? Only the people who clean or cook. That is huge, a major problem, that we are reproducing." This "major problem" points to the role of "necessary compromises" in the reproduction of class and race power relations of greater US society at the school. Over the years, African Americans have overwhelmingly filled only low-wage positions at the school, at best. The school offers almost no middle-class, educated, professional role models for African American students, but rather only the traditional semi-skilled or unskilled labor roles of cleaning and cooking. This fundamentally undermines one of the school's key founding rationales: challenging oppression and racism in US society in general and specifically the segregation and discrimination in its own city and in the school itself (see Apple 2013; Lipman 2011).

Again, the needs of the bilingual program were presented by school administrators as producing this marginalization. Priority in hiring teachers was given to bilingual candidates, in a context where it is difficult to find qualified African American teachers who are fluent in Spanish. Teachers expressed awareness of this deep-rooted problem and admitted the choice not to compromise the bilingualism at the school by hiring insufficiently bilingual teachers: "That's a problem [no African American teachers]. We had a couple in the past, but they have to speak Spanish ... Not making excuses, it's just the way it is." The result was a failure to recognize and serve African American students' need for role models and representation. In a reality in which over 80% of public school teachers in the United States are White (US Department of Education 2016), clearly it is challenging for the school to find qualified African American teachers, let alone Spanish–English bilingual ones.

Given this, the overriding identity of the school as bilingual partly interrupts the critical dimensions of cultural diversity at the school, trapping it in a sort of bicultural paradox. It creates a dichotomy between Spanish-speaking communities and English-speaking communities as almost exclusively definitive of diversity, "otherness," in the school. This has left little room to cultivate a more critical multiculturalism in practice, not only in the program but in the student body itself, in order to recognize in more powerful ways a diversity of cultural groups and communities.

Similar problems arise in the context of politics of recognition and cultural diversity at the school. Many noted in interviews the all-embracing atmosphere of diversity, cultural and otherwise, due to the multicultural and antiracism program, and this was clearly observable in the student artwork on the walls, extracurricular cultural events, and overt discourse in school signs and notices. Yet there is a clear marginalization of non-White, non-Hispanic groups, most particularly the African American community. African American enrollment has dramatically declined with time, while White English-speakers and native Spanish-speakers have been courted and their enrollment has consistently risen. Thus, the needs of two-way bilingualism have effectively stripped the African American community of its recognition as a distinct political and cultural (including linguistic) group at the school.

The impact of this on linguistic politics has been profound. While not a conscious choice, this has meant that the school overlooks cultural aspects of the African American English dialect, as well as the community's cultural distinction beyond mere language. In the framework of the Spanish/English dichotomy, the African American community belongs to (or is considered part of) the majority in terms of first language; they are uncritically put together with Whites who speak Standard English.

One further accompanying factor in the blurring of the African American community's identity as a distinct cultural group within the school is the need to maintain a balance between native Spanish-speaking and native English-speaking students for the two-way bilingualism program to work. This has resulted in a dichotomous—rather than multicultural—approach to diversifying the student body. As the pressures for the bilingual program to succeed intensified, a prominent concern became how to attract more Spanish-speaking students to balance English-speaking students. Moreover, from a class perspective, attracting a balance of White middle-class students was vital for a real attempt at achieving redistribution and recognition (Fraser 1997). Preventing the reproduction of social and material inequalities requires the production of transformed students (Apple 2013). But transformation must occur at both ends of the spectrum—the privileged and non-privileged/less privileged, the oppressed and oppressors. Thus White, English-speaking, middle-class students are critical for both their own transformation and the transformation of non-White, Spanish-speaking, working-class students.

In saying this, we want to stress that despite the strong correlation between race and class position, we do not want to essentialize all Spanish-speakers as lower class, but rather want to present the different ends of the spectrums: White and non-White, English-speakers and Spanish-speakers, middle class and working/lower class. But still, it should be clear that this, again, has come at the expense of African American students and their place in the school as a distinct group and culture.

Conclusion

There is so much about this school that is worthy of respect and support. But what emerges from our analysis here is a story of complexity and contradictions, a mixture of hope and worry. Even in this school—whose vision, collaborative ethos, and curriculum contents embody recognition, redistribution, and equal representation (Fraser 2010)—inequalities and racializing power relations have been produced in important ways. In these circumstances, what was meant to be a powerful educational challenge to dominance is significantly weakened.

The school is to be commended for its goal of interrupting such relations in the larger society and in the school itself. But the effects of neoliberal policies, the realities of who teaches at the school, the constraints on time and resources, the tensions between the sometimes contradictory progressive programs, the multiplicity of racialized groups, and the ability of middle-class parents to re-occupy or "appropriate" (Reay et al. 2007) the space of critical educational reform for their own purposes—all of these and more have created a set of conditions and dynamics that "interrupt the interruptions."

In many ways, this school is a powerful example of the impact of the ongoing neoliberal assault, both direct and indirect, not only on public education in general, but most specifically on schools that aim to be counter-hegemonic. This has been experienced on a number of levels and in various defining aspects. The school emerges as no less a site of conflict and compromise between different powers and interests—even if all valid and equally desirable from the school's perspective—which has led to concessions most significantly in the sphere of race, representation, inclusion, recognition, and redistribution, with surprising implications for the struggle to equalize social, cultural, and racial power relations.

Promoting social justice and challenging society's power structures are undoubtedly major constituents of the school. This manifests in its structure, governance, and curriculum and pedagogy. The school has had broad success in transforming the public education system in its district and city. Over the years, it has formed important alliances with social groups and movements, other district schools, the teachers' union, and progressive activists and scholars, in an effort to introduce more critical multicultural antiracist policies into the public system. This is a story that needs to be told as well.

Alongside these successes, however, the school, like many others in the United States, has had to contend with the major challenges brought on by neoliberal policies such as NCLB. "Certainly the NCLB and the testing regime and the push to assess districts, to assess schools, to assess students, to assess on the basis of narrow test scores are a huge problem," a teacher noted. This should remind us that neoliberalism in education is more than mere economic policy and more than an attempt to impose audit cultures on the public sector and the schools within that sector. Neoliberalism seems to be inherently racializing in its assumptions and foundations as well as its effects (Apple 2006, 2013; see also Lipman 2011; Buras 2014). In its destruction of what might be best seen as "thick democracy" and its recreation of the citizen as a consumer, a "chooser," it makes full, collective participation by an engaged community more difficult (Apple 2006, p. 15).

The school in our study exemplifies the depth and breadth of this effect. Daily life in the school is still partly transformative. But the compromises that "need to be made" and the school's increasing role as a site for middle-class conversion strategies lead to the reproduction of the unequal structure of race relations and a loss of the resources and time needed to maintain the critical work that makes the school a site of counter-hegemonic possibilities.

When the critical multiculturalism program has been set at odds with other fundamental goals or interests pursued by the school, the balancing process has seemed to unevenly weigh against the needs of antiracism. The concessions and compromises that were made—giving up paraprofessionals, but keeping a full-time librarian, choosing a Latino/Latina parent coordinator over an African American representative—had differentiating effects. The tensions between the conflicting needs of its programs (e.g., sustaining diverse antiracist multiculturalism in and from the neighborhood versus the need to bus-in Spanish-speaking students for two-way bilingualism) had similar hidden effects. Thus, the school has had mixed results in challenging racial and social inequalities.

In terms of the politics of official knowledge (Apple 2014), the multicultural antiracist curriculum is no longer uniformly conceived and applied. Some teachers succeed at only expanding the borders of hegemonic domination, struggling to challenge it beyond the limited understanding of racism. A deeply counter-hegemonic orientation seems to be very challenging to fully implement.

This is evident also in the politics of representation. As described, a major shortcoming at the school is its inadequate representation of the African American community: their unequal representation on the professional staff and in parental participation, and the "swallowing up" of their culture, language, and identities as a distinct community. Along these two trajectories, the school has paradoxically reinforced the cultural marginalization and, at times, exclusion of African Americans in US society and has reproduced its unequal and racialized social structure. This was admitted in interviews as a tragic "price" for the successful implementation of the bilingual agenda. A choice had to be made.

But to call this a "choice" risks reinstalling neoliberal forms. Why are such choices forced on so many schools? What is the social and economic context of such choices? Who ultimately benefits in the creation and enforcement of such a context?

The school in no way pretends to be a utopian radical school. But it is "directed toward transcending and fundamentally transforming an unequal and undemocratic society in the here and now" (Tannock et al. 2011, p. 941). Given this, we need to ask some crucial questions: in choosing the compromises to be made, who is compromised, at whose expense? Is the social price too heavy, and does it undermine the project as a counterhegemonic endeavor? Finally, in a context of neoliberal restructuring of the ends and means of schooling, we need to think about what can be done to protect the space that schools like this aim to produce and occupy. Is it inevitable that when faced with the ideological and economic conditions now confronting such schools, these are the only results we should expect? We hope not.

Notes

1   The analyses presented in this chapter are from a larger study on multicultural, bilingual schools educating for democracy and social justice in different national, political, and cultural contexts (Meshulam 2011). The school was selected for the study based on its reputation as an example of "thick" democratic education pursuing social justice and equality. The names of the school and participants are withheld to protect their anonymity. Ethnographic methods were used to collect data during two months of intense research in the school in 2009. Twenty semi-structured, open-ended individual interviews with the school's principal, teachers, a multi-racial group of parents, and founding members, past and present, were conducted. The research also included in-class and out-of-class observations (classroom activities, teacher meetings, school council meetings, recess activity, field trips, and various extracurricular activities) and document

analysis, in particular a number of books composed by school staff and community activists summarizing the first four years of the school's operation. All interviews were audio-recorded and transcribed, and all collected data were triangulated and organized to attain a thick description of the central themes of the study. The interviews focused broadly on questions about: the socio-political and historical contexts of the school's establishment; its structure and governance; its vision and goals, especially regarding bilingualism, multiculturalism, and antiracism; its pedagogy and curriculum; and the kind of critically democratic identity the school seeks to cultivate. Augmenting the interviews and observations was a detailed examination of documents related to the history of the school and the social context of the city in which it is located

2   Currently, there is only one African American on the school's teaching staff.

References

Apple, M. W. (2004). *Ideology and Curriculum* (3rd ed.). New York: Routledge.

Apple, M. W. (2006). *Educating the "Right" Way: Markets, Standards, God, and Inequality* (2nd ed.). New York: Routledge.

Apple, M. W. (2012). *Education and Power* (Revised Routledge Classic ed.). New York: Routledge.

Apple, M. W. (2013). *Can Education Change Society?* New York: Routledge.

Apple, M. W. (2014). *Official Knowledge* (3rd ed.). New York: Routledge.

Apple, M. W., and Beane, J. A. (Eds.). (2007). *Democratic Schools* (2nd ed.). Portsmouth, NH: Heinemann.

Baker, C. (2006). *Foundations of Bilingual Education and Bilingualism* (4th ed.). Clevedon: Multilingual Matters Ltd.

Ball, S. (2003). *Class Strategies and the Education Market*. New York: RoutledgeFalmer.

Banks, J. A. (1981). *Multicultural Education. Theory and Practice*. Boston, MA: Allyn & Bacon.

Banks, J. A., and Banks, C. A. M. (Eds.). (1997). *Multicultural Education. Issues and Perspectives* (3rd ed.). Boston, MA: Allyn & Bacon.

Bhopal, K., and Preston, J. (Eds.). (2012). *Intersectionality and 'Race' in Education*. London: Routledge.

Billingham, C., and Kimelberg, S. M. (2013). Middle-class parents, urban schooling, and the shift from consumption to production of urban space. *Sociological Forum 28* (1): pp. 85–108.

Bourdieu, P. (1984). *Distinction: A Social Critique of the Judgment of Taste*. Cambridge, MA: Harvard University Press.

Buras, K. (2014). *Charter Schools, Race, and Urban Space: Where the Market Meets Grassroots Resistance*. New York: Routledge.

Center for Applied Linguistics. (2016). *Directory of Two-Way Bilingual Immersion Programs in the U.S.* Available at: http://www.cal.org/twi/directory.

Cucchiara, M. (2013). *Marketing Schools, Marketing Cities: Who Wins and Who Loses When Schools Become Urban Amenities*. Chicago, IL: University of Chicago Press.

Fraser, N. (1997). *Justice Interruptus*. New York: Routledge.

Fraser, N. (2010). *Scales of Justice*. New York: Columbia University Press.

Freire, P. (1970). *Pedagogy of the Oppressed*. New York: Herder and Herder.

Hall, S. (1996). Gramsci's relevance for the study of race and ethnicity. In *Stuart Hall: Critical Dialogues in Cultural Studies*. D. Morley and K. H. Chen (Eds.). pp. 411–441. New York: Routledge.

History of Bilingual Education. (1998). *Rethinking Schools 12* (3): pp. 1–2.

Ladson-Billings, G. (1995). "Toward a theory of culturally relevant pedagogy." *American Educational Research Journal* 32(3): pp. 465–491.

Ladson-Billings, G. (2003). New directions in multicultural education: Complexities, boundaries, and critical race theory. In *Handbook of Research on Multicultural Education: Issues and Perspectives*. J. A. Banks and C. A. M. Banks (Eds.). pp. 50–66. San Francisco, CA: Jossey-Bass.

Ladson-Billings, G. (2004). Culture versus citizenship: The challenge of racialized citizenship in the United States. In *Diversity and Citizenship Education*. J. A. Banks (Ed.). pp. 99–126. San Francisco, CA: Jossey-Bass.

Ladson-Billings, G., (2014). "Culturally relevant pedagogy 2.0: a.k.a. the remix." *Harvard Educational Review* 84(1): pp 74–84.

Lipman, P. (2011). *The New Political Economy of Urban Education*. New York: Routledge.

McLaren, P. (1994). White terror and oppositional agency: Towards a critical multiculturalism. In *Multiculturalism. A Critical Reader*. T. H. Goldberg (Ed.). pp. 45–74. Cambridge, MA: Blackwell.

Meshulam, A. (2011). *What Kind of Alternative? Bilingual, Multicultural Schools, as Counterhegemonic Alternatives Educating for Democracy*. PhD diss., University of Wisconsin–Madison.

Meshulam, A., and Apple, M. W. (2010). Israel/Palestine, unequal power, and movements for democratic education. In *Global Crises, Social Justice, and Education*. M. W. Apple (Ed.). pp. 113–161. New York: Routledge.

Mills, C. (1997). *The Racial Contract*. Ithaca, NY: Cornell University Press.

Miner, B. (1991). Taking multicultural, anti-racist education seriously: An interview with Enid Lee. *Rethinking Schools 6* (1): pp. 19–22.

Miner, B. (2013). *Lessons from the Heartland: A Turbulent Half-Century of Public Education in an Iconic American City*. New York: The New Press.

Nieto, S. (2004). *Affirming Diversity. The Sociopolitical Context of Multicultural Education* (4th ed.). Boston/New York: Pearson.

Orfield, G. (2009). *Reviving the Goal of an Integrated Society: A 21st Century Challenge*. Los Angeles, CA: The Civil Rights Project/Proyecto Derechos Civiles at UCLA.

Peterson, B. (1995). A journey toward democracy. In *Democratic Schools*. M. W. Apple and J. A. Beane (Eds.). pp. 58–82. Alexandria, VA: ASCD.

Posey-Maddox, L. (2014). *When Middle-Class Parents Choose Urban Schools: Class, Race, and the Challenge of Equity in Public Education*. Chicago, IL: University of Chicago Press.

Reay, D., Hollingworth, S., Williams, K., Crozier, G., Jamieson, F., James, D., and Beedell, P., (2007). "A darker shade of pale?" Whiteness, the middle classes and multi-ethnic inner city schooling. *Sociology 41* (6): pp. 1041–1060.

Skutnabb-Kangas, T., and García, O. (Eds.). (1995). *Multilingualism for All? General Principles*. Lisse, The Netherlands: Swets and Zeitlinger.

Tannock, S., James, D., and Torres, C. A. (2011). Radical education and the common school: A democratic alternative. Review Symposium. *British Journal of Sociology of Education 32* (6): pp. 939–952.

Thomas, P. W., and Collier, P. V. (2002). *A National Study of School Effectiveness for Language Minority Students' Long-Term Academic Achievement*. Santa Cruz, CA: Center for Research on Education, Diversity and Excellence, University of California-Santa Cruz.

Tolan, T. (2003). *Riverwest: A Community History*. Milwaukee, WI: Past Press and COA.

US Census Bureau. (2008). State & County Quickfacts. http://quickfacts.census.gov/qfd/states/. Accessed 09/05/09

US Department of Education. (2016). The State of Racial Diversity in the Educator Workforce. www2.ed.gov/rschstat/eval/highered/racial-diversity/state-racial-diversity-workforce.pdf. Accessed 01/20/17

Wong, T-H. (2002). *Hegemonies Compared*. New York: RoutledgeFalmer.

Year One. (1989). Unpublished School Document.

3

STRUGGLING FOR THE LOCAL

Money, Power, and the Possibilities of Victories in the Politics of Education

Eleni Schirmer and Michael W. Apple

Introduction

The struggles over the meanings of democracy not just in theory but in actual practice occur at multiple levels and in multiple sites. But in all too many places these battles do not take place on a level playing field. Increasingly, their money and power give advocates of "thin" democracy an advantage that is difficult to overcome. The focus of a good deal of critically oriented work has been larger arenas of contest. Yet, one thing that the Right has been teaching us is that the *local* is equally as important, especially in building "new common-sense" understandings of democracy as individual choice in a competitive market. The significance of this focus on the local is the subject of this chapter. We tell the stories of local defeats and victories on the terrain of democratic representation and voice in key educational bodies. And we ask ourselves to think more seriously about the role of mobilizations and who the actors are in these contests. But in order to understand this, we also need to remember that the local does not stand alone; it has very real ideological and economic relations that surround it. Thus, our first task is to situate the local in this larger context.

Hegemony, Money, and Power

The dueling requirements of capitalism and democracy narrate one of history's most vibrant threads. Especially since the economic slump beginning in the 1970s, the snarl between these forces have migrated from one sector to another, like a recess brawl rolling across a playground (McNally 2011). The crisis of one decade lurches into the next, effectively delaying the fundamental conflict that undergirds each crisis: capitalism's needs for market liberation and democracy's needs for social liberation, forces often at direct odds with each other (Fraser 2015; Streeck 2014). Thus, billowing inflation rates of the 1970s gave way to public debt crises the next decade; and by the 1990s, private credit seemed to flow without limits, until the global economic collapse of 2008. How have these crises impacted education, and what have they meant for the struggle for democracy?

Since the 1970s, each shift in the economy ushered in a collapse; the welfare state seemingly cannot hold. First, labor markets buckled.[1] Then public institutions, choked off from revenue and saddled with rising debt, began to wither. Then the private credit market sputtered and, in 2008, crashed, as those dispossessed from the welfare state scrambled to shelter themselves from the mercurial economy by purchasing homes, health care, higher education—resources the state no longer provided. Yet, the unregulated credit system that enabled this spending was shoddily managed and hardly regulated; its breakdown caused the "Great Recession" of 2008. To mitigate the worst of the ensuing economic collapse, policy actors rigged a "trickle-up" system to prevent the viscous tide of the free market from sweeping away those firms "too big to fail" (Prasad 2012). Meanwhile millions, apparently too poor to matter, watched their homes, savings, and pensions wash away (Grusky 2011). Perhaps most significantly, those dispossessed lost their trust in a government that supposedly concerned itself with their well-being (Fraser 2015).

Over the next decade, when presented with opportunities to elect self-proclaimed "radical outsider" candidates, many voters, discouraged by both capitalism and democracy, seized the chance to do so (e.g., Cramer 2016). Yet, despite a new vintage of political leadership at the helm, little evidence suggests the transmuting crises have stopped unfolding (e.g., Streeck 2017). As we shall see in this chapter, the crises of democracy has shifted out of the global financial markets and increasingly into local-political contests, such as small town school board elections. Examining how political crises have migrated into these spaces offers rich lessons for future struggles for democracy, especially in education.

As the economy has changed, so have the identities of the populace. Even to themselves, workers became citizens became taxpayers became consumers became debtors. Simultaneously, the identities of capital shifted; legal rulings give corporations the power of personhood (Brown 2015). And the animus of late capitalism—often called neoliberalism—formed alliances with neoconservative and authoritarian populist forces, infusing a religious ethos into its austere regime (Apple 2006). By the Great Recession in 2008, the key protagonists of the conflicts between capitalism and democracy were no longer workers versus employers or citizens versus bankers, as they had been in previous decades, but rather a complex tangle of global financial firms, governments, and occasionally, the electorate (Ferguson et al. 2015; Hacker and Pierson 2010; Streeck 2011). Thus, on all sides, the struggle for democracy is both a political project, involving the terms of economic and material distribution, and a subjective project over the terms of personhood and social meaning.

Education, of course, is a central arena for these snarls. Because of its character as both a political and ideological project, it provides a particularly important site for the struggle over democracy. What's more, as a project of the state, the shifting political economy has significantly impacted the contours of education (Althusser 1971; Apple 2012). The onslaught of budget cuts has forced school districts to financialize their assets, ranging from intricate investment schemes, as we shall see in the next few pages, to the privatization of services from supplementary education services to full-blown takeovers (Ball 2007; Ball and Junemann 2012; Burch 2006; Lipman 2011).

Though the influence of corporate and conservative forces in education represents a growing trend, it is far from inevitable. Too often, analyses critical of the growing conservative agenda in education depict an overly deterministic model of the politics of education, in which financial influence necessarily determines political outcomes (e.g., Anderson and Donchik 2014; Reckhow and Snyder 2014; Scott and Jabbar 2014; Scott 2009). While such models offer crucial explanations of the mechanics of the growing corporate influence in education politics, they often minimize the contingent nature of power, thus presenting a highly deterministic model of politics. In doing so, these analyses misrepresent the central calculus of political dominance, what Antonio Gramsci calls "hegemony" (Gramsci 1971), and therefore overlook possibilities for interruption.

Briefly put, Gramsci understood hegemonic control as a key way in which dominant groups maintain control of power through not only economic and political mechanisms, but also through cultural and ideological means, by constructing "common sense." Common sense, for Gramsci, is not an objective or universal set of truths, but rather a dominating system of logic that is developed and presented by dominant groups in conjunction with specific interests that speaks to real needs or fears of people. Therefore, hegemony is in some essence contractual, in that it fulfills certain needs of people, and it makes sense for people to subscribe to it, even if that choice is not fully conscious. Yet, it is possible for people to move out of hegemonic control, politically, culturally, and ideologically by gaining consciousness. As Gramsci states, "the conscious realization of being part of particular hegemonic force which is the first stage towards a further progressive self-consciousness" (Gramsci 1971, p. 333). Power, therefore, becomes a contest and process, not a static product yielded by one force alone. In fact, the subtle and contingent forms of power are part of what entails Gramsci's "war of position"—the slow, continuous, and often hidden efforts to gain influence, power, and to construct the elements of common sense. This differs from Gramsci's "war of maneuver," the outright blows that occur between competing forces.

The subtle and seemingly invisible infrastructure of politics, especially those in education, has provided a crucial source of strength for rightist movements over the past four decades, as evinced by its high-profile leaders, such as the oil mogul billionaires Koch brothers and the US Secretary of Education Betsy DeVos (e.g., Mayer 2016). The Koch brothers, DeVos, and others have led the charge to invest in research centers, university posts, policy think tanks, and media outlets as a means to develop the ideological agenda necessary to achieve their political goals—what Gramsci would call investing in the "war of position." Through this system of research, legal architecture, policy advocacy and media aims, these groups take seriously the importance of developing an ideological agenda in order to establish political dominance. For them, no space has been too small or too ephemeral to be of import (see also Schirmer and Apple 2016a).

Of course, these strategies couple with more overt and direct tactics to gain political influence, such as lobbying, campaign work, and political organizing to achieve short-term electoral victories. Yet here too, conservative movements have attended to small political spaces as a means to develop their influence. Despite losing the president's office in 2008, over the following years, conservatives in the United States turned their focus to down-ticket, local level elections. This strategy, coupled with leveraging economic anxieties and racial antagonisms heightened by President Barack Obama's election from two years before, allowed conservatives to gain control of state houses, governors' seats and legislatures across the country in 2010 (Skocpol and Hertel-Fernandez 2016). Indeed, the process of focusing on the local did not stop at the state level. Over the past seven years, school boards, particularly in small towns, have provided an important site of skirmish for forming the common sense of education (Reckhow et al. 2016; Schirmer and Apple 2016b). The following analysis of two small town school board elections in politically mixed counties, in "purple" states, show just how important these local levels are for building common sense.

In this chapter, we examine two school boards elections in politically mixed, mid-sized US cities, one in Kenosha, Wisconsin in 2013 and another in Jefferson County, Colorado in 2016. Both of these school board elections defied the traditional school board electoral processes, which are typically somewhat sleepy, nonpartisan, parochial affairs, with low voter turnout and minimal campaign financing. Yet in both Kenosha and Jefferson County, the school board elections became high-profile arenas of struggle for the larger political and economic battles endemic to state and national politics. In Kenosha, Wisconsin the 2008 economic recession caused a financial collapse of the school district, making it vulnerable to neoliberal reformers inside the school district, as well as outside the school district, thanks to conservative Governor Scott Walker's election in 2010. When Walker curtailed the collective bargaining power of teachers' unions and issued further budget cuts to public education, an activist-minded school board took it upon themselves to protect the district's public education system by continuing to recognize teachers' contracts, thereby defying key provisions of Walker's assault on public education. This triggered the attention of nationally grounded conservative groups, such as Americans for Prosperity, who quickly jumped into the election and backed a conservative challenger to the incumbent school. Armed with corporate financial reserves, the conservatives in Kenosha seized control of the school board.

In Jefferson County, Colorado progressive forces similarly challenged the rising conservative agenda, again attracting the attention of corporate political action committees (PACs), such as Americans for Prosperity. However, unlike Kenosha, Wisconsin, progressives in Colorado defeated conservative forces—at least temporarily. What made Jefferson County, Colorado different from Kenosha? As we shall see, progressives in Jefferson County were able to form broad-based coalitions, rooted in cultural and ideological commitments to democracy, as well as economic distribution. In this way, the struggle for justice grounded itself in systems of recognition *and* redistribution (Fraser 1997). Unlike Kenosha, teachers, parents, and students in Jefferson County developed activist networks and engaged in widespread mobilization to defend not just the structure of public education, but also its contents. These two cases reveal the deep war of position adopted by the conservatives. But it also shows the fragile and conditional alliances that these power bases are formed upon, and how they can be interrupted.

Kenosha, Wisconsin

Kenosha, Wisconsin is a small Midwest city whose economy has long depended on its automobile industry. Its relative prosperity and its respect for the economic and cultural rights of workers disintegrated due to the repeated economic crises that "rust belt" cities have experienced. In the past decade, a bad situation became worse. Global political-economic changes had major effects in Kenosha following the 2008 financial collapse. And a crisis in school funding and the politics surrounding it came center stage. Kenosha offered a situation ripe with possibilities for a successful neoliberal intervention at the local level. Understanding how this happened requires that we look more closely at the politics of local corporate involvement.

In the early 2000s, declining state aid to public education, coupled with rising health care costs, ushered school districts such as Kenosha into unstable financial markets of private investment. Facing rising health care costs and declining state aid, the Kenosha school district eagerly sought solutions for its budget shortfalls. When the district's trusted financial advisor, David Noack, presented collateralized debt obligations (CDOs) as the alleged best investment possible to the school board in June 2006, members listened eagerly. As Noack explained, this investment would require the district to borrow large amounts of money from an overseas bank, and then purchase a "collection of bonds from 105 of the most reputable companies that would pay the school board a small return every quarter" (Duhigg and Dougherty 2008). These collections of corporate bonds would be sold to the school district by the Royal Bank of Canada, which had a relationship with Noack's company (Duhigg and Dougherty 2008). The more than 300 pages of documents presented to school board members on this complicated financial mechanism seemed impenetrable. But board members quickly became convinced to accept the plan, given both the financial success such mechanisms had yielded for New York investment bankers and the assurance presented by Noack to the school board that it would take "15 Enrons" for this investment to fail (Flores 2011c). As Kenosha school board member Marc Hujik told the *New York Times*, "Everyone knew New York guys were making tons of money on these kinds of deals. It wasn't implausible that we could make money, too" (Duhigg and Dougherty 2008).

What could go wrong? Unfortunately, all too much. Mr. Noack's description of CDOs failed to encompass an accurate portrayal of the risks at hand, nor did it account for the growing instabilities of global capitalism. If only a mere 6% of the bonds defaulted, the school district would lose all its money (Duhigg and Dougherty 2008, para. 22). What's more, Noack and his employing investment firm, Stifel, Nicolaus and Company, failed to communicate how risky the school district's actual investments were. The investments performed poorly from the outset; within the first 36 days of closing the account, 10% of the investments were placed on negative watch. None of this information, however, was communicated to the Kenosha school board or the four other Wisconsin school districts that had collectively invested $200 million dollars in Noack's plan. As Hujik, himself a financial advisor in addition to his role on the school board, told the press, "I've never read the prospectus. ... We had all our questions answered satisfactorily by Dave Noack, so I wasn't worried" (Duhigg and Dougherty 2008). This statement makes evident the assumption of expert knowledge bestowed to financial elites, obviating local and democratically elected decision makers of their own deliberations—a hallmark feature of managerial regimes (Apple 2006; Clarke and Newman 1997). More significantly, the school board's pursuit of high-risk, speculative investments to finance the school district's operating budget revealed the larger trend of neoliberalism: state divestment from public institutions. Declining state aid to public education, coupled with rising health care costs, ushered school districts such as Kenosha into unstable financial markets of private investment.

After several months, administrators at Kenosha Unified School District (KUSD) and the other districts began receiving notices that their investments had suffered a series of downgrades and were on the verge of failure. By 2010, the remaining investments lost all value, and the lender seized the trust's assets. The financial management firm was charged with fraud; it was the first time a private securities firm had been charged for fraudulent dealings with a government entity. The US Securities and Exchange Commission alleged that David Noack in particular had "misrepresented the risk of [the CDOs] and failed to disclose 'material facts' to the districts" (Flores 2011c). The school districts had not only lost all of the $200 million they had invested, including the $163 million they had borrowed. They also suffered severe credit rating downgrades. This loss of funds, in addition to the massive shortfalls in state aid of 2011, painted a bleak financial picture for KUSD. The financial crisis also provided extremely fertile ground for more conservative policy changes in the district. As the school district scrambled for financial restitution, they became more willing to embrace further funding cuts and program streamlining. They searched for a new superintendent of schools who could handle this crisis.

Economic Crisis Meets Education Reformer

When Michele Hancock, the new superintendent, arrived at Kenosha in 2010, the district was still financially wobbling from its 2008 collapse. Hancock, a former "human capital officer" from the Rochester, New York school district, was immersed in the corporate management of education (see e.g., Ravitch 2013). Within a few months of the start of her tenure as superintendent, Hancock issued her "Transformation Plan" to KUSD. This several hundred page document offered an analysis and roadmap for Hancock's education vision, largely centered around education reform buzzwords such as building "life and career skills," deploying "relevant global knowledge," and increasing the use of technology in the classroom (Clegg et al. 2013, p. 40).

Yet the gap between Hancock's rhetoric and the actual practices in schools felt jolting to many teachers and community members in Kenosha. "It was simply too much at one time," proclaimed an incumbent school board member (Flores 2013). Though the school district was still struggling from the disastrous financial investments it had been advised to make, the Transformation Plan proposed investing in increased technology for the school district, such as laptops, tablets, and online textbooks (Hallow 2011). Meanwhile, Hancock called for massive staff layoffs. Although Hancock herself earned a salary over $320,000, near the end of the 2010–2011 school year Hancock issued layoff notices to over 300 teachers in the district (Flores 2011a; Smith 2014). In addition to providing devastating job losses to the town's largest employer and unionized workforce, the reduction in staff changed the education provided across the district. Class sizes rose. Foreign language teachers were replaced by the online instruction program, Rosetta Stone (Flores 2012; McDarrison 2013). In a school district with a very quickly growing Spanish-speaking population, the decision to eliminate foreign language instructors and replace them with computer programs signaled a sharp divestment from some of the community's key resources. The loss of jobs, increased class sizes, and changes to curriculum priorities frustrated parents and teachers alike.

Furthermore, Hancock's Transformation Plan had few positive effects on educational outcomes. An independent curriculum audit conducted in 2013 (Clegg et al. 2013) revealed very little progress in the actual adoption of technology by students or in pursuit of the district's educational goals. More seriously, the curriculum audit suggested that the Transformation Plan did very little to address the significant race and class inequalities in the school district. (Clegg et al. 2013, p. 25). The audit of the Transformation Plan revealed that teachers and administrators disproportionately suspended Black and Latino students while under-enrolling them in special curricular offerings or advanced programs. Programs specifically designed for English Language Learners (ELLs)—largely Latino students—were grossly under-resourced (Clegg et al. 2013, p. 2015).

What's more, students of color and low-income students had less access to the district's school choice program. KUSD had developed a well-respected district sponsored school choice program, offering several public charter schools, an open-enrollment policy, and an in-district transfer policy (Flores 2013). However, the school choice programs were not equally accessible to all Kenosha families. First, many of the public charter schools were not served by the district's school bus system. Second, selection into choice programs was determined by an elective lottery, which imposed a language and education barrier to underrepresented families who did not have sufficient background information necessary to participate (Clegg et al. 2013; Brighouse and Schouten 2014). To summarize, under Hancock's leadership, racial and class inequalities in the school district got no better or even worsened. While Hancock and her administration did not independently cause any of the economic preconditions for this reorganization—in either the economic collapse or the district's financial response—they responded with the inflection of what one of us has called the "new managerial" class (Apple 2006), prioritizing efficiency over equity.

Kenosha's Education Reformer and the Neoliberal State

The KUSD administration's adoption of an austerity regime—laying off staff, while simultaneously increasing investments in technology and administration, all the while using the economic downturn to justify the rollback of public services, had other very significant effects. Rather than defending schools as vital social institutions, public education became defined in terms of efficiencies, returns on investment, and profit margins (Lipman 2011; Saltman 2007, 2009).

Between 2010 and 2013, the Kenosha school district followed the classic neoliberal roadmap: financial collapse provided justification to reorganize elements of the state, altering both the content of the social services and their organization. This reorganization placed new premiums on efficiency, market nimbleness, and choice as the central mechanisms of social provision.

In the meantime, the dissatisfaction with Hancock's leadership dovetailed with rising discontent about Governor Walker's cuts to public sector institutions and workers' rights (Hallow 2011). In the first month of his term as governor, Governor Walker enacted an aggressive neoliberal reform across the state of Wisconsin, stripping all but the most basic collective bargaining rights of nearly all public sector unions in the state, and imposing rigorous—and often prohibitive—requirements for union recertification. Despite a fervent fight-back and a historic uprising, Walker and his administration eventually forced the bill through the Senate and the Assembly. Within weeks, Walker issued the 2011–2013 budget, which imposed more cuts to public services, more cuts to public protections, and more cuts to public employees. While the swiftness and severity of Wisconsin Act

10 and the 2011–2013 budget were unique, the tenor and direction of the attacks paralleled national and international trends which curtailed public sector employees, institutions, and education.

Alarmed by the direction of both Walker and Hancock, the Kenosha school board stepped forward to protect the rights of teachers. Mobilized labor and public education supporters took action themselves in the Kenosha school board in 2011. Yet the mobilization against Walker also galvanized conservative forces in Kenosha. The statewide campaign to "Recall Walker" spread to recalling other conservative legislators around the state, in order for Democrats to regain a majority in the State's House and Senate. However, conservatives mobilized their own defensives, and also began recall campaigns of their own. One of their targets was Kenosha's Democratic state senator, Bob Wirch, a lifelong Kenosha resident who had served as a public official in the district for the past 20 years (Olson 2011). Wirch had been an outspoken opponent of Walker's school voucher plan, which had targeted Kenosha as a site for expansion. "By proposing to expand the school voucher plan," Wirch stated, "the Governor is ignoring the voices of people of Kenosha" (Steinkraus 2011). When it became clear that Walker and his administration were unwilling to negotiate the extreme budget cuts and legal changes to public employees' rights proposed in the bill first called the Budget Repair bill, now known as WI Act 10, Wirch and 12 other Democratic state senators left the state for nearly two weeks (Nichols 2012).

Unsurprisingly, this tactic enraged conservatives around the state. As a response, a group of conservative citizens in Kenosha, dubbed "Taxpayers to Recall Robert Wirch," began a recall campaign of their own (Steinkraus 2011). The campaign to recall Wirch attracted the first out-of-state groups to Kenosha. More than half of the campaign donations came from out-of-state organizations (Olson 2011). Though Wirch survived his attempted recall election, the campaign itself made conservatives even more active in the area and stimulated national interest in Kenosha politics.

Meanwhile, members of the Kenosha school board took careful note of the unfolding state-level political drama. After the failed attempts to recall both the governor and enough Republican senators to reclaim Democratic control of the state legislature, liberal political elites shifted their strategy to the legal overturn of Act 10, the law that curtailed collective bargaining. In September 2012, municipal judge Juan Colas ruled that portions of Act 10 were indeed unconstitutional. This meant that municipal employers, such as school boards, were no longer legally prohibited from bargaining with teachers' unions, as Act 10 mandated. This fact is crucial to understanding conservative national groups' focus on Kenosha.

Members of the Kenosha school board seized this opportunity to restore bargaining with their district teachers' union. In October 2012, they approved employment contracts, rather than mandating teachers' adherence to the employee handbooks, which had become the common replacement. Whereas handbooks unilaterally dictated teachers' employment conditions, contracts were produced through mutual negotiations between teachers and the school board. In a climate of increasing conservative legal hostility to public education and labor unions, the Kenosha school board's willingness to bargain contracts with the teachers' union went against the political current and challenged the "new common sense" that conservative modernizers were seeking to create as the dominant forms of social and educational understanding.

In addition to preserving teachers' rights to a union, the school board also opposed Walker's plans to expand school voucher programs across the state. This too was crucial. Kenosha was one of nine school districts in the state that Walker targeted for a voucher expansion plan in February 2013 (Flores 2013). Despite the governor's proposal, the board unanimously passed a resolution opposing any expansion of vouchers to the district, declaring that voucher programs circumvented important mechanisms of public accountability, such as school boards. Expanding vouchers, school leaders declared, would take money away from public schools and siphon these funds to private schools. These schools, they continued, were not subject to the same curricular standards, regulation, or accessibility requirements as were public schools (Beebe 2013). In the face of conservative legislative attacks on teachers' unions and aggressive expansion of school choice programs, the Kenosha school board members took it upon themselves to defend these institutions. However, their decision made them political targets for the growing conservative movement in the state.

Ideological Clash in School Board Elections

School choice supporters and anti-collective bargaining forces coalesced in Kenosha. Both programs attracted the Koch-funded organization Americans for Prosperity to Kenosha. In the winter of 2013, Americans for Prosperity held a panel discussion promoting school choice in Kenosha. Though their previous activity in Wisconsin largely related to the 2011 state senate recall elections, now the group turned their attention to shifting the agenda around public schools. In essence, Americans for Prosperity argued that both the "public" and teachers' unions were jointly threatening "democracy," and school boards were key participants in this threat ("Board Opposed to Private School Voucher Proposal" 2013). Americans for Prosperity turned to Kenosha to form new "commonsense" links between school choice politics and reduced union rights for public sector employees.

At the same time, the Right also pursued legal sanctions against the resistant school board. Within a few months of the school board's approval of teachers' collective bargaining agreements, the board came under fire. The school district's legal standing for bargaining with the teachers' union was shaken in September 2013, when the Wisconsin Supreme Court overturned Judge Colas's ruling against the constitutionality of Act 10. Immediately, two anti-union teachers in the district sued the school board and Kenosha's teachers' union, the Kenosha

Education Association (KEA), for violating Act 10. The conservative, libertarian public interest law firm Wisconsin Institute for Law and Liberty (WILL), funded by the conservative Bradley Foundation, backed the anti-union teachers' lawsuit (Murphy 2011). The teachers, one of whom had recently left her job teaching in the school district, sued the school board and the union for collecting union dues through automatic dues withdrawal. Overlooking the fact that teachers' unions have been among the strongest supporters of teachers in their historical struggle to be treated as professionals, one of the anti-union teachers, Kristi Lacroix, wrote in an op-ed to the *Milwaukee Journal Sentinel* that "teachers are not blue-collar laborers; they are academic professionals like lawyers, scientists and engineers. Industrial-style union representation does not advance the respect that educators deserve in Wisconsin or nationwide" (Lacroix 2013, para. 7). In addition to deeming the class associations of labor unions irrelevant, Lacroix disputed the political direction of the union, particularly its opposition to Act 10 and Governor Walker ("Former Teacher: I Know My Own Worth" 2015).

In their case against the school district, these teachers claimed legal standing as "taxpayers." Notably, this legal standing positioned the plaintiffs as pseudo-employers of the district teachers, authorized to audit and direct salary funds. As "taxpayers," the teachers positioned themselves as customers, entitled to public benefits in a fee-for-service model. This framework renders an individual as sole proprietor of his or her skills and resources, with the unfettered right to market these skills. The individual owes nothing to society, but rather is entitled to dictate the terms of one's social participation based on responsibilities as a taxpayer. Furthermore, the possessive individual seeks freedom from state-enforced regulations. Kenosha displays the ways that neoliberal ideology does not simply follow the interests of corporate actors and their commitment to profit. It also restructures the common-sense notions of teachers about their rights as workers.

Yet, in spite of the plaintiffs' extensive backing from outside conservative organizations, the courts initially denied WILL and Lacroix's attempt to void the union contract. Having failed to legally overturn the school board's decision to continue to extend teachers' contracts, right-wing groups looked to take over the school board itself. After a court-ordered injunction stalled WILL's lawsuit, Lacroix's father, Dan Wade, former Kenosha chief of police, decided to run for a seat on the district's school board. In the February primary, Jo Ann Taube, the incumbent board president and union-supported candidate, earned the most votes. Yet, the tide turned between the February primary and the April election. During those weeks, Wade and fellow conservative candidate Gary Kunich received support from the Koch-funded conservative organizations American Majority and Americans for Prosperity (Smith 2014). Almost overnight, glossy flyers and yard signs for Wade and Kunich appeared on the streets of Kenosha. In addition to providing campaign contributions directly to the candidates, these groups conducted their own organizing, bringing in outside staff to carry out door knocking and phone calling to Kenosha voters.

Despite the dissent among some Kenosha voters, the conservatives defeated Taube and the other union-supporting candidate in the April 2014 elections. The increase in advertising, phone banking, and outside field organizers changed the nature of the district's elections, from a neighbors-voting-for-neighbors brand of politics to one in which major corporate and philanthropic money continually transformed the politics. This not only affected the 2014 school board race, but also generated a far more conservative common sense. The school board's willingness to take a politically oppositional stance threatened conservative organizations, triggering their interest and persistence in the district's political affairs. What started out as a local issue became a national testing ground for conservative mobilizations (see Apple 1996, for other examples). And the conservative mobilizations won. But such victories are not always guaranteed, as exemplified in Jefferson County, Colorado.

Curriculum Control in Colorado

For Americans for Prosperity, their victory in Kenosha only marked the beginning of their interest in school board elections. In late summer of 2015, field organizers for Americans for Prosperity marched through the streets of Jefferson County, Colorado (known as Jeffco), knocking on doors and leafleting voters about the upcoming school board recall election. Like Kenosha, Jeffco had become deeply entangled in political battles, and the school board became a key site for these struggles. Indeed, the similarities between Kenosha and Jeffco were notable. Like Kenosha, Jeffco had a mix of conservative and liberal tendencies. But unlike Kenosha, public school supporters in Jeffco successfully fought back American for Prosperity's hold on the elected school board. What happened?

Jefferson County spans nearly 800 miles in the center of Colorado. It abuts Denver to the east, its northern border opens to the Rocky Mountains, just south of Boulder, and its southern border dips below Buffalo Peaks. The county encompasses urban, suburban, and rural parts of Colorado, as well as growing Latino populations east of Denver, wealthy suburban communities in the southern stretches of the county, and small mountain towns in its northern edge. Its geographic and demographic mix provides a political template for the state as the whole. As one political analyst told news reporters, "As Jefferson County goes so goes the state of Colorado, that's why the stakes are so high here because it is a leading indicator or a bellwether … it is ground zero for all kinds of political wars but at the moment that political war is over the public education system" (*CBS Denver* 2015). And the political indeterminacy of Colorado as a state has made it a key battleground state, especially in national election years.

What Jeffco is to Colorado, Colorado is to the nation. Like Jeffco, Colorado bobbles between red and blue. Its possibilities of purple are foreign to many beyond the state's borders, as political polarization across the country heightens.

Though the state voted respectively for Democrats Barack Obama and Hilary Clinton in the three most recent presidential elections, it has provided fertile incubation for Tea Party movement leaders (Colorado State Election Results 2017; *New York Times* 2010). The state as a whole has a fierce and long-lasting libertarian streak that bends towards fiscal conservatism and social liberalism. By and large, Coloradans want their government to do two things: keep taxes low and keep marijuana legal, regardless of whether Democrats or Republicans are at the helm.

Hence, when a proposal to increase school funding bubbled up across the state in 2013, a commotion ensued. That fall, the big ticket item on the Colorado ballot was a proposition to increase funding for the state's public education system. The proposed measure, known as Amendment 66, would alter the state's flat 4.6% income tax system into a two-tiered system based on income. Residents making $75,000 per year or less would see their tax burden increase to 5% of their income; taxes would rise to 5.9% of the income of residents with incomes above $75,000 a year. If passed, this increase in tax revenue would provide increased funding for high-poverty urban and rural schools, expand pre-kindergarten options, create more support English language learners, extend the school day and school year, and update technology in schools (Brown 2013).

Regardless of funding realities, the measure faced an uphill battle. Similar measures proposed in 2008 and again in 2011 were soundly defeated, revealing Colorado's deeply entrenched small-government and anti-tax character (Healy 2013). In the early 1990s, Colorado passed a Taxpayer Bill of Rights that limits government growth and tax increases, and mandates that all budget surpluses get sent back to taxpayers in rebate checks. This measure has provided a national model for small government and conservative groups nationwide. And it has infused "citizen as taxpayer" sentiments into the common sense of the state, blurring the boundaries between liberalism and conservatism (Policy Basics: Taxpayer Bill of Rights (TABOR) 2015). In 2013, neither conservatives nor the state's liberals could be convinced to vote for Amendment 66. As a university student at liberal University of Colorado-Boulder and a registered Democrat told the *New York Times*, "I felt a little guilty when I voted against [Amendment 66]. It tugged at my heartstrings," she confessed. "I just don't always believe that money solves problems. It's difficult for me to write a blank check to the government" (Healy 2013). Her sentiments spoke to many across the state.

Despite a plague of cash-strapped schools, the measure to increase their budgets failed across the state by high margins. It failed in liberal leaning areas like Telluride that had voted for President Obama the year before and against Tea Party attempts to take over the Democratic controlled legislature. It failed in financially struggling areas where the amendment's victory would have increased funds for the public schools. And, unsurprisingly, it failed in conservative areas. The state's anti-tax ethos proved more durable than the state's recent drift towards liberal politicians on the national level.

Despite its failure, Amendment 66 nonetheless yielded electoral consequences in 2013. As the big-ticket item in an otherwise small-stakes election, voters turned out to the polls to register their refusal to be taxed more, casting "no" votes on Amendment 66. But down-ticket races, like local school board elections, bore the windfall. This is what happened in Jefferson County, Colorado, when three conservative school board members were elected to the school board. Though the election of a conservative school board was a shift in direction for the county, it was consistent with the state's electoral winds. It was also congruent with the growing conservative strategy to look to municipal and county elections, frequently in suburban areas beyond the purview of urban political forces.

For example, in the neighboring Douglass County, a county packed full of wealthy Denver suburbs, conservative school board reformers took over the school board in 2009. In only a few years' time, the Douglass County school board deployed an increasingly common sequence: it sidelined the teachers' union, expanded vouchers and charters, enacted market-based pay for teachers, and encouraged schools to compete for students. These changes disturbed a number of parents and community members, who tried to elect pro-public education candidates to the school board to replace the conservative stronghold. The possibility of losing control of this model conservative district caught the attention of national groups, such as Americans for Prosperity, who donated more than $350,000 to the school board campaign. Douglass County's conservative school board was subsequently re-elected (Simon 2013).

Therefore, given the conservative energy roused by Amendment 66 across the state and the example of neighboring Douglass County, it perhaps wasn't surprising that Jefferson County's school board flipped to a conservative majority. The newly elected members, Ken Witt, John Newkirk, and Julie Williams, ran on a conservative slate and won their races by high margins. Their election created a new majority on the board, and with it, the promise of changes for the district (*Colorado Public Radio* 2013). The new members campaigned on their opposition to Amendment 66, as well as proposals to expand charter options in the district and move teacher salaries to pay-for-performance models. The new school board members in Jefferson County, in other words, wanted their districts to become more like Douglass County.

Yet, the change in school board leadership did not sit well with many teachers and community members in Jefferson County. Two days after the election, Jefferson County's beloved superintendent, Cindy Stevenson, announced she would retire at the end of the year. Stevenson began working in Jeffco schools as a first grade teacher in 1971, and had served as Jeffco superintendent for 12 years. She had won state and national recognition for her work in the district, and was admired and respected by many teachers and staff (Vaccarelli 2013). Audience members rose twice to give her a standing ovation for her work. Stevenson wept while she announced her decision and thanked the community for all their support. Her decision to leave worried many teachers, who were sad to lose a respected leader and troubled by the new management at the helm. One principal told the *Denver Post* that he was sad to see Stevenson go, as she had been an important mentor to him. He was also worried about the direction of the new board. "I'm concerned what the real agenda is with the new board members" (Torres 2013). Though many teachers felt wary and uncertain about the new board's vision for the school district, they were willing to keep an open mind. Stevenson said she would spend the remainder of her time as superintendent helping to establish transition teams to a new leader and to work with the board. The president of the teachers' union, too, expressed an openness to work with the new board, despite concerns. "There is a lot of apprehension about the changes that are going on in Jeffco," she said. "But as an association, our position has been that we believe in collaboration" (Vaccarelli 2013).

Indeed, cooperation characterized the relationship between the previous board and the teachers' union. Teachers endured pay cuts with little pushback during the tough budget cycles of the previous years. And although the broader political and economic climate of the state didn't seem to value teachers, in Jeffco teachers at least were shown the dignity of collaboration. Though they hadn't had a raise since 2010, Jeffco teachers had worked closely with the board and Superintendent Stevenson to develop a new teacher compensation model. Watching the changes happen in the neighboring Douglass County, however, made clear to teachers in Jeffco just how easily working conditions can change. When the new Jeffco school board was elected in November, teachers were open, but apprehensive. Would the new board continue to work collaboratively to develop a teacher evaluation program and negotiate a new contract, or would the interests and concerns of teachers get tossed aside as the new board charged forward on its own path?

It didn't take long for teachers to determine the answer to these questions. Just three months after the election of the new school board to office, the superintendent announced at a packed school board meeting she would be leaving, not at the end of the year, but in the next few weeks. She turned to face the audience and spoke with a tear-choked voice, "Superintendents need to be able to lead and manage. ... I can't lead or manage because I'm not trusted or respected by this board of education. ... I can't make decisions and I can't lead and I can't move the district forward. ... I will be gone before the end of month." The crowd rose to stand as she spoke, giving her a standing ovation. Someone at the back of the room yelled, "The board's a piece of crap!" and people standing nearby nodded, as if the man had spoken their mind. Stevenson thanked the community, and reiterated her connection to them. "And I just want you to know how much your being here and how much our years together have mattered to me." Following her decision, a member of the board minority stood up and questioned the new direction of the board. She said, "I want to know, and let's be really clear: this is about the three-board majority. And I want to ask the three members of the board, how this decision is good for 85,000 kids?" The dozens of people standing in the room cheered at this statement (Transparency Jeffco 2014).

Though the teachers and community members may have lost a trusted leader, they did not lose their voice. Over the next weeks, a vocal group of concerned parents and residents began to publicize the growing chasm between the board majority's direction and the community's will. In early February, the district published the results from a community outreach survey, which queried Jeffco community members about their budget priorities. The survey, which the school district posted online for roughly a week, garnered 13,000 responses, predominantly from parents in Jeffco, as well as teachers and community members. The survey asked questions about the community's budget priorities—what programs and initiatives the community most supported. The responses to the survey were overwhelming and nearly unanimous. The top initiatives community members most strongly supported were increasing pay for teachers, lowering class size in primary schools, maintaining curriculum electives, and funding an all-day kindergarten for low-income families. The initiatives the community most strongly disapproved of were expanding charter and options schools (Community Outreach Survey Information 2014).

The unanimity of the survey results assured many in the community that they were not alone in their vision for building strong Jeffco public schools. Yet, community members feared the board was not taking their concerns and priorities seriously. They began to organize. A small group of parents and community members formed a non-profit group called "Support Jeffco Kids" to communicate to the public what was happening in the board. As one member described their work, "SJK was formed from strong volunteers … with a desire to keep those who supported public education in constant communication and not have to continually rebuild the network each year when we need to take action. We recognized that it was difficult to participate and stay informed with the many meetings on top of parenting and other life obligations" ("Why 3A & 3B?" 2016). According to these parents, they had "learned the necessity of staying involved after the results of the 2013 election where not many volunteers showed up to help." They began actively blogging, writing letters to the school board, and coordinating community meetings to inform people what was happening in the district. As the board began to act with less transparency and democratic engagement, this group became a vital organ for public schools in Jeffco. They monitored meeting agendas, queried the board's secretive tactics, and notified the public of their events (Klemaier 2014).

The group was not short on material to cover. Behind closed doors, the board majority had begun privately and secretively hiring a special attorney for the board. This raised eyebrows for a number of reasons—why did the board need their own attorney? How much would it cost, and why were all of the salary negotiations redacted in the public records? And why did the board select this particular pro-charter attorney, and why were the non-majority board members not included in the hiring decisions? As one of the non-majority board members reported her frustration: "There was no public process. I did not get to see a résumé. I did not get to see references" (Caldwell 2013). Upon securing their own attorney, the board majority pushed ahead to hire a superintendent of their choice: Douglass County's former superintendent, Dan McMinimee.

Though the school board had been unable to secure a contract with the Jeffco teachers, they whisked McMinimee into a five-year contract, subverting the normal hiring processes. Furthermore, McMinimee's starting salary of $280,000 was well above the previous superintendent, who had won national awards, held the position for more than a decade, and possessed a PhD (McMinimee had none of the above). McMinimee's starting salary made him one of the highest paid education employees in the state (Garcia 2014a). Parents and teachers in Jeffco were concerned by the secrecy of his hiring, the size of his salary, and his affiliation with conservative Douglass County. A number of parents circulated a petition to reconsider the appointment. The petition stated: "it has become apparent to us that the superintendent search was not completed in a manner that would result in objectively finding the best candidate for the job in a fair, transparent, and accountable manner. In our opinions, the board majority has placed their own personal biases over the needs of this district and the community" (Clark 2014). Their concerns over the hiring process were not taken into consideration. Nor were their concerns over McMinimee's background as a former charter school board member, guest of a right-wing talk radio show, or previous position in the neighboring conservative district of Douglass County.

The contradictions between the board's hiring of McMinimee and contract negotiations with teachers were glaring. One community member wrote a letter urging that the board should adopt the same performance pay measures for top administrators as they were pushing for teachers. The letter stated:

> Since Mr. McMinimee, [school board majority members] Mr. Witt, Mr. Newkirk, and Ms. Williams have all touted the value of performance based pay, I look forward to hearing the discussion and seeing changes to Mr. Mc Minimee's contract in order to provide him with performance based pay. He should be offered a base salary of $200,000 a year. The rest of the proposed salary should only be available to him based on district wide student test scores, district wide teacher evaluations, and his own evaluations. If students in Jeffco meet the Board's academic goals, if enough teachers in Jeffco are performing as "Effective" and "Highly Effective," and if Mr. McMinimee is himself deemed "Highly Effective," Mr. McMinimee should be rewarded for his leadership and accomplishments with financial incentives. If these goals are not met, Mr. McMinimee should not earn these financial incentives. I cannot imagine a leader who could possibly advocate this type of pay system for the employees whom he is charged to lead, and not happily embrace a similar pay system for himself.
>
> *(Murphy 2014)*

Amidst the board's backroom personnel decisions to hire an attorney and new superintendent, teachers in the district were trying to negotiate their contract with the board during the spring of 2014. Among the issues on the table were class sizes—Jeffco faced serious overcrowding issues—and teacher evaluation criteria, since the district had squarely shifted towards performance pay. Negotiations were slow and unproductive. Although the teachers' union had agreed to compromise to meet some of the board's interests, the board would not accept a contract. As a result, in April 2014 the teachers' union declared a bargaining impasse. They sought a third party independent fact finder as a bridge to cross the growing gulf between the school board and the teachers' union. Over the summer, an independent review team worked to create a fact-finding report, focusing especially on the contentious issue of how to determine the criteria for teachers' performance pay. The report found "that the current evaluation system lacks sufficient validity and reliability as a basis for setting salaries." The fact finders, therefore, recommended that the board and teachers hold off on denying teachers' raises based on the current system and next year, work to "jointly develop an improved evaluation system for the 2014–15 school year" (Snider 2014).

The board, however, did not agree. At their meeting on September 4, 2014, they rejected the independent fact-finders' report. The conservative majority voted 3-2 to not follow the recommendations, and instead approved a proposal developed singlehandedly by conservative board member Witt to determine teachers' raises (Gorski 2014). The new plan would give some teachers a 5% percent raise, others a 2.4% raise, and others a 1% raise; the old plan would have given all teachers a 2.8% raise. What's more, Witt's proposed plan did not clarify the evaluation standards, which remained fuzzy (Garcia 2014b). School board member Jill Fellman, one of the two dissenting members, raised her concerns about passing a pay proposal plan created without teacher input. She said, "We need to be very clear— this is your model, Mr. Witt," Fellman said.

Teachers, unsurprisingly, were not pleased with the new plan. The following week, on September 9, 2014, the Jeffco Education Association Council, the teachers' union, issued a no-confidence vote in the school board. The vote took place at a representative council meeting, in which nearly every school was represented, and was based on similar surveys that previously took place at the school level. As the president of the teachers' union John Ford told the press, "Teachers absolutely put kids first, but it's really difficult to do that if you have a board majority and president that continue to put their agendas before kids" (Garcia 2014c). Although the teachers' no-confidence vote didn't come with clear next steps, it formalized the gravity and unanimity of their frustration.

Things boiled over at the next school board meeting the next week. Few teachers were present at the meeting, as many had begun knocking on doors to let the community know about their frustration with the board. That Thursday night, however, the school board finalized the district's performance pay measures, rejecting the previous teacher salary schedule that compensated teachers according to years of experience and education level.

Perhaps most surprising, however, was the central role that the conservative politics of "official knowledge" also began to play (see Apple 2014). Conservative majority board member Julie Williams made a proposal to change the Advanced Placement US History curriculum to promote more "positive" aspects of national heritage by eliminating histories of US social movements. The curriculum changes were designed to "promote citizenship, patriotism, essentials and benefits of the free-market system, respect for authority and respect for individual rights" while minimizing and discouraging the role of "civil disorder, social strife or disregard of the law" (*CBS News* 2014). In a press release defending her proposed curriculum changes, Williams derided the AP curriculum for its "emphasis on race, gender, class, ethnicity, grievance and American-bashing while simultaneously omitting the most basic structural and philosophical elements considered essential to the understanding of American History for generations" (Williams 2014). She also doubled-down on her proposal by reminding the concerned public that similar changes have taken place in Texas, and that the top three things for students "graduating from an American school" to know are: American exceptionalism, US history, and the Constitution.

On Friday September 19, 2014, the day after the school board meeting, approximately half of the teachers at two high schools called in sick, forcing the high schools to close for the day. Students at these two high schools also joined in. They held sing-ins and chanted phrases such as, "my school, my voice." As one student told *The Denver Post,* "We are supporting the teachers. We think they should get paid more." Many parents, too, were supportive of the teachers' actions and empathized with their frustration with the school board and the board's lack of trust in teachers. One parent said that the school closures, "makes teachers' annoyances louder. It causes more people to pay attention" (Nicholson and Gorski 2014).

What's more, students began to develop their own voice on the issue. They were concerned not only about their teachers' treatment but about the proposed changes to their curriculum. They put out calls for organizing meetings on Facebook over the weekend, and that Sunday night they got together a plan. That Monday morning, several hundred students gathered outside of two high schools, holding signs that read sayings such as, "There is nothing more patriotic than protest," "People didn't die so we could erase them," "My education is not your political agenda," and "I got 99 problems and the B.O.E. is all of them." Over the next two days, students at high schools throughout the district joined in the protests and marches.

Parents and teachers supported and encouraged the students' protests, despite criticism issued by the superintendent as well as conservative groups who accused the teachers' union of using the students as "props." As a parent of one protesting high school student told the *Washington Post,* "I am very proud and think that having young people involved in their community and to feel strongly about education and teachers is a positive thing" (Strauss 2014). Using the energy generated by the students, teachers, and concerned parents, community members quickly sprang into action. In a few weeks, they gathered thousands of signatures to petition for a recall election of the conservative school board.

But the active support of parents, teachers, and community members was not a sufficient guarantee that the conservative candidates would be successfully recalled. In fact, the community support triggered an opposite reaction: it spurred nationally conservative groups, like Americans for Prosperity, once again to defend the conservative school board members. Unwilling to see the conservative majority lose the ground they had won, the national organization poured hundreds of thousands of dollars into the recall campaign. They hired field organizers, bought TV and media ads, and sent out pamphlets. As the Colorado state director of Americans for Prosperity candidly declared, "We advocate competition. Education shouldn't be different. ...Competition really raises the quality of education. ...Where you get the best solutions is through free market principles" (Robles 2015). Despite their heavily financed campaign to protect the conservative school board, Americans for Prosperity were not successful. In November 2015, the people of Jeffco voted to recall all three of the conservative candidates. Whereas in Kenosha, Wisconsin, the school board candidates backed by Americans for Prosperity won their elections, in Jefferson, County, they lost. What explains the difference?

Jeffco versus Kenosha

The differences between the struggles of Kenosha and Jeffco offer three key lessons. *First, what we struggle for matters.* Conservative forces in Jeffco expanded their agenda to issue key educational policy forms, such as teachers' contracts and school choice proposals, as well as educational content itself—the knowledge, values, and stories that get taught in schools. This recognition of the cultural struggles at stake in educational policy signaled their engagement in a deeper level of ideological reformation. By overtly restricting the curriculum to supposed "patriotic" narratives and excluding histories of protest and injustice, the conservative school board majority attempted to exercise their power to create ideological dominance (see Apple 2014). Yet, despite the school board's attempt to control the social narratives of meaning, they missed a key component of ideological formation: meaning is neither objective nor intrinsic. Meaning cannot be mandated, not by a school board majority or any other organization, no matter the campaign financing. Rather, meaning is constantly constructed, contested, and co-constructed, determined by its social surroundings. In the case of Jeffco, this meant that students' responses to the curricular changes became quite significant. Struggles over what should be taught that felt culturally relevant to students and parents galvanized them into action. Students were summoned to participate in the Jeffco battle for public schools because they wanted to protect the traditions of social protests and social movements that are fundamental to the project of democracy in the United States (see Foner 1998).

This has important implications for how we think about what struggles can generate progressive transformations. As Nancy Fraser reminds us, a politics of recognition as well as a politics of redistribution is crucial (Apple 2013; Fraser 1997). In Kenosha, on the other hand, the struggle for public schools was undertaken by foregrounded redistributive and representational rights—such as teachers' rights to unions—and positioned questions of recognition, such as racial justice, as secondary. What's more, as the struggle for public education in Jeffco broadened to include cultural questions as well as concerns over school funding and teachers' rights, so did the coalitions of forces working to oppose these forces.

This marks the second key difference between Kenosha and Jeffco: *how struggles cohere–or fail to—matters.* In Jeffco, teachers, parents, and students alike *all* found common ground and unification between their concerns, and used that as a basis for mobilization. Teachers, students, and parents saw themselves united on multiple fronts. Teachers' working conditions became a point of concern for parents and students alike; teachers were concerned with equitable funding for programs like all-day kindergarten. Their mutual connections became the basis of their organizing (see Apple 2013). Slowly, they built up enough actions to develop not only their political analysis, but also their power. This mobilized coalition had sufficient popular support and power to successfully recall the conservative candidates. In Kenosha, however, progressives were not able to mobilize a broad-based coalition to defend against the changes to public education. Instead, conservatives in Kenosha managed to suture together seemingly disparate programs into a unified political program. Whereas progressives in Jeffco were able to form a powerful alliance that addressed multiple registers of the impending conservative reforms, in Kenosha it was conservatives who formed such alliances. The Kenosha school board became a site for the Right to closely connect school choice arguments with anti-union arguments. Because of the school board's capacity to articulate policy priorities, it became attractive to both school choice proponents and those opposed to teachers' unions.

Finally, *how* we struggle matters. In Jeffco, community members, teachers, and students developed a more active model of mobilizing. They built up a series of actions, starting with low-stakes actions and moving to higher stakes ones that allowed for a wide range of participation, but developed increasing levels of engagement. They wrote letters, they attended school board meetings en masse, they door-knocked, they circulated petitions. They issued a no-confidence vote. They protested. They coordinated mass sick-outs. They walked out of school. Eventually, community members in Jeffco were able to *withhold* their participation, a critical mechanism for transferring power from elite minorities to majorities (McAlevey 2016). As Gramsci insightfully recognized, hegemony requires consent; exit, therefore, constitutes a fundamental means for non-dominant forces to build power (Gramsci 1971; Hirschman 1970). Building a series of escalating direct actions proved to be a vital strategy for community success in Jeffco.

In Kenosha, by contrast, little to no community or teacher organizing took place. Instead, the school board took on the job of protecting the teachers; the teachers themselves had little infrastructure to organize themselves, much less unite with community members or students. The school board members became the sole *advocates for* public education, rather than having public education *organized by* teachers and community members. Ultimately, it rendered the pro-public education forces in Kenosha weaker and more brittle in the face of corporate interest and a state antagonist to public education and workers' rights. Furthermore, in Kenosha, neither students, parents, nor teachers engaged in direct action. Rather, the struggle between conservative and progressive visions of education occurred either through electoral organizing, or through skirmishes amongst institutional elites, staged in board meetings and legal courts. This restricted the capacity for participation, engagement, and deliberation among Kenosha teachers, students, and community members. As a result, public school supporters in Kenosha failed to develop the dialogic power necessary for democratic transformation (Offe and Wiesenthal 1980).

The differences between the two models of struggle—one more passive and led by external advocates positioned somewhat above the terms of struggle, and one more active and led by members of the community embedded within the struggles—have profound implications. Not only did Jeffco produce better policy results, but the long-term changes are far different from active forms of struggle versus passive ones. As social movement scholars inform us, the most significant impacts of social movements are often not changes to social policy or programs, but rather the personal consequences of participating in activism. Once engaged with networks of other activists, participants have both attitudinal willingness and structural resources and skills to participate again in other activist efforts (e.g., McAdam 1989). Organizing and participating in a series of effective walk-outs created activist identities for Jeffco high schoolers, a change that may impact them for decades forward. By contrast, in Kenosha, neither students, nor community members, nor parents pursued active organizing, and therefore had fewer opportunities for the subjective changes to their sense of self, resulting from their participation.

What Is to Be Learned?

The story in Jeffco, however, did not end with the recall of the conservative school board members. After the recall election, many of the basic problems in Jeffco public schools remained. The high schools were still overcrowded. The teachers were still underpaid. The infrastructure and technology were still out of date. Fixing these problems required not only leadership, but also resources and political will. The newly elected school board needed more funds to create a school, but could only raise more money if voters across the state agreed to raise taxes. The same law that prevented tax increases and brought voters to the polls to elect Jeffco's conservative school board also prevented the newly elected school board from creating necessary changes to strengthen the public schools. In 2016, under a new school board, voters in Colorado once again voted down proposals to increase taxes to fund public schools.

While the details of this campaign are beyond the scope of this chapter, they shed light on an important dilemma in the struggle for a more democratic public education. Community members, teachers, and parents concerned with public education must transition from engaging in short-term mobilizations around specific campaigns, towards the long-term, deep work of movement building to defend not only public education, but a robust democratic state. Although a clear understanding of what we're fighting against often provides important material for mobilizations, it is not a substitute for building a progressive vision, much less the strategies to get there. Electoral strategies, too, may constitute an important part of this work, but they alone cannot provide the exclusive domain of struggle. Rather, as the students in Jeffco made clear, struggles must unite with deeper currents of social, cultural, and economic programs.

Again, struggles over school board elections in Kenosha, Wisconsin and Jefferson County, Colorado yield insights into the broader social movements. The triumph of conservative actors in Kenosha and their failure in Jeffco reveals three key lessons in the strategies of rightist movements. First, these cases highlight the Right's growing commitment to small political spaces, and the political persistence necessary to take control of them. As these cases show, the Right successfully occupied micro political spaces by waging lawsuits against the liberal school board, running political candidates to take over the school board, and providing large amounts of financial support for these candidates. Second, conservative movements offer identities that provide attractive forms of agency to many. For example, as "taxpayers" individuals are able to position themselves as entitled to public benefits *and* authorized to dictate the terms of these benefits. Finally, effective movements combine multiple ideological elements to form a more unified movement. In Kenosha, the Right did this work by suturing the efforts of anti-collective bargaining mobilizations with pro-vouchers programs. In Jeffco, progressives did it by uniting students with parents and teachers around curricular changes, anti-school choice plans, and against merit pay for teachers.

The triumph against conservative alliances in Jeffco, Colorado provides important lessons for those of us committed to a critically democratic education for all of our children. As economic crises roll into education, the democratic accords of public education have come under new threat. In the decade since the 2008 economic recession, conservative leaders have cited declining public funds as a justification to further demolish democracy's key pillars, such as labor rights of teachers, democratic governance of school boards, and socially just curricula. But such attempts to establish the conservative common sense are not without opposition, as we've seen in Jeffco and Kenosha. Resistance to these conservative movements is a crucial part of the "war of position."

Defenders of democratic institutions must understand the acute vulnerability of things that we too often take for granted—such as local democratic control through school boards. But we must do more than simply defend these spaces. As the students and teachers in Jeffco remind us, we need to continue the long and never-ending struggle to build an education that does not divide us by class and race (see Apple 2013), that is equally respectful of the teachers who now labor so hard in uncertain conditions in our public schools, and that presents histories of social struggle. More than defend, we must construct, co-construct, and reconstruct schools as meaningful spaces. We must connect our mobilizations for public education with movements for structural, long-term transformation of the larger, social democratic conditions. This work begins closer than we may think: in our school boards, no matter the size.

Note

1 Beginning in the late 1970s, labor markets took the brunt of the struggle. Social movements demanded higher wages and more equal employment, driving up inflation as capitalists continued to hold on to their need for marginal productivity. In an effort to tamp down the billowing economy, conservative government regimes enacted a politically costly assault on labor, beginning with US President Ronald Reagan's defeat of the Professional Air Traffic Controllers Organization (PATCO) in 1981 and spreading to UK Prime Minister Margaret Thatcher's defeat of the miners' strike in 1984, and beyond. Yet the contradictions between the needs of capital and democratic society were not abated, lurching next into the electoral arena. States and countries faced rising public spending, but dwindling revenue capacity, as the public became increasingly hostile to taxation in the face of their own declining incomes. As a result, public debt rose, pushing these struggles into the arena of private credit; regulations to access credit were relaxed as a way for citizens to maintain the level of economic security and prosperity that the state could no longer guarantee(Dumenil and Levy 2005; McNally 2011; Prasad 2012; Streeck 2011).

References

Althusser, L. (1971). Ideology and ideological state apparatuses (Notes towards an investigation). In *Lenin and Philosophy and Other Essays* (pp. 127–186). New York: Monthly Review Press.

Amendment 66: Crucial school overhaul or pricey tax hike. *Colorado Public Radio* (November 19, 2013). www.cpr.org/news/audio/amendment-66-crucial-school-over haul-or-pricey-tax-hike

Anderson, G. and Donchik, L. M. (2016). Privatizing schooling and policy making: The American Legislative Exchange Council and new political and discursive strategies of education governance. *Educational Policy* pp. 1–43. Available at: http://doi.org/10.1177/0895904804270777

Apple, M. W. (2006). *Educating the "Right" Way: Markets, Standards, God and Inequality* (2nd ed.). New York: Routledge.

Apple, M. W. (2012). *Education and Power* (2nd ed.). New York: Routledge.

Apple, M. W. (2013). *Can Education Change Society?* New York: Routledge.

Apple, M. W. (2014). *Official Knowledge* (3rd ed.). New York: Routledge.

Apple, M. W. and Oliver, A. (1996). Becoming right: Education and the formation of conservative movements. *Teachers College Record* 97(3): pp. 419–445.

Ball, S. (2007). *Education plc: Understanding Private Sector Participation in Public Sector Education*. New York: Routledge.

Ball, S. and Junemann, C. (2012). *Networks, New Governance and Education*. Bristol: Policy Press.

Beebee, T. (2013). *Kenosha school board unanimous in opposition to private school vouchers. Education in the News.* Available at: http://wisconsinsfuture.org/kenosha-school-board-unanimous-in-opposition-to-private-school-vouchers/. Accessed 19/05/2015.

Board opposed to private school voucher proposal. (2013). *Channel 3000* (February 22). Madison. Available at: http://www.channel3000.com/news/Board-opposed-to-private-school-voucher-proposal/-/1648/19046792/-/100trmd/-/index.html. Accessed 30/06/2015.

Brighouse, H. and Schouten, G. (2014). To charter or not to charter: What questions should we ask, and what will the answers tell us? *Harvard Educational Review 84*(3): pp. 341–365. Available at: http://hepg.org/her-home/issues/harvard-educational-review-volume-84-number-3/herarticle/to-charter-or-not-to-charter

Brown, T. H. (2013). Colorado voters rally for a flat tax, reject Amendment 66. *Forbes. com* (November 15). Available at: www.forbes.com/sites/travisbrown/2013/11/15/colorado-voters-rally-for-a-flat-tax-reject-amendment-66/#255980d67aa3

Brown, W. (2015). *Undoing the Demos: Neoliberalism's Stealth Revolution*. New York: MIT Press.

Burch, P. E. (2006). The new educational privatization: Educational contracting and high stakes accountability. *Teachers College Record 108*(12): pp. 2582–2610. Available at: http://doi.org/10.1111/j.1467-9620.2006.00797.x

Caldwell, A. (2013). Jeffco school board didn't take long to raise eyebrows. *Denver Post* (December 16). Available at: www.denverpost.com/2013/12/16/caldwell-jeffco-school-board-didnt-take-long-to-raise-eyebrows/

Clark, M. (2014). Petiton for Jeffco BoE to reconsider McMinimee. *Change.org*. Available at: www.change.org/p/the-jefferson-county-board-of-education-colorado-we-want-the-jeffco-boe-to-reconsider-the-announcement-of-daniel-mcminimee-as-the-sole-superintendent-finalist-we-request-that-the-board-reexamine-the-candidate-pool-and-announce-3-4-new-finalists-2

Clarke, J., & Newman, J. (1997). *The Managerial State*. London: Sage Publications.

Clegg, R., Kulas, O. M. A., Proffitt, E., Shidaker, S., Tuneberg, J., and Van Hoozer, S. (2013). *A Curriculum Audit of Kenosha Unified School District*. Bloomington, IN: International Curriculum Management Audit Center, Phi Delta Kappa International.

Colorado State Election Results. (2017). www.270towin.com/states/Colorado.

Community Outreach Survey Information. (2014). www.jeffcopublicschools.org/community/documents/02132014_CommunitySurveyResults.pdf

Cramer, K. (2016). *The Politics of Resentment: Rural Consciousness and the Rise of Scott Walker*. Chicago, IL: University of Chicago Press.

Dr. Stevenson Forced Out. (2014). Transparency Jeffco. Retrieved from www.youtube.com/watch?v=zS3OytSHb1Y&t=337s Transparency Jeffco. (2014). Dr. Stevenson Forced Out. [Online Video]. 8 February 2014. Available at: www.youtube.com/watch?v=zS3OytSHb1Y&t=337s

Duhigg, C. and Dougherty, C. (2008). From Midwest to M.T.A., Pain From Global Gamble. *The New York Times* (November 2), p. A1. New York. Available at: http://www.nytimes.com/2008/11/02/business/02global.html?pagewanted=all&_r=0

Dumenil, G. and Levy, D. (2005). The neoliberal (counter)-revolution. In *Neoliberalism: A Critical Reader*. A. Saad-Filho and D. Johnston (Eds.). London: Pluto Press.

Ferguson, T., Jorgensen, P., and Chen, J. (2015). How money drives US congressional elections: More evidence. In *Institute for New Economic Thinking* pp. 1689–1699. Paris. Available at: www.ineteconomics.org/uploads/papers/WP_48_Ferguson_et_al.pdf

Flores, T. (2011a). Unified layoffs affect nearly every school. *Kenosha News* (April 28). Available at: www.kenoshanews.com/home/unified_layoffs_affect_nearly_every_school_136429303.html. Accessed 19/06/2015.

Flores, T. (2011b). SEC charges Stifel with fraud. *Kenosha News* (August 10). Available at: http://www.kenoshanews.com/home/sec_charges_stifel_with_fraud_207348082.html. Accessed 19/06/2015.

Flores, T. (2012). KEA leader: Teacher morale falls as class sizes rise. *Kenosha News* (September 20). Retrieved from www.kenoshanews.com/news/kea_leader_teacher_morale_falls_as_class_sizes_rise_440076013.html. Accessed 19/06/2015.

Flores, T. (2013). Transformation plan comes under fire at unified forum. *Kenosha News* (March 20).

Foner, E. (1998). *The Story of American Freedom*. New York: Norton.

Former teacher: I know my own worth. (2015). *Wispolitics.com*. Available at: http:// quorumcall.wispolitics.com/2015/02/former-teacher-i-know-my-own-worth.html. Accessed 20/05/2015.

Fraser, N. (1997). *Justice Interruptus: Critical Reflections on the "Postsocialist" Condition*. New York: Routledge.

Fraser, N. (2015). Legitimation crisis? On the political contradictions of financialized capitalism. *Critical Historical Studies* 2(Fall): pp. 157–189. Available at: http://doi. org/10.1086/683054

Garcia, N. (2014). In split vote, Jeffco board hires new superintendent. *Chalkbeat Colorado*. (May 27). Available at: www.chalkbeat.org/posts/co/2014/05/27/jeffco-board-expected-to-hire-new-superintendent-dan-mcminimee-tonight/

Garcia, N. (2014a). Jeffco board majority OKs tentative compensation plan for teachers. *Chalkbeat Colorado* (September 4). Available at: www.chalkbeat.org/posts/co/2014/09/04/ jeffco-board-majority-oks-tentative-compensation-plan-for-teachers/

Garcia, N. (2014b). Jeffco union votes no confidence in board chair Ken Witt. *Denver Post* (September 10). Available at: www.chalkbeat.org/posts/co/2014/09/10/jeffco-union-votes-no-confidence-in-board-chair-ken-witt/

Gorski, E. (2014c). Jeffco board restricts pay raises for "partially effective" teachers. *Denver Post* (August 28). Available at: www.denverpost.com/2014/08/28/jeffco-board-restricts-pay-raises-for-partially-effective-teachers/

Gramsci, A. (1971). *Selections from The Prison Notebooks of Antonio Gramsci*. New York: International Publishers.

Grusky, D. B. (2011). *The Great Recession*. New York: Russell Sage Foundation.

Hacker, J. S. and Pierson, P. (2010). Winner-take-all politics: Public policy, political organization, and the precipitous rise of top incomes in the United States. *Politics & Society* 38(2): pp. 152–204. Available at: http://doi.org/10.1177/0032329210365042

Hallow, L. (2011). "We need to be optimistic": Unified superintendent encourages parents, teachers to stay positive. *Kenosha News* (August 29). Available at: www.kenoshanews. com/home/we_need_to_be_optimistic_221238606.html

Healy, J. (2013). Defeat of school tax stings Colorado Democrats. *New York Times* (November 6). Available at: http://www.nytimes.com/2013/11/07/us/politics/loss-on-school-tax-stings-colorado-democrats.html

High schoolers protest conservative proposal. (2014). *CBS News* (September 24). Available at: www.cbsnews.com/news/colorado-high-schoolers-protest-conservative-proposal/

Hirschman, A. O. (1970). *Exit, Voice, and Loyalty: Responses to Decline in Firms, Organizations, and States*. Cambridge, MA: Harvard University Press.

In "Purple District," Jeffco school board recall could have big influence. (2015). *CBS Denver* (August 26). Available at: http://denver.cbslocal.com/2015/08/26/ jeffco-school-board-recall-could-influence-other-districts-stakes-so-high/

Klemaier, J. (2014). Group aims to inform Jefferson County residents about school board. *Denver Post* (February 17). Available at: www.denverpost.com/2014/02/17/ group-aims-to-inform-jefferson-county-residents-about-school-board/

Lacroix, K. (2013). Association offers fresh start for Wisconsin teachers. *Milwaukee Journal Sentinel* (September 2). Available at: www.jsonline.com/news/opinion/association-offers-fresh-start-for-wisconsin-teachers-b9985309z1-221866951.html. Accessed 11/03/2015.

Lipman, P. (2011). The *New Political Economy of Urban Education: Neoliberalism, Race and the Right to the City*. New York: Routledge.

McAdam, D. (1989). The biographical consequence of activism. *American Sociological Review* 54(5): pp. 744–760.

McAlevey, J. (2016). *No Shortcuts: Organizing for Power in the New Gilded Age*. New York: Oxford University Press.

McDarrison, K. (2013). Sign of the times: Protest at Kenosha Unified School District, continued. Available at: http://wisconsinhappyfarm.com/sign-of-the-times-protest-at-kenosha-unified-school-district-continued/. Accessed 11/03/2015.

McNally, D. (2011). *Global Slump: The Economics and Politics of Crisis & Resistance*. Oakland, CA: PM Press.

Mayer, J. (2016). *Dark Money: The Hidden History of the Billionaires Behind the Rise of the Radical Right*. New York: Doubleday.

Murphy, E. (2014). No responses and superintendent comments. *Support Jeffco Kids*. Available at: www.supportjeffcokids.org/2014/05/page/5/

Murphy, K. (2011). Kenosha teacher backs governor in fight over collective bargaining. *Kenosha News* (July 12). Available at: www.kenoshanews.com/home/kenosha_teacher_backs_governor_in_fight_over_collective_bargaining_178420122.html. Accessed 19/06/2015.

Nichols, J. (2012). *Uprising: How Wisconsin Renewed the Politics of Protest, from Madison to Wall Street*. New York: Nation Books.

Nicholson, K. and Gorski, E. (2014). Two Jeffco high schools close Friday after teachers are absent. *Denver Post* (September 19). Available at: www.denverpost.com/2014/09/19/two-jeffco-high-schools-close-friday-after-teachers-are-absent/

Offe, C. and Wiesenthal, H. (1980). Two logics of collective action: Theoretical notes on social class and organizational form. In *Political Power and Social Theory*. M. Zeitlin (Ed.) pp. 67–116. Bingley, UK: JAI Press.

Olson, M. (2011). Wirch recall group has received nearly $11,000. *Kenosha News* (March 30). Available at: www.kenoshanews.com/home/wirch_recall_group_has_received_nearly_11000_118415117.html. Accessed 12/05/2015.

Policy Basics: Taxpayer Bill of Rights (TABOR). (2015). Available at: www.cbpp.org/research/state-budget-and-tax/policy-basics-taxpayer-bill-of-rights-tabor

Prasad, M. (2012). *The Land of Too Much: American Abundance and the Paradox of Poverty*. Cambridge, MA: Harvard University Press.

Ravitch, D. (2013). Meet the Broad Superintendents. Available at: http://dianeravitch.net/2013/08/15/meet-the-broad-superintendents/. Accesssed 15/05/2015.

Reckhow, S., Henig, J. R., Jacobsen, R., and Litt, J. A. (2016). "Outsiders with deep pockets": The nationalization of local school board elections. *Urban Affairs Review* 5(53): pp., 1–29. Available at: http://doi.org/10.1177/1078087416663004

Reckhow, S. and Snyder, J. W. (2014). The expanding role of philanthropy in education politics. *Educational Researcher* 43(4): pp. 186–195. Available at: http://doi.org/10.3102/0013189X14536607

Robles, Y. (2015). Americans for Prosperity group plans to stay in Jeffco. *The Denver Post* (October 29). Available at: http://blogs.denverpost.com/coloradoclassroom/2015/10/29/americans-for-prosperity-group-plans-to-stay-in-jeffco/5440/

Saltman, K. J. (2007). Corporatization and the control of schools. In *The Routledge International Handbook of Critical Education*. M. W. Apple, W. Au, and L. A. Gandin (Eds.) (pp. 51–63). New York: Routledge.

Saltman, K. J. (2009). The rise of venture philanthropy and the ongoing neoliberal assault on public education: The Eli and Edythe Broad Foundation. *Workplace: A Journal for Academic Labor 16:* pp. 53–72.

Schirmer, E. and Apple, M. W. (2016a). Capital, power, and education: "Dark Money" and the politics of common-sense. *Education Review 23:* pp. 1–13.

Schirmer, E. and Apple, M. W. (2016b). Teachers, school boards, and the power of money: How the right wins at the local level. *The Educational Forum, 80*(2): pp. 137–153. Available at: http://doi.org/10.1080/00131725.2016.1135384

Scott, J. (2009). The politics of venture philanthropy in charter school policy and advocacy. *Educational Policy. 23*(1): pp. 106–136. Available at: http://epx.sagepub.com/content/23/1/106.short

Scott, J. and Jabbar, H. (2014). The hub and the spokes: Foundations, intermediary organizations, incentivist reforms, and the politics of research evidence. *Educational Policy 28*(2): pp. 233–257. Available at: http://doi.org/10.1177/0895904813515327

Simon, S. (2013). Kochs vs. unions in schools race. *Politico* (November 2). Available at: www.politico.com/story/2013/11/koch-group-unions-battle-over-colorado-schools-race-099252

Skocpol, T. and Hertel-Fernandez, A. (2016). The Koch network and Republican Party extremism. *American Political Science Association 14*(3): pp. 681–699. Available at: http://doi.org/10.1017/S1537592716001122

Smith, D. (2014). Proposed charter bill worries Kenosha Unified principals. *Kenosha News* (January 10).

Snider, M. A. (2014). *Report and Recommendations of the Fact Finder between Jefferson County Public Schools and Jefferson County Education Association.* Available at: http://www.jeffcopublicschools.org/human_resources/negotiations/Jeffco_fact_finding_report.pdf. Accessed 23/03/2017.

Steinkraus, D. (2011). Angry volunteers rally at Wirch recall drive. *The Journal Times* (February 26). Available at: http://journaltimes.com/news/local/angry-volunteers-rally-at-wirch-recall-drive/article_6d6a3a8e-4231-11e0-a7df-001cc4c03286.html

Strauss, V. (2014). Colorado student protest leader: "I'm learning how people need to act to make a democracy function'. *Washington Post.* (October 2).

Streeck, W. (2011). The crises of democratic capitalism. *New Left Review.* 71: pp. 5–29. Available at: https://newleftreview.org/II/71/wolfgang-streeck-the-crises-of-democratic-capitalism

Streeck, W. (2014). *Buying Time: The Delayed Crisis of Democratic Capitalism.* New York: Verso.

Streeck, W. (2017). The return of the repressed. *New Left Review* 104: pp. 5–18. Available at: https://newleftreview.org/II/104/wolfgang-streeck-the-return-of-the-repressed

Tea Party fatigue in Colorado. (2010). *New York Times* (October 26). Available at: www.nytimes.com/roomfordebate/2010/10/26/tea-party-fatigue-in-colorado

Torres, Z. (2013). Election brings new direction for Jefferson County schools. *Denver Post* (November 19) Available at: http://www.denverpost.com/2013/11/19/election-brings-new-direction-for-jefferson-county-schools/

Vaccarelli, J. (2013). Jefferson County Schools chief Cindy Stevenson to retire after school year. *Denver Post* (November 7) Available at: www.denverpost.com/2013/11/07/jefferson-county-schools-chief-cindy-stevenson-to-retire-after-school-year/

Why 3A & 3B? (2016). *Support Jeffco Kids.* Available at: www.supportjeffcokids.org/2016/09/page/2/

Williams, J. (2014). Press Release for AP US History. *Support Jeffco Kids.*

4

HOW "DEMOCRACY" CAN LEAD TO INEQUALITY

Class Relations and the Realities of Educational Reform

Shuning Liu and Michael W. Apple

Introduction

At the very core of this book's arguments is the fact that not only is democracy what Raymond Williams would call a "key word" in the debates over what kind of society we should strive for (Williams 2014), but it is also a sliding signifier. It is a *contested* concept. It has multiple meanings and is used to legitimate very different visions of the ways in which our institutions should function and how individuals and groups should participate.

This is especially important today. We are living in a time of what has been called "conservative modernization" (Apple 2001; Dale 1989), where the "thick" meaning of democracy based on fully participatory citizenship is being replaced by the "thin democracy" of markets and consumption practices (Apple 2014, 2006; Apple et al. 2003).[1] Such ideas of democracy are best demonstrated in an increasing adoption of school "choice" policies in many nations of the world. While the specific genesis of the arguments employed by the advocates of such policies may partly differ for reasons of region and history, most often they claim that by placing schools into the market and giving parents more choices among schools, schools will improve their competitiveness and become more responsive to the needs of students and parents (see, for example, Apple 2006; Chubb and Moe 1990; Friedman and Friedman 1980; Henig 1994; Lauder and Hughes 1999; Whitty et al. 1998). Embracing this idea, many governments around the world have adopted school choice policies as a supposedly effective solution to national and local educational problems (Adamson et al. 2016; Forsey et al. 2008; Plank and Sykes 2003; Whitty 1997). Marketization, parental choice, and competition are thus viewed as key strategies of such varied programs (Buras and Apple 2005).

Despite the often overly romantic assertions made by proponents of school choice, there has been substantial and growing research on these policies that questions and complicates the logic of so-called "rational choice" models by critically examining the practices and effects of them in a wide variety of educational settings. These critical studies contribute to our understanding of the ideology of the choice agenda in education, grounded as it is in the idea that the ability to choose a school both promotes the personal freedom of individuals and improves school effectiveness and the quality of an educational system (Apple 2006; Ball 1998; Forsey et al. 2008; Olssen et al. 2004). This idea derives from the ideologically, politically, economically intertwined paradigm most commonly known as neoliberalism. Although neoliberalism has a complex history and is inflected by a number of other movements and tendencies (Apple 2006), by and large it came to prominence in the 1980s (Harvey 2005). As David Harvey (2005) puts it,

> Neoliberalism is in the first instance a theory of political economic practices that proposes that human well-being is best advanced by liberating individual entrepreneurial freedoms and skills within an institutional framework characterized by strong private property rights, free markets and free trade. The role of the state is to create and preserve an institutional framework appropriate to such practices.
>
> *(p. 2)*

Choice then acts as a neoliberal imperative. The development and spread of neoliberalism in the global context over time and space has gone hand in hand with "the globalization of school choice" since the 1980s as well (Forsey et al. 2008). In the process, market-oriented educational reforms treat education as a private consumption good and reduce citizen rights to mere individual consumer rights. This reduction of education to a private consumption good has been rigorously criticized (see, for example, Apple 2006, 2010; Whitty 1997). Although it has raised powerful questions about the neoliberal agenda in education and the larger society, much of this critical research draws on the experiences of the Western countries. Yet, given the increasingly global nature of marketized school choice policies, this geographic fact makes it even more crucial to investigate how the multiple scales, forms, and emphases of school choice in different countries are influenced by particular political, economic, and cultural conditions. Broadening and internationalizing our analyses will enable us to develop a considerably deeper understanding of various forms and effects of neoliberal educational reforms.

This chapter examines the practices and effects of parent-initiated school choice in China, a program that has significant differences from government-led parental choice in the West. Using Pierre Bourdieu's (1984) theory of the ways in which various forms of capital enable conversion strategies by differently positioned class actors, the chapter will reveal the ways in which such market-oriented practices primarily advantage the rising Chinese middle- and upper-class families who possess more economic capital, cultural capital, and social capital than working-class and low-income migrant families. Drawing on Stuart Hall's (1980, 1985; see also Grossberg 1986) concept of articulation, which underscores that different social forces, discourses, and practices can be contingently (re)articulated and disarticulated around contradictions under certain historical conditions to constitute particular social formations, this chapter will illuminate school choice as a site of contestation by linking the specificity of choice practices in China to its historical, social, political, ideological structures.[2] We will also connect the analysis of contradictory effects of school choice in China with Apple's (2013, 2016) notion of "epistemological fog" to explore the cultural politics of educational reforms. Furthermore, the chapter will take up what Nancy Fraser (2005, 2009) calls the politics of "redistribution," "recognition," and "representation" to uncover how the (re)articulation of school choice practices and Chinese social and educational reforms also entails social injustice. In doing such critical analyses, this chapter will not only document how "thin" democracy leads to educational inequality and social injustice, but it also will "point to contradictions and to *spaces of possible action*" (Apple 2016, p. 511, emphasis in original).

In the following sections, we shall first go into detail about the complex and at times contradictory sociopolitical and educational contexts of Chinese policies on choice. Then we will employ recent research on middle school choice in China by analyzing school choice as a middle-class conversion strategy and the contradictory effects of choice practices. We will then map a new configuration of school choice by examining the complexities of parental choice of emerging international high school curriculum programs newly established by Chinese key public high schools. Through connecting the practices and effects of school choice in the compulsory education sector with a new trend of high school choice, this chapter will track the development of the school choice movement in China genealogically and map the play of some particularly profound social forces in this process (Slack 1996, p. 115).

The Recontextualization of School Choice in China

As discussed above, school choice policies are in essence market-oriented education reforms. Although, in general, market mechanisms are the same in most nations, choice within local education markets is often different, given the history of that particular nation or region. This is especially the case for school choice in China. The school choice movement has become apparent in China since the 1990s. Previous studies, such as Tsang (2003), Qin (2008), and Wu (2008, 2011, 2014), have pointed out four unique features of school choice practices in the Chinese context. First, school choice is officially banned by the Chinese central government. Second, parental choice of school is a bottom-up movement that is initiated by Chinese parents "who want to select a good school for their children as early as preschool (kindergarten)" (Wu 2014, p. 1). Third, key state schools (*zhongdian xiao*, 重点校) are the desired choice schools. Fourth is the involvement of choice fees that refer to "all those additional costs associated with parental choice" (Wu 2008, p. 605). To better understand these unique characteristics, we would need to look carefully at the Chinese context that leads to such differences. In this section, we will discuss the recontextualization of school choice in China, which is an important way to look at historical and social specificities in relation to education. As one of us has argued at much greater length elsewhere (Apple 2006, 2014; Apple et al. 2003), thinking relationally about educational issues enables us to pay attention to the power dynamics created by particular social contexts.

Basic education in China covers grades 1–12 education, including a six-year elementary education, a three-year middle school education, and a three-year high school education. However, only nine years of elementary and middle school education are designated as compulsory. This was articulated in the *Compulsory Education Law of the People's Republic of China* passed in 1986 and amended in 2006. The law stipulates the principles of compulsory education, including the provision of free education, exemption from entrance examinations, enrollment "in a school near the places where their residence is registered," and equality (National People's Congress of the People's Republic of China 2006). This means that school choice is not officially permitted in the compulsory education sector. However, it is crucial to understand that these rules have been and are challenged by contesting social forces, such as the Chinese government's insufficient investment in education, the existing key school system, China's selective examination system, and significant social class changes in contemporary China, under historical conditions where decentralization of authority, devolution of responsibilities, and marketization have been adopted to reform education, health, housing, and other social services with the goal of improving economic development, efficiency, and effectiveness (Liu 2015; Liu 2016; Mok et al. 2009; Wu 2014). These conditions and changes were complexly articulated to form the school choice market in China while making school choice policies a field of contestation.

Decentralization and Financial Diversification of Education: The Rise of the Neoliberal Approach to Chinese Educational Reforms

The educational landscape in China has been changed since the 1980s. The market-oriented economic reforms that aim to modernize Chinese society have profoundly influenced Chinese educational reforms. Education for economic development has become the dominant discourse that guides educational reform in contemporary China, as it does in many other countries (Apple 2006; Ball 2013; Mok et al. 2009). The Chinese government's efforts to improve the modernization of its education system began with the reform of decentralization and financial diversification in education. This reform was initially issued by the *Decision of the Central Committee of the Chinese Communist Party of China on the Reform of the Educational System* in 1985 and was restated in the *Outline for Reform and Development of Education in China* in 1993 (Mok et al. 2009; Ngok 2007; Central Committee of the Chinese Communist Party and State Council 1993). The reform emphasizes that the central government devolves financial responsibility and management of education to local governments. This education reform calls for local governments and state schools to utilize multiple channels to improve their education services and resource provision (Cheng 1997; Liu and Dunne 2009; Ngok 2007; Tsang 1996). Such school autonomy reforms encourage state schools with quality educational resources to generate additional revenues through expanding their educational services to meet social needs. This reform led to the marketization of education in China (Mok 1997; Mok et al. 2009).

The Chinese Government's Insufficient Investment in Education

The recent three decades have witnessed tremendous economic growth in China associated with the "Reform and Opening Up" policy initiated in 1978. As Mok, Wong, and Zhang (2009) note, since the 1980s the Chinese economy has grown at an average rate of 9–10% annually (p. 506). However, the rate of the Chinese government expenditures in education was low. For instance, empirical evidence reveals that less than 3% of gross national product (GNP) has been spent on education in contemporary China, with spending at 2.86% in 1991, 2.41% in 1995, 2.49% in 1997, 2.79% in 1999, 3.14% in 2001, and 2.81% in 2005. Even though the number increased to 3.48% in 2008, Chinese government expenditures on education are still below the average level in East Asia and the Pacific region and far lower than in those "developed" countries which spend 6% or more of GNP on education (Mok et al. 2009; Wu 2014). On the one hand, along with insufficient education investment, the Chinese central government devolves the responsibilities of educational provision to local governments. On the other hand, it encourages various types of public organization and individuals to make donations to education (National People's Congress of the People's Republic of China 1986, 2006). These historical and political realities highlight the challenges that schools face. Such conditions have driven schools to move in the direction of marketization, putting a price on educational services that they can provide for families and raising funds by taking choice students and charging high choice fees. Hence, for many schools, marketization of education seems an appropriate way to deal with the challenge of insufficient government investment because it not only allows schools to update equipment, improve teachers' welfare, and maintain routine operations, but it also eases the financial pressures on local governments (Qin 2008; Tsang 2003; Wu 2014). The political context described here helps us understand why the government has felt that it had to compromise and to basically give a green light to school choice, even though choice practices are indeed still officially banned in the compulsory education sector.

The Key School System in China

The existing key school system is another important factor for the creation of the school choice market. Citing Yuan (1999), Xiaoxin Wu (2014) traces the history of the key school system to "the early 1940s in the Communist-controlled area of Yan'an, where primary schools were divided into central primary schools and regular primary schools with more attention being given to the former" (p. 22). A series of government educational policies promulgated in the early 1950s led to the nationwide establishment of the key school system. The overall policy was based on two rationales. First, it was regarded as the most effective way to "produce maximum educational returns in the shortest possible time to meet the immediate growing manpower needs of the country" when the Chinese government faced the challenges of scarce educational resources and a limited education budget in the early stage of the People's Republic of China (p. 22). Second, key schools were expected to act as teaching and learning models for regular schools. Since then, key schools have gained priority in the assignment of sufficient government funding, good facilities, qualified teachers, and top-performing students on standardized tests. The unequal distribution of educational resources has existed not only between key schools and non-key schools but also between urban and rural areas because key schools have been concentrated in urban regions. Yet, even among key schools, there are still disparities based on which level of administration they embody: district, country, municipal, provincial, or national level. The higher the level, the better a key school is in terms of reputation, government support, academic achievement, and so on.

In addition, the key school system has permeated all levels of Chinese public educational institutions, from preschool education to tertiary education. Influenced by a series of educational reforms, key state educational institutions have changed their names. Whether they are *demonstration schools* for former key state high schools, *converted schools* for former key state middle schools, or "211 project universities" for former key public universities, key schools and universities still represent the image of high quality of education in the eyes of the Chinese public. Attending key schools is seen as an ideal pathway to elite universities and then elite social positions (Liu 2015; Liu 2016; Shao and Zhang 2013; Wang, H. 2011; Ye, H. 2015; You 2007). Key schools and universities are at the top of a steep pyramidal educational structure and account for only a very small percentage of state educational institutions. Because of this, such schools serve as an important field for positional competition (Brown 2003).

China's Educational Examination System

China's selective examination system has a very long history (Niu 2007, cited by Liu and Dunne 2009). Chinese students' promotion to the next level of schooling is largely determined by their performance on entrance examinations. Before the implementation of the 1986 *Compulsory Education Law*, there was a Middle School Entrance Examination administrated by Chinese local educational authorities. Along with the open enrollment in the compulsory education sector designated by the law, the Middle School Entrance Examination has been cancelled (Wu 2012). However, there are still entrance examinations for post-compulsory education, including High School Entrance Examination (*zhongkao*, 中考) and College Entrance Examination (*gaokao*, 高考). The former is set by local educational authorities while the latter is subject to national enrollment planning. Both high school and college entrance examinations serve as crucial gatekeepers in the Chinese educational system because the examination results play a key role not only in determining transitions to high school and tertiary education, but also in determining the type of education received—such as academic or vocational education, regular or key high schools, which types of key high schools, and what kinds of Chinese universities (Hannum et al. 2011, p. 299). Chinese key middle and high schools are well known in preparing students for achieving high scores in these entrance examinations, which is an important reason why the key schools are perceived as precious educational resources by many Chinese parents. Quantitative studies from D. Yang (2005) and Y. Wu (2013) point out that students from higher socio-economic status families are more likely to attend key high schools, while attending a key school at one educational stage increases students' opportunities to enroll in a key school at the next level of schooling. Clearly, the high-stakes testing system articulated with the existing key school system enhances the tracking system in China, which further leads to differentiated educational opportunities and mobility.

Social Class Changes in Contemporary China

The official position on banning school choice practices is challenged not only by political and historical conditions but also by substantial economic and social changes. The Reform and Opening Up policy has brought about rapid economic development and improved the material conditions for many Chinese people. However, it has also led to significant rates of social stratification and has transformed class structures, particularly since the 1990s (Harvey 2005; Yan and Chang 2009). The rise of the new middle classes, who mostly concentrate in urban China, is fundamentally tied to "the post-Mao market reforms and economic liberalization that set the condition for the growth of private businesses and the accumulation of private wealth" (Zhang 2010, p. 5–6). The Chinese middle-class urbanites are more able to invest in their children's education—most often, the education of their only child given the one-child policy in China.[3] Their desire for "quality education" for their own children means that focusing on middle-class Chinese families is crucial because they are key actors in parental school choice in China.

Parental Choice of Middle Schools: School Choice as a Middle-Class Conversion Strategy

School choice issues in all transitional educational stages deserve critical studies (Ball 2003). In this section, we will focus on examining parental choice of middle schools because this is the most intensive field where parental choice practices are subject to the most maneuvering. Our analysis draws on Xiaoxin Wu's (2014) fine book, *School Choice in China: A Different Tale?* which explores middle school choice issues in Nanning, the capital city of Guangxi Zhuang Autonomous Region/Province in southern China. As a metropolitan city in China, Nanning shares many similarities to other Chinese cities. Many of the forces, practices, and discourses identified in Xiaoxin Wu's study are also applicable to school choice issues in the compulsory education sector elsewhere in urban China.

Although focusing on middle-class parental choice of school, Xiaoxin Wu is conscious of other classes and their position in an increasingly marketized situation for advancement. With increasing urbanization and the influx of millions of migrant workers into Chinese cities, it is also of considerable importance to show how the school choice situation of migrant workers is markedly different from that of middle-class families. Thus, Xiaoxin employs a comparative perspective in his research design and data collection. He chose three state middle schools with different tiers in Nanning: Schools A and B are key schools and more likely to have choice students who come from privileged families, whereas School C is a below-average school that tends to serve working-class families such as migrant workers. Using a range of data, his study provides us with a holistic picture of parental school choice and how it does indeed serve both to reproduce existing inequalities and to actually produce new ones. Just as importantly, his focus on unpacking the practices of middle-class, parent initiated school choice documents the process of the recontextualization of school choice in China. As we will see, the definition of "democracy as choice" clearly advantages particular class actors.

Xiaoxin Wu draws on Pierre Bourdieu's theory of capital formation, accumulation, and mobilization to demonstrate the practices of market-based parental choice in China. In doing so, he also provides us with an example of how even the most detailed empirical analyses can be enriched by the use of substantive theoretical resources. As many readers may know, Bourdieu's work has become a powerful theoretical framework to unravel the complex processes of school choice in the education market in Western contexts (Ball 2003; Ball et al. 1995; Ball and Vincent 1998; Rollock et al. 2014). Bourdieu (1986) has described three major forms of capital (economic, cultural, and social) and emphasized that these different types of capital can be converted into other forms. Drawing on these distinctions, Xiaoxin Wu (2014) insightfully applies Bourdieu's theory to the specific conditions of school choice issues in China, again with an emphasis on uncovering the practices of middle-class families.

It is widely recognized that there is a special relationship between the middle class and education; the middle class is more dependent on educational qualifications than other social classes (Apple 2006; Ball 2003; Bernstein 1977; Bourdieu 1984; Power and Whitty 2006). Like their counterparts in the West, middle-class Chinese parents are also actively involved in their children's education by taking them on cultural trips and helping them acquire cultural capital, including the accumulation of educational credentials in such things as mathematics contests and English language contests. Not surprisingly, Xiaoxin Wu's study reveals that a majority of parents at both Schools A and B and only a few at School C sent their children to extracurricular activities. This disparity is consistent with the difference in parents' educational levels among the three schools because, again not surprisingly, parents of children in the two key schools (Schools A and B) are better educated than those in non-key schools (School C).

Besides hiring private tutors, middle-class Chinese families send their children to various types of after-school classes in the compulsory education stage. The purpose of doing so is not just for simply cultivating their children's special talents but also for accumulating cultural capital for "*zhankeng*" (占坑, place-holding). *Zhankeng* means that if a student attends extracurricular classes run by key schools or by private tutoring institutions with close relations with key schools (what are called *zhankeng* classes, 占坑班), he or she will have more opportunities to be admitted to these key schools. There is part of a hidden game under the "*zhankeng*" phenomenon. Although the *Compulsory Education Law* has exempted students from entrance examinations and restricted schools from holding entrance exams, key schools still want to recruit top performing students to maintain their reputation. *Zhankeng* classes not only allow key schools to evaluate students' academic performance and potential and find those students that they prefer, but these classes also provide students with possible entry into their desired key schools.

In cosmopolitan cities such as Beijing, school choice competition is even more fierce. To increase the opportunities for their children to attend key schools, many parents register for *zhankeng* classes in several target schools. When there are time conflicts for their children to take classes in certain schools, parents attend training classes, take notes, and then tutor their children at home. Such practices require parental investment of both money and time. *Zhankeng* becomes a vivid metaphor for positional competition in the school choice market.

The payoff of parental involvement in the acquisition of cultural capital can be shown in the conversion of cultural capital into economic capital in the school choice competition. For instance, a son of one of Xiaoxin Wu's parent interviewees has more than 20 certificates in mathematics and English contests. Acquiring such cultural capital allowed this student to attend a key state middle school with a waiver of the choice fee and an award of ¥500. As the parent commented,

> It is obvious now that the most valuable investment for the family is to invest in the child. His success in study can win him a place in the preferred

school and save the choice fee for the family, a situation of killing two birds with one stone.

(pp. 65–66)

However, *zhankeng* does not stand alone. It is closely connected to something else of considerable significance. In the process of school choice, privileged Chinese parents' deep motivation for acquiring valued forms of cultural capital is similar to the investment and mobilization of their social capital. To understand this, we need to say something about its linkages with the concept of *guanxi* (关系) in the Chinese context.

In Xiaoxin Wu's words:

> *Guanxi* is regarded as a form of social capital, and the network consists of the ties between people and the access to the resources. The amount of social capital one possesses depends on the size of his *guanxi* networks and the amount of the social capital that each … member of the network possesses.

(p. 69)

Given the history of the hierarchal political system in China, *guanxi* networks play an important role in the school choice process. In the face of fierce competition for limited spaces in oversubscribed schools, choice students with a "leader's memo" are more likely to enter their target schools than those without strong relationships with the leaders who are in powerful and/or influential positions. In addition, because the Chinese government officially bans school choice practices, the lack of open application and transparent screening requires parents to seek effective ways to obtain insider information about both admission policies and the amount of choice fees at their desired schools. Who you know matters because to a large extent it will determine how much insider information you may get and whether it is possible for you to make an exceptional entry into a desired school.

The most interesting part about the role of *guanxi* is that it can be converted in conjunction with economic capital. As Xiaoxin Wu points out, the use of *guanxi* can be to reduce or waive the choice fee if *guanxi* is very strong. Given the importance of *guanxi*, advantaged Chinese parents usually begin to make early investments in developing their *guanxi* networks and accumulating their social capital networks for potential use in the future. The construction and mobilization of *guanxi* networks in the Chinese context is closely connected to the use of economic capital, as money must be paid to chosen schools (choice fees) during the school choice process and a good deal of money is needed for the investment in preparatory activities, including taking extracurricular classes, hiring tutors, and participating in various contests (p. 82).

The social and economic strategies and capital conversions we have described above are crucial. Choice fees constitute one of the striking features of parental school choice in the Chinese context. These fees vary depending on the locations and reputations of schools, students' academic performance, the influence of *guanxi*, and so on. With the widespread growth in parental choice of schools since the early 1990s, choice fees have increased sharply. Xiaoxin Wu notes that the highest choice fee in Beijing rose from ¥50,000 in 1995 to ¥120,000 in 2007. Payment for the choice of desired schools has become "a hidden rule" in China, a fact that has unfortunately led to the growth of choice fee-related corruption. Because of this, the requirement of a choice fee in the compulsory education sector has become one of the most contested issues in Chinese education because it conflicts with the mandate of "free education" articulated by the law. "Democracy" is, hence, definitely *not* free.

Economic capital works in ways other than the hidden rule of choice fees as well. Like many parents in the West, Chinese parents often try to buy a house in the catchment area of preferred schools, what is called a "catchment house," because it is the most reliable and legitimate way to achieve choice of school. As we noted in an earlier part of this chapter, the *Compulsory Education Law* underscores that students should enroll in schools near the places where their residence is registered. In many cases, by purchasing a "catchment house," the *hukou* (household registration) certificate of a family can be changed to show an address in the catchment area. This basically guarantees that a child attends the desired school affiliated with the neighborhood even if he or she does not possess sufficient cultural and social capital.

However, we need to be honest here. As is often the case internationally, by and large only affluent people are able to relocate their families by buying "catchment houses," given the current real estate market in China. "Catchment houses" have become too expensive for ordinary middle-class Chinese families to afford. To a large extent, then, once again economic capital determines the ability of a Chinese family to operate effectively on the terrain of school choice.

However, parents are not the only main actors in the school choice process. Schools and the Chinese government themselves at many levels are also deeply involved in the economics of school choice. This involvement of multiple actors in the school choice market makes the picture of parent-initiated choice more complicated. By connecting to Xiaoxin Wu's examination of who benefits from choice practices, particularly choice fees, we need to discuss a number of the additional and quite complicated effects of school choice policies and parental school choice in the Chinese context. This too provides a more nuanced understanding of how choice actually works and once again may lead us to have a less romantic sense of its effects and of the social realities it both responds to and creates.

Contradictory Effects and the Politics of "Not Seeing"

As we have seen, *School Choice in China* gives a well-balanced description of the (seemingly) positive and negative effects of school choice policies and parental school choice in China. But Xiaoxin Wu's analysis does not end there. He points out that both schools and the Chinese state also benefit from choice fees. Given the reality of insufficient government investment in education, choice fees have become an important source of non-budgetary income for schools. As Xiaoxin Wu has found, "Choice fees have made it possible [for schools] to update teaching facilities, purchase new equipment, construct new buildings, refurbish old buildings and maintain the campus" (p. 101). Some teachers also become the beneficiaries of parental choice of school because choice fees are used to increase their income and improve their welfare. The flight of highly qualified teachers is often accompanied with the flight of top-performing teachers from non-key schools to key schools. As one might expect, this actually increases (rather than reduces) existing disparities among schools.

Choice fees are also a significant source of funds for the Chinese government. In many places, schools need to submit the choice fees they collect to the local government; the government usually keeps 30% while returning the rest to schools. The share of choice fees by the local government is used to build new schools and/or is redistributed to non-key schools or poor schools to update educational equipment and help them catch up with those key schools. In this sense, such a policy allows the local government to cash in on the emergence of parental school choice and generates additional funds for state education through parental contributions.

Xiaoxin Wu emphasizes that economic interests are not only the driving force for Chinese state schools to take choice students, but they also have influenced the central government's policy making and implementation of school choice policies. For instance, for a period of time, the Chinese government accommodated middle-class parents' demands for quality education by converting state schools in the compulsory sector into quasi-public institutions. These "converted schools" could charge choice fees and high tuition fees without violating the *Compulsory Education Law* (Wu 2008, p. 608). As Z. Wu and Shen (2006) comment, while government policy officially has banned school choice practices in the compulsory education sector on one hand, it has tended to accommodate it on the other. "Gray markets" were constructed due to the conflicts between the official discourse of banning school choice and the actual practices of the participation of parents, schools, and local governments in the school choice process. The result has been that the collection of choice fees is basically removed from the budget audit system.

In essence, the situation is one of what might best be called an "epistemological fog." Knowledge is dangerous. Not seeing what is actually happening is the wiser choice for dominant groups and government officials because knowledge may require action (see Apple 2013, 2016). Thus, choice fee-related corruption has become a common problem, with serious issues such as the embezzlement and misuse of choice fees and abuse of political power for private interests by sending "leader's memos" or accepting bribes for school admission. This puts the state in a deeply paradoxical position, for it then is constantly struggling with school choice-related policies and their consequent complicated and often contradictory outcomes. In the process, the state's legitimacy can be called into question.

As Xiaoxin Wu notes, in the Chinese context, parental choice of school has been from the bottom-up. His study reveals that based on their self-interests, parents, schools, and local governments have all become actors in the practices of school choice in the compulsory education sector. Although there are clear tensions and conflicts between these interest groups, as he mentions, current school choice-related policies seem to be pragmatic solutions to meet the needs of dominant interest groups. Given this, it is even more imperative that we ask in whose interests they are carried out, who are included, and who are excluded (Apple 2004, 2006). As *School Choice in China* powerfully shows, middle-class families are included into, and working-class and migrant families are excluded from, choice practices. Although we wish that research such as that done by Xiaoxin Wu and others would have provided us with more voices from the disadvantaged groups, even their limited presence helps us to better understand the realities of parental school choice (see also Yu 2016).

As demonstrated so far, parental choice of middle school in urban China is "an articulated combination" of multiple social forces (historical, political, economic, ideological), discourses (such as promoting the modernization of Chinese society and pursuing "quality" education), and choice practices of rising Chinese middle classes (Hall 1980). The market-oriented social and educational reforms created the seemingly potent possibility of these (re)articulations. However, the contradictory effects of school choice in the compulsory education sector reveal the struggles of dominant social groups, such as the Chinese state, local governments, key schools, and middle-class families, in the process of legitimating their dominant positions during the shift between a socialist egalitarian mode of education and a liberal competitive model. Similar struggles play out in the field of high school choice in Chinese urban areas, but with a new configuration.

Mapping the Context of the Choice of Internationally Focused High Schools

High school education is not compulsory in China. There are two major types of high schools in this post-compulsory education sector—general high schools (*putong gaozhong*, 普通高中) and vocational high schools (*zhiye gaozhong*, 职业高中). General high schools are divided into ordinary and key high schools. As aforementioned, there are different tiers of key high schools—national, provincial, municipal, country, or district. The higher the level, the better a key school is. The high school choice phenomenon concentrates on the choice of those general public high schools, particularly key public high schools.

The market-oriented educational reforms and contesting social, political, historical, and ideological forces that we have discussed above also play out in the high school choice market. The close link between high school admission and China's selective examination system formed a unique configuration of high school choice process, particularly surrounding the issue of choice fees. In China, the high school that students attend among their desirable ones largely depends on their scores on *zhongkao* (中考, High School Entrance Examination). *Zhongkao* and high school admission policy is administrated by local educational authorities. As Xiaoxin Wu (2008) describes, "Each public school is given a certain quota of enrolment called plan or compulsory enrolment. After they complete this enrolment, they are allowed to take students whose scores are usually lower than the threshold score" (p. 605). Such students are called "choice students" (*zexiao sheng*, 择校生). Schools charge choice fees (*zexiao fei*, 择校费) from choice students. The choice fees vary depending on regions, types of public high schools, students' *zhongkao* scores, and changing policies on choice. For instance:

> In 2003, a school in Beijing made it clear in its policy of taking choice students; for those choice students whose test scores are lower than the threshold score, ¥10,000 for one point (F. Chen 2003). That is, if you are five points below the threshold score, you have to pay extra ¥50,000.
>
> In Jiangxi Province, the annual choice fee for provincial key senior middle school rose from ¥1289 in 1997 to ¥10,000 in 2004. The annual average savings per capita of the lower and lower-middle income families in that province was only ¥1010.5 in 2002 (Leng and Leng 2004). For a family of three people (Chinese families normally have only one child), the potential saving is about ¥3000. Therefore, it will take them 10-years of savings to cover the cost of a child's three-year study in such school, which we know is not possible because the savings also have to be used to cover housing, medical and other expenses, etc.
>
> *(Wu, Xiaoxin 2008, p. 605)*

The intake of choice students and charge of choice fees are controversial, a fact that is demonstrated by the changing policy on these issues. The Chinese government's policies on choice of public high schools have gone through three main stages. First, from the 1990s to 2000, the government tended to "accept" the emergence and development of public high school choice and there were no clear regulations on this issue. The fast growth of a high school choice market caused chaos. In addition to charging choice fees, high school choice practices also involved the use of other strategies such as "sponsor fees" and "co-founding fees," which were also popular in school choice at the compulsory education sector. Sponsor fees (*zanzhu fee*, 赞助费) mean "the large sum of extra money one is supposed to 'willingly give to the destination school to secure a school place'" while co-founding fees (*gongjian fee*, 共建费) refer to "the money given to preferred schools by work units to ensure that children from the work units can attend their co-founding schools, which are, in most cases, the best local schools"

(Wu, Xiaoxin, 2008 p. 600). Such arbitrary fees and charges involve the power of using political and economic capital in the school choice market, which leads to educational inequality (Yang, D. 2006; Yang, P. 2009; Ye, X. 2012).

The second stage was from 2001 to 2011. In face of the increasingly chaotic collection of school choice-related fees and the rise of public complaints about this issue, the Chinese central government promulgated the *Opinions of the State Council Rectification Office and the Ministry of Education on Further Curbing Arbitrary Fee Collection* in 2001. Focusing on the issue of school choice fees in large and medium-sized cities, the document makes explicit provisions on the recruitment of high school choice students, which is called the Three-Restriction Policy (restrictions on student numbers, the amount of choice fees, and enrollment scores). Since 2001, the Chinese government has issued an updated implementation guideline on the "Work of Curbing Arbitrary Fee Collection" every year. The enactment of these policies has involved the participation of seven key departments of the central government, including the Ministry of Education, the State Council Rectification Office, Ministry of Supervision, National Development and Reform Commission, Ministry of Finance, National Audit Office, and General Administration of Press and Publication, which shows the government's seriousness about this educational issue. According to the Three-Restriction Policy, the maximum percentage of choice students that a school can recruit each year is 30% (Ministry of Education 2006). However, "this restriction is not always rigorously observed" (Wu, Xiaoxin, 2008, p. 605). The Three-Restriction Policy also requires that the standards of choice fees are proposed by local educational authorities and approved by provincial-level Chinese governments, and then will be made public to the society. Despite these efforts of the Chinese government to regulate public high school choice, one of the most significant complaints against this choice policy is that the key high schools' intake of choice students adversely affects the educational opportunities of other students who also desire to attend quality schools.

Given the controversial issues surrounding high school choice students, the Chinese central government stipulated that starting from the fall of 2012, the percentage of choice students a school can accept should not exceed 20%. The government planned to cancel the recruitment of choice students at public high schools within three years (Ministry of Education 2012). Up to 2015, Beijing, Guangdong, and Anhui were among the many cities and provinces that had implemented the cancellation of high school choice students. The practices and effects of these choice policies deserve further in-depth investigation. However, interestingly, a new trend of parental choice of high school has been emerging in China as the Three-Restriction Policy was strictly regulated by the Chinese central government. This is the focus of our next discussion which will closely examine the ways in which the international as well as national conversion strategies now have increasingly rearticulated "democracy as choice" to benefit particular class actors. In this case, the curriculum itself and the politics of "official knowledge" (Apple 2014) plays a large role.

The Rearticulation of Global Education Markets and Chinese Education Markets

Since 2010, the number of urban Chinese high school students applying to US universities has rapidly grown. Many of these students have chosen the emerging international curriculum programs established by Chinese key public high schools in big cities. These programs are designed to prepare Chinese students for the US college application process by exposing them to an internationalized curriculum—an integration of the Chinese national curriculum with various imported international curricula, such as Advanced Placement (AP) and Global Assessment Certificate (GAC). These emerging curriculum programs are ostensibly public, but tuition is expensive—from about ¥60,000 to ¥120,000 (about $9,600 to $19,000) each year, which is far more expensive than that of any state high school as yearly tuition for these institutions is approximately ¥1,000 to ¥2,000 (Li 2008; Liu, J. et al. 2012; Shen 2006; Xue and Tang 2016). Compared with the average annual family income in China in 2012—¥13,033 (Xie et al. 2013), it is clear that only wealthy Chinese families can send their children to these new fee-charging high school programs. The "public" programs exclude disadvantaged students and create unequal access to internationalized curriculum and education. This phenomenon presents a new configuration of high school choice in China. The effects and implications of how these new international curriculum programs have changed school access deserves serious study.

Shuning Liu's recent research project takes a closer look at this educational phenomenon. One part of her research focuses on the complexities of urban Chinese students' choice to attend emerging internationally focused public high schools. The data discussed in this section is derived from her larger research project on educational experiences of Chinese students who choose to go to US colleges. In this large study, Shuning used multi-sited ethnography as a systematic data collection approach to explore various sites within the social, economic, and political landscapes of privileged Chinese young people's lives. In addition to analyzing policy documents, Shuning conducted an intensive fieldwork in 2013 in an internationally focused public high school in Moon City (pseudonym), a cosmopolitan city in China. This school is called Sunny High (pseudonym) International Division that offers an International curriculum program named International Access Project (pseudonym) (IAP). Sunny High is a reputational key high school in Moon City. The Sunny High IAP Program is the largest among the 24 government-approved international high school curriculum programs in the city. Shuning employed participant observation, informal conversations, semi-structured interviews, a survey at the field study school, and site document collection to generate rich descriptions. She conducted in-depth interviews with students, parents, as well as school teachers and administrators.

As discussed in the beginning of this section, there are "disjunctures, contradictions, antagonisms and tensions" in the internal organization of the evolving high school choice market in China. In what follows, we shall look at how "their external conditions of existence created the possibility of 'disarticulation and rearticulation' in the formation of the internationally focused high school choice movement" (Clarke 2015, p. 277). We shall also link the exploration of the internal contradictions and tensions in the choice practices to the analysis of external conditions. Specifically, we will examine how the new configuration of high school choice is constructed by the combination of the (re)articulation of global and Chinese education markets, the discourses of the internationalization of education and the cultivation of "international talents" highlighted in recent Chinese educational reforms, and choice practices of Chinese middle-upper and upper classes. We will also discuss the contradictory effects in the process of articulation, rearticulation, and disarticulation, as well as the politics of neoliberal educational experiment.

As one of us has argued elsewhere (Liu 2015; Liu 2016), the international high school curriculum programs in China emerge at a particular time when Chinese education markets connect with global education markets. China's entry into the World Trade Organization (WTO) in 2001 opens up spaces for the infiltration of the global education services industry into Chinese education markets, and create opportunities for wealthy Chinese families to mobilize their capital in the international education market. Particularly since 2008, the year of a global financial crisis, many universities in the United States have faced budget cuts. US universities have become increasingly open to wealthy Chinese students who can afford international tuition for their college education. Meanwhile, the Chinese government's tightening policies on public high school choice narrow the opportunities for privileged Chinese families to send their children to elite Chinese schools and universities. The high demand of quality educational resources from privileged Chinese social classes was articulated with the trend of global higher education, which created a potential market for international education business. In addition, the neoliberal approach to trade in educational services embedded in the WTO's General Agreement on Trade in Services (GATS) (Robertson 2003) provides an opportunity for Chinese high schools to enter into that global education market because high school education is not compulsory and educational service at the high school level can be traded in the global education market. These conditions created the possibility of the disarticulation of college choice and the choice of Chinese key high schools, and the rearticulation of choice of world-class universities abroad and the emerging internationally focused high school market.

The Discourses of the Internationalization of Education and the Cultivation of "International Talents"

Following the market-oriented educational reforms, such as the decentralization and financial diversification of education, three major educational reforms and policies in the 2000s have provided new conditions and discourses for the development of international high school programs in China. These educational reforms and policies include the *New Curriculum Reform of Chinese Basic Education*, the *Chinese-Foreign Cooperation in Running Schools (CFCRS) policy*, and the *National Guidelines for Medium- and Long-term Educational Reform and Development (2010-2020)*. The articulation of these educational policies foregrounds the discourses of the internationalization of education and the cultivation of "international talents," which constitute the formation of internationally focused high schools in China.

The *New Curriculum Reform of Chinese Basic Education* was initiated in 1999 and implemented in the 2000s. This curriculum reform was expected to transform Chinese education from *yingshi jiaoyu* (应试教育, examination-oriented education) to *sushi jiaoyu* (素质教育, quality education) (Guan and Meng 2007; Zhong 2006). The New Curriculum Reform emphasizes improving the global competence of the Chinese population in the face of challenges arising from the knowledge-based economy. This educational reform reflects the fact that the Chinese government connects the nurturing of "talents" (*rencai*, 人才, i.e., human capital) with the building of a competent nation-state as a response to the requirement of international economic competition. However, the New Curriculum Reform has encountered many "bottlenecks," which made the Chinese government seek solutions via external forces. In particular, the state places hope in the introduction of high-quality foreign educational resources through new international collaborative program modes. This solution to the challenges of the New Curriculum Reforms point to the articulation of the *Chinese-Foreign Cooperation in Running Schools (CFCRS) policy* and the curriculum reform.

The new version of CFCRS policy was promulgated in 2003 and enhanced in 2004 (MOE 2003, 2004). The practices of CFCRS have been extended from Chinese universities to high schools and involves the exploration of new talent-cultivating patterns. Since 2008, the Chinese government had gradually approved CFCRS High School programs, which are commonly called international high school curriculum programs. As of 2014, there have been 90 high school international programs approved by the Chinese government (NetEase Education 2015).[4] The majority of these programs were newly created by Chinese elite public high schools in big cities through supposedly cooperating with foreign education institutions. This is the focus of Shuning's research. The unique institutional structure of the CFCRS policy brings private education companies into the development of international programs for profit making. Take the Sunny High IAP international curriculum program as an example. Shuning's study points out that according to the government document, Sunny High and a US private high school are partner schools in creating this international curriculum program. However, a for-profit Chinese education company is a de facto partner with the Chinese key public high school to develop the Sunny High IAP program. The education company helped with making connections between Sunny High and the US high school in dealing with the partnership required by the CFCRS policy while the company also imported an international curriculum program from the United

States and collaborated with Sunny High to integrate the imported international curriculum with Chinese high school curriculum (for details see Liu 2015). To a large extent, the interventions of these private institutions into Chinese public education reforms are tacit business practices. Choice programs hence not only advantage more affluent Chinese, but also provide a space for profit (see also Ball 2007, 2012).

In addition, the *National Guidelines for Medium- and Long-term Educational Reform and Development 2010-2020* (MOE 2010), abbreviated as "The Guidelines," create the historical and policy context that also constitutes the formation of internationally focused Chinese public high schools. This new education policy puts the internationalization of high school education on the agenda. It highlights the importance of diversifying Chinese high schools, the school-running system, and the modes of education. It also encourages Chinese key public schools to expand their high-quality education resources to meet the needs of students with differing potential. The Guidelines marked a new development in the internationalization and modernization of the Chinese education system. It provides a normative discourse for legitimating the market-oriented international high school programs.

Shuning's study reveals that the emerging public international high school curriculum programs are supported by the *Chinese-Foreign Cooperation in Running Schools (CFCRS) policy* and legitimated by the Chinese government. In the legitimation process, these international programs are framed as the experiment of the Chinese New Curriculum Reform by key state high schools and local educational authorities. The state seems to "accept" the discourse of educational experiment. To further legitimate these new international programs, the dominant social groups connect the educational programs with the cultivation of "international talents" (*guoji rencai,* 国际人才, i.e., international human capital), a discourse articulated by the *National Guidelines for Medium and Long-term Education Reform and Development (2010-2020).* Specifically, the international programs are framed as a way to foster students with international perspectives and cross-cultural understanding for Chinese economic development.

Neoliberal globalization of education policy provides the conditions and possibilities for dominant social groups to build connections between practices, interests, rhetorical discourses, common senses, and social forces. The practice of articulation is not fixed; it is fraught with contradictions, contradictions that can be better understood by looking at the practices and effects of parental choice of internationally focused public high schools.

Internationally Focused High Schools: New Parental Choice of Schools in China?

In this section, we will examine how parental choice of the Sunny High IAP International Curriculum Program reflects the interests and strategies of burgeoning Chinese elite classes in the struggle for legitimation and recognition.[5] This section is intended to uncover the complexities of students' choice to attend internationally-focused high schools.

Shuning's study finds that students enrolled in Sunny High IAP International Curriculum Program are all urban-*hukou (户口*, household registration) holders. They are divided into three groups. The majority of them are Moon City residents. About one-fourth of the students did not have Moon City *hukou*. Among the latter group, half of them have received elementary and middle school education in this cosmopolitan city. Another half have completed their pre-high school education from provinces outside Moon City. Despite the difference in having or not having Moon City *hukou*, the students have similar family backgrounds. Their parents are higher managerial and professional people, business owners, or government officers who have high economic capital, social capital, and/or cultural capital. In the language of the school teachers and administrators whom Shuning interviewed, these parents are "successful people" (*chenggong renshi*, 成功人士). In other words, they belong to an interest group that tends to benefit a good deal in contemporary Chinese society (Yan and Chang 2009). Based on family incomes, these socially elite groups would be considered middle-upper and upper classes. In addition, the survey data conducted at the school also shows that 80% of the students in the school have attended public key middle schools.

The interview data reveal the complexity of the motivations and contextual factors that influenced the high school choice of these socially elite Chinese students. The parents of these students were highly engaged in the processes and decision-making behind choosing a high school. Student choice of a high school is indeed a parent-initiated school choice. For the majority of the students attending Sunny High IAP, failure to get admitted to public key high schools due to their low test scores on *zhongkao (*中考, High School Entrance Exam) is the most important reason why they chose international divisions or international curriculum programs created by public key high schools. Like their academically elite Chinese counterparts, these students preferred attending key high schools because usually only excellent students could be selected by such schools and also the schools act as a symbolic threshold to access top universities in China. As a parent interviewee explained,

> There are too many thresholds in the Chinese education system. Why? It is because we have too many people in China. The expansion of college enrollments has led to the result that many Chinese college graduates cannot find jobs. The labor market is extremely competitive. The key school system could keep you on the elite track—entering a key elementary school, a key middle school, and then a key high school and an elite Chinese university. If you have no access to the key school system, there is no hope to get in a good university and get a good job. If you are not on the (elite) track, then there is less probability for you to succeed and find a job.

This excerpt highlights the importance of entering the elite track in the Chinese education system. This finding resonates with the literature that despite the substantial expansion of educational opportunities in high school education and higher education in China since the 1990s, the competition of key public high schools has become more intense because attending such schools increases one's likelihood of entry into Chinese top universities (Wu, Xiaogang 2010; Wu, Xiaogang and Zhang 2010; Ye, H. 2015). Like their parents, many students at the Sunny High IAP program recognized that in the Chinese context, educational qualifications from elite institutions serve as "a screening device" and elite education acts as "an arena of competition and social exclusion" (Ball 2003, p. 15). Thus, competing for access to the traditional elite track is taken for granted by the students. However, their low scores on *zhongkao* jeopardized their access to Chinese elite education. But the international curriculum programs created by public key high schools open up an alternative elite pathway for them—not to the Chinese elite universities that they originally preferred, but to the world-class universities that are even more valued than the former. This is exactly true for many students at the Sunny High IAP program, who have studied in key middle schools. Their high school choices were oriented toward elite college education.

For many parent interviewees, sending their children to the emerging internationally focused high schools was a "back-up" plan. Knowing that their children might not be able to achieve enough high scores on *zhongkao* to be admitted to key public high schools, some parents started early to collect information about these new types of high schools. Their social and cultural capital played an important role in the information gathering process. Asking friends whose children attended similar schools often provided trustworthy "grapevine" or "hot" knowledge about "best" schools. Attending information sessions organized by schools helped parents gather "objective" data and "cold" formal knowledge (Ball and Vincent 1998). These choice activities show that these parents are "active choosers" of high schools.

Although originally not interested in attending internationally-focused high schools, student informants who received their *zhongkao* results and knew that they were not eligible to enter a key high school accepted and appreciated their parents' back-up option of school choice. In making sense of their high school choice for their children, many parents also noted that Sunny High IAP curriculum program was appealing to them in that compared with the test-driven teaching and learning in regular Chinese high schools, such a school was intended to help students pursue a personalized study plan. As one parent commented, "It sounded that students enrolled in such schools had a relaxing school life and also could easily go to US colleges." The first class of students from Sunny High IAP graduated in 2011. The school reported that all of the graduates were admitted by the top 50 US universities. This school outcome excited prospective parents. They knew that the first class of students at the school were not high academic achievers because many of them entered the Sunny High IAP Program with much lower test scores on *zhongkao* in 2008. Many parents believed that if such students went to the top 50 US universities, their own children could easily reach these goals because their children were higher academic achievers than those students.

For those students who received their compulsory education in Moon City, but did not have Moon City *hukou*, choosing to attend an internationally focused high school was a "reluctant" choice. The students without the *hukou* of this city could not attend *gaokao* (高考, College Entrance Examination) in Moon City. As a female parent, who migrated to the city and became a successful business woman, shared in the context of her experiences of school choice, the household registration system restricted her son's entry to middle school, high school, and *gaokao*-taking in Moon City. With the help of friends, she found an appropriate person and paid ¥150,000 (approximately equal to $23,000) school choice fees for her child to enter Sunny Middle School, the Middle School Section of Sunny High. She didn't even know the distribution of the choice fee and how much money was actually paid to the school, a fact that reflects the choice fee-related corruption that we discussed earlier in this chapter. She noted that she didn't need to know because what she cared about was the result. Paying the choice fee did help her son go to the desired key middle school. She mentioned that she could also use this social network (of course, along with the need to pay choice fees or sponsor fees) to help her child enter Sunny High.

However, knowing that her son was not a top student academically, she was worried that he would not be as competent as elite students at Sunny High and thus might be looked down on by others. She worried that such a stressful experience would make him lose his confidence. More importantly, she mentioned that due to the lack of a Moon City *hukou*, her son could not attend *gaokao* in the city. She couldn't send him to go back to his home province to take the *gaokao* because what he studied in Moon City was different from the one there. In addition, the cut-off points of the *gaokao* scores in their home province were particularly high. She emphasized that there was too much uncertainty if her son chose to take *gaokao* in the home province. Therefore, she had to choose a "smooth pathway" for her son by sending him to Sunny High International Division because this way could enable him to access elite college education overseas.

For such high-income migrant families, choosing internationally focused high schools does seem like a "reluctant" choice. However, it is also a strategic choice. Despite the restriction of the household registration system, these families were able to utilize their economic, social, and cultural capital to help their children navigate the process of seeking access to alternative pathways to elite education. Compared with millions of children from low-income migrant families, who face similar difficulties in accessing educational resources and opportunities in China (Yu 2016), high-income migrant elites were able to overcome or circumvent the barriers using their various types of capital.

Our analysis of privileged parents' choice of high school demonstrates how their educational practices were shaped by struggles for elite positions through access to elite education. When they encounter the constraints of the elite education system in China, such as high-stakes testing and the restriction of the household registration system, Chinese middle-upper and upper classes struggle to maintain and enhance their positions in the social order through access to Chinese elite higher education institutions. Thanks to neoliberal globalization, world-class universities in the West open opportunities for these social groups to access the field of international elite education. The newly-established international high school programs in China provide these Chinese elite classes with a new educational pathway to elite education in an international context. The international programs become an intersection of the field of elite education (in both Chinese and international contexts) and the field of social classes, which constitutes a new field of power relations and also a field of struggle. Thus, these social actors "unwittingly reproduce or change those class distinctions simply by pursuing their own strategies within the sets of constraints and opportunities available to them" (Swartz 1997, p. 134). Clearly then, these Chinese middle-upper and upper classes' field-specific practices are related to class strategies and the field of power. Let us say more about this.

The choice practices of these growing Chinese elite classes in the high school international education market were interest-driven. Their aspirations for either Chinese or international elite higher education institutions represented their struggle over important forms of cultural capital—including educational capital, which is often translated into elite educational credentials, an institutionalized form of cultural capital (Waters 2006). Whether for "reluctant choosers" or "active choosers," accumulating more valuable forms of cultural capital was a taken-for-granted strategy to secure a dominant position in the field of power.

The parents of these privileged students were highly strategic in their decisions to engage with an international education market. Capital conversion was used to transfer strategic advantage from these privileged parents to their children. Shuning's study reveals how the new Chinese elite families utilize various type of capital—economic, cultural, and social capital—in the process of choice and decision-making. Particular attention should be given to the use of economic capital because it acted as a precondition for the educational choice of the Chinese middle-upper and upper classes. Some of the parent participants have tabulated the cost of attending an international high school program and a US university— it was about ¥2,000,000 (approximately $300,000). The "volume" of economic capital (material resources) needed for this educational choice excluded the families who do not have the ability to pay the educational cost.

The taste for this new elite education is not cheap (Ball 2015). Only wealthy Chinese families are able to buy access to international educational resources and opportunities for their own children, and convert their economic capital into cultural and social capital that could be further converted into financial capital. As a male parent who was a director of a Chinese national science laboratory highlighted, "The classmates and schoolmates who you study with matter a lot because you study in this school for preparation for the US college application and also for building a social network for the future use." The social capital accumulated through the construction of social connections made at this internationally-focused high school has the potential to be converted into economic capital through access to valued information and resources. Class strategies used by these Chinese middle-upper and upper-class families lead to social production.

In summary, this section examines the complexities of students' choice to attend international high school curriculum programs. It demonstrates the practices of market-based parent-initiated school choice in China. We argue that the rising Chinese middle-upper and upper classes mobilize various types of capital and power in an international education market to pursue their class interests. Their educational practices, whether their deployment of class strategies or their unconscious acceptance of the rules of the game in which they play, constitute the production of the fields of international high school curriculum programs and international elite education, which overlap with multiple other fields, such as social class. Through the realization of social advantages in education, the practices of parent-initiated choice of internationally focused Chinese public high schools enhance the marketization and privatization of education, which exacerbates existing educational and social inequality. In this process, fields and field-specific practices also shape the identity formation of these social classes.

Contradictory Effects and the Politics of "Educational Experiment"

The analysis of parental choice of internationally focused high schools points out the class interests, struggles, and strategies of new Chinese elite classes. The connection between this analysis and the analysis of the external conditions of existence outlines the objective structure of the relations between the positions occupied by key stakeholders, including the middle-upper and upper-classes, Chinese public key high schools, the Chinese state, and various domestic and international for-profit education businesses.[6] Each stakeholder has their own interests and competes for the legitimation of their power within the particular fields where their practices occur. However, the marketization and privatization of education facilitated by neoliberal globalization and market-oriented education policies and practices open up space for them to articulate and rearticulate, which maximizes their own interests and realizes their common interests. Shuning's study points out that the interests of public key high schools, the Chinese state, and various domestic and international for-profit businesses are coordinated with the interests of the new Chinese elites. This coordination process is fraught with contradictions.

The stretch of neoliberal education policies and practices into international spaces provides the possibility for students from wealthy Chinese families to pursue international education as a form of capital conversion for occupying dominant positions in a globalizing world. The emerging international high school programs created by Chinese key public high schools meet the private needs and interests of these privileged classes—upward social mobility. Chinese middle-upper and upper classes became key actors in the international high school curriculum program market. As a parent commented, "Compared to the grey markets of parental choice of Chinese public key schools, the international high school curriculum program market is a transparent market because it lists the price [tuition] I need to pay for service provision." The emerging international high school curriculum programs are demanded by and cater to rising Chinese elite classes.

For public key high schools like Sunny High, developing an international high school curriculum program has educational, social, political, and economic meanings. As school administrators emphasized, such a program met a social need and provided those students who could not access Chinese elite universities with an opportunity to make their college choice globally. The international program was framed as having great potential to improve Chinese education reforms. It helped leverage its international profile and enhanced the school reputation in order to occupy a competitive position among key schools. In this sense, establishing an international high school curriculum was for the maintenance and production of the school's eliteness. As school administrators repeatedly emphasized, the market of international high school curriculum programs was very competitive. The school needed to compete for students in the recruitment markets.

More importantly, the high tuition-charging international program generated important revenue for school survival and development. As Mrs. Zhao, an administrator of Sunny High International Division, noted:

> Sunny High IAP Program is an experimental project. It plays a leading role in developing international high school curriculum programs in Moon City. It is on the cutting edge of Chinese educational reforms. If this program is well developed, the State would popularize our successful reform experience. In fact, the international program is a new growth point. It is a new point of educational growth. It is also a new economic growth point. We indeed need to run this program. The government didn't invest in the program. Thus, students and families themselves need to make investments in it. This program helps improve Sunny High's and our teachers' economic and living conditions because the 15% annual increase in teacher salary largely depends on the economic efficiency of this program. Therefore, this program is a new economic growth point of our school. It is a growth point of Sunny High.

This statement highlights the economic interests that the international program brought to Sunny High. The curriculum program became a crucial source of nonbudgetary income for the school.

From another perspective, the profits that the program made for the public key school alleviate the financial burdens that the Chinese government bears in term of its investment in public schools.

For various educational businesses, profit-making is the main interest that drove them to engage with the development of international high school programs. The involvement of the US private high school and other international education services in the development of the Sunny High IAP Program indicates their interests in expanding their education business in the US into a global education market. "Collaboration" and "partnership," advocated by the *Chinese-Foreign Cooperation in Running Schools (CFCRS) policy*, allow these educational businesses to pursue their own interests in the field of international high school curriculum programs.

For the Chinese government, the newly-established international high school curriculum program is an educational experiment to explore diverse approaches to running schools and to improving Chinese high school curriculum reform. The discourse of educational experiment provides the Chinese government with policy space and flexibility. From a pragmatic point of view, however, creating these international programs catered to social needs, particularly the needs of growing Chinese middle-upper and upper classes while avoiding a drain of capital from China by keeping them consuming high school education within a domestic market. Neoliberal definitions of democracy, hence, "solved" the problems faced by multiple actors and institutions.

To be sure, the emergent international high school curriculum programs are socially produced through the interactions between these dominant interest groups. And there are tensions between these dominant interest groups. For instance, the school's pursuit of quality curriculum development and its emphasis on the long-term development of the program were conflicted with Chinese educational companies' focus on profit-making and lack of dedication to student learning. The privileged Chinese students complained that Sunny High allocated the high tuitions that they paid to the main campus where their academically elite Chinese counterparts study rather than investing more resources in the International Division that they attended. The distribution of students' tuitions was willfully opaque by dominant groups. This secret was kept from "public view," which is part of what Apple (2013, 2016) calls an epistemological fog. Maintaining the fog allows the dominant practices to go forward.

In addition to the interfield contradictions, there are internal tensions within each field. For example, the school struggled with balancing its economic interests and educational commitment to students. The Chinese state itself was struggling with advocating socialism's egalitarian ideas, the ideology of the Chinese Communist Party, while dealing with the inequalities and other problems that the "public" international high school curriculum programs created. When more and more voices were raised in criticism of these programs using public educational resources to provide study-abroad services, the epistemological fog of the international education programs was gradually unveiled.

These criticisms in the populist public sphere pushed the Chinese government to respond. Since 2014, the municipal government of Moon City stopped approving more international high school curriculum programs. The guidelines on the education charges of the CFCRS High School programs was added in the 2014 Chinese government's policy on high school recruitment (Ministry of Education 2014). The issue of international high school curriculum programs became a "hot" educational topic in 2015 national *Lianghui* (全国两会, annual sessions of the National People's Congress and the National Committee of the Chinese People's Political Consultative Conference).[7] Wei Hu, a deputy director of the Shanghai Academy of Educational Science and also a member of the National Committee of the Chinese People's Political Consultative Conference (CPPCC), proposed to regulate the high school international education market. According to the Ministry of Education's (2016) Letter on Reply of Proposal No. 0140 (Education No. 029) of the Fourth Session of the 12th National Committee of the CPPCC, the Chinese central government has been drafting a policy on high school international programs based on conducting an in-depth investigation and extensively solicited the advice of educational experts and the schools that established such programs. This evidence suggests that the Chinese government constantly struggles with the policies on internationally-focused high school choice and their consequent complicated and contradictory outcomes. The evidence also foregrounds the space to intervene in the market-oriented educational reforms. Particular attention should be paid to the state's strategic position on these reforms, which is reflected by the use of the discourse of "educational experiment." Our critical analysis shows that this discourse allows the Chinese state to distance itself from the realities of educational reforms while providing it with greater opportunity for enforcing its legitimacy and capacity to govern education.

Conclusion and Implications

In this chapter, we tracked the formation and development of the "thin democracy" of the school choice movement in China. We mapped the way in which some particularly profound social forces, moments, discourses, and practices are articulated to produce a school choice fever in China. This approach of "thinking relations and connections" (Slack 1996, p. 115) allows us to see school choice as a developing articulated practice. By looking at what has been articulated and rearticulated in the changing configurations of the school choice movement in China, our analysis foregrounds the role of market-oriented educational reforms in "leading to the old linkages being dissolved and new connections—rearticulation—being forged" (Hall 1985, p. 113).

Using Bourdieu's concepts of capital and conversion strategy, we examined choice practices of middle and upper Chinese classes in the school choice markets at the compulsory and post-compulsory education sectors. Our analysis illustrates how these privileged classes strategically utilize various kinds of capital in their choice processes to realize their advantage in education. This analysis points out that the (re)production of advantage through school choice practices leads to educational and social inequalities. Linking critical research on parental choice of middle schools to Shuning's study on the choice of internationally-focused high schools, the chapter shows differential consumption of different volumes of capital, which marks out class fractions among the privileged Chinese social groups.

Through analyzing how market-oriented educational reforms articulated, rearticulated, and disarticulated with Chinese historical, political, and social specificities, this chapter reveals the participation of dominant groups, including Chinese middle, middle-upper, and upper-class families, key state high schools, for-profit educational institutions, local Chinese governments, and the Chinese state, in the changing of the school choice market in China and the creation and maintenance of consensus among them. In this very process of disarticulation and rearticulation, educational resources are redistributed and students from privileged Chinese families are more able to access quality educational resources and opportunities. The educational needs of Chinese middle and upper classes are more recognized and met by Chinese key schools, the Chinese government, and education policies. The exclusion of Chinese working-class and low-income migrant families in the school choice market points out the politics of representation. The politics of redistribution, recognition, and representation, Fraser (2005, 2009) suggests, means that the parent-initiated school choice not only leads to educational inequalities, but also creates social injustice.

In this chapter, we illustrated many of the contradictory effects of school choice policies and practices in Chinese compulsory and post-compulsory education sectors. We highlighted the fact that school choice is a site of contestation. For instance, the conflicts between a central government that calls for the prohibition of school choice practices and local governments that may encourage schools to charge unauthorized choice fees reflect the contradictions between the central government and local governments. Capturing the field of contest is especially important in terms of understanding the crisis of both education and the state. When market-oriented educational reforms are part of a process of opening up the economy, they also can create a powerful ideological crisis.

There are other possible ideological crises to which we need to pay close attention. As the chapter highlights, the bottom-up movement of parental school choice contributes to different ideological forms, such as parents' ever-increasing desire for quality education for their only child. These new ideological forms are often in conflict with the ideological formation that the Chinese Communist Party wants. In such ideological tensions, what do schools stand for? How can the Chinese government covertly support the growth of school choice, a position that privileges democracy as consumer choice based on "possessive individualism" (see, for example, Apple 2006) and at the same time keep the ideology of the Communist Party alive and relevant in daily life? This question goes to the core of the Chinese ideological and social project of building socialism with Chinese characteristics.

In addition, our political analysis of the Chinese state's constant struggles with the choice-related policies and their complicated effects points out the contradictions within the state. Our examination suggests that market-oriented educational reforms such as the policy of decentralization and devolution in education don't necessarily mean that the power of the state was weakened. Rather, such educational reforms imply the shift from state control to governance in education (Mok 2001). As Clarke and Newman (1997) argue, "decentralized authority," "conditional empowerment," and "structured autonomy" shape the managerial state (p. 105). Understanding the role of the state is crucial for exploring the complex relationships between the state and civil society, which is "the cornerstone of democracy" (Castells 2008).

Thinking comparatively about school choice policies, particularly parental choice of school, we hope that this chapter deepens our knowledge of the similarities and differences between choice policies in China and those in the West. The recontextualization of school choice within the Chinese historical, political, economic, and social landscape demonstrates how choice policy is interpreted differently in the Chinese context. The use of Hall's theory of articulation in the critical analysis of school choice issues has methodological and political implications. It provides a powerful research approach to thinking relations and connections in critical educational studies. More importantly, it directs us to the spaces in which more progressive and counter-hegemonic actions can go on.

Directing our attention to such spaces is crucial. Our analysis documents that the current policies and the practices of parental choice of school in China not only exacerbate existing educational and social inequalities, but also lead to social injustice. This is significant not only for China but also for global educational policy. This chapter reminds us of one of the most serious questions we must constantly ask: "What are the *long-term* implications of the current school choice fever and school choice policies in China and elsewhere?" This is one of the major questions that future researchers on neoliberal policies will need to continue to take very seriously. The future of more "thick" versions of democracy in education will depend on answering it.

Notes

1 For details on the values and principles of "thick" democracy, see Apple and Beane (2007), p. 7.
2 Hall (1985) explains his concept of articulation: "By the term 'articulation,' I mean a connection or link which is not necessarily given in all cases, as a law or a fact of life, but which requires particular conditions of existence to appear at all, which has to be positively sustained by specific processes, which is not 'eternal' but has to be constantly renewed, which can under some circumstances disappear or be overthrown, leading to the old linkages being dissolved and new connections—rearticulations—being forged.

It is also important that an articulation between different practices does not mean that they become identical or that one is dissolved into the other. Each retains its distinct determinations and conditions of existence. However, once an articulation is made, the two practices can function together, not as an 'immediate identity' (in the language of Marx's '1857 Introduction') but as distinctions within a 'unity'" (p. 113–114). Slack (1996) further notes that "articulation can be understood as a way of characterizing a social formation without falling into the twin traps of reductionism and essentialism" (p. 113).

3   The one-child policy has recently been altered to some degree.

4   According to NetEase Education (2015), there are only 90 high school international programs approved by the Chinese government. However, up to 2013, the number of Chinese schools that established international high school programs has increased from 22 to 338 within 12 years. These statistic data show the rapid growth of high school international education market in China.

5   Here, we adopt Khan's (2012) definition of "elites," which refers to "those with vastly disproportionate control over or access to a resource" (p. 362). There has been a debate on whether elites are a distinct social class (Maxwell 2015). In this chapter, we use the term of Chinese elite classes interchangeably with Chinese middle-upper and upper classes.

6   For how various social actors were involved in the development of the Sunny High IAP Program, see Liu (2015).

7   Annual *Lianghui* often make national-level political decisions in China.

References

Adamson, F., Astrand, B., and Darling-Hammond, L. (Eds.). (2016). *Global Education Reform: How Privatization and Public Investment Influence Education Outcomes*. New York: Routledge.

Apple, M. W. (2001). *Educating the "Right" Way: Markets, Standards, God, and Inequality* (1st ed.). New York: Routledge.

Apple, M.W. (2004). Creating difference: Neo-liberalism, neo-conservatism and the politics of educational reform. *Educational Policy 18*: pp. 12–44.

Apple, M. W. (2006). *Educating the "Right" Way: Markets, Standards, God, and Inequality* (2nd ed.). New York: Routledge.

Apple, M. W. (Ed.). (2010). *Global Crises, Social Justice, and Education*. New York: Routledge.

Apple, M. W. (2013). *Can Education Change Society?* New York: Routledge.

Apple, M. W. (2014). *Official Knowledge: Democratic Education in a Conservative Age* (3rd ed.). New York: Routledge.

Apple, M. W. (2016). Challenging the epistemological fog: The roles of the scholar/activist in education. *European Educational Research Journal 15*(5): pp. 505–515.

Apple, M.W., and Beane, J.A. (Eds.). (2007). *Democratic Schools: Lessons in Powerful Education* (2nd ed.). Portsmouth, NH: Heinemann.

Apple, M. W., Aasen, P., Cho, M. K., Gandin, L. A., Oliver, A., Sung, Y. K., and Wong, T. (2003). *The State and the Politics of Knowledge*. New York: RoutledgeFalmer.

Ball, S. J. (1998). Big policies/small world: An introduction to international perspectives in education policy. *Comparative Education 34*: pp. 119–130.

Ball, S. J. (2003). *Class Strategies and the Education Market: The Middle Class and Social Advantage*. New York: Routledge.

Ball, S. J. (2007). *Education plc: Understanding Private Sector Participation in Public Sector Education*. New York: Routledge.

Ball, S. J. (2012). *Global Education Inc.: New Policy Networks and the Neo-Liberal Imaginary.* New York: Routledge.

Ball, S. J. (2015). Elites, education and identity: An emerging research agenda. In *World Yearbook of Education 2015: Elites, Privilege and Excellence: The National and Global Redefinition of Educational Advantage.* A. van Zanten, S. Ball, and B. Darchy-Koechlin (Eds.). pp. 233–240. New York: Routledge.

Ball, S. J. (2013). *Education Debate* (2nd ed.). Bristol: The Policy Press.

Ball, S. J., Bowe, R., and Gewirtz, S. (1995). Circuits of schooling: A sociological exploration of parental choice of school in social class contexts. *Sociological Review 43: pp.* 52–78.

Ball, S. J. and Vincent, C. (1998). "I heard it on the grapevine": "Hot" knowledge and school choice. *British Journal of Sociology of Education 19: pp.* 377–400.

Bernstein, B. (1977). *Class, Codes and Control, Vol. 3: Towards a Theory of Educational Transmissions.* New York: Routledge.

Bourdieu, P. (1984). *Distinction: A Social Critique of the Judgement of Taste.* Cambridge, MA: Harvard University Press.

Bourdieu, P. (1986). The forms of capital. In *Handbook of Theory and Research for the Sociology of Education.* J. G. Richardson (Ed.) pp. 241–258. New York: Greenwood Press.

Brown, P. (2003). The opportunity trap: Education and employment in a global economy. *European Educational Research Journal 2*: pp. 141–179.

Buras, K., and Apple, M. W. (2005). School choice, neoliberal promises, and unpromising evidence. *Educational Policy 19*: pp. 550–564.

Castells, M. (2008). The new public sphere: Global civil society, communication networks, and global governance. *The ANNALS of the American Academy of Political and Social Science 616*(1): pp. 78–93.

Central Committee of the Chinese Communist Party. (1985). *The Decision of the Central Committee of the Chinese Communist Party of China on the Reform of the Educational System* [in Chinese]. Available at: www.moe.edu.cn/publicfiles/business/htmlfiles/moe/moe_177/200407/2482.html. Accessed 02/10/17.

Central Committee of the Chinese Communist Party and State Council. (1993). *Outline for Reform and Development of Education in China* [in Chinese]. www.moe.edu.cn/publicfiles/business/htmlfiles/moe/moe_177/200407/2484.html. Accessed 02/10/17.

Chen, F. (2003). School choice: Global investigation report. *Xinhua Digest* 11: pp. 178–179.

Cheng, B. (1997). Exploring the practice and theory of Chinese private schools. *Chinese Education & Society 30*(1): pp. 23–37.

Chubb, J. E., and Moe, T. M. (1990). *Politics, Markets and America's Schools.* Washington, DC: The Brookings Institution.

Clarke, J. (2015). Stuart Hall and the theory and practice of articulation. *Discourse: Studies in the Cultural Politics of Education 36*(2): pp. 275–286.

Clarke, J., and Newman, J. (1997). *The Managerial State: Power, Politics and Ideology in the Remaking of Social Welfare.* Thousand Oak, CA: Sage.

Dale, R. (1989). The Thatcherite project in education: The case of the City Technology Colleges. *Critical Social Policy 9*(27): pp. 4–19.

Forsey, M., Davies, S., and Walford, G. (Eds.). (2008). *The Globalization of School Choice?* Oxford, UK: Symposium Books.

Fraser, N. (2005). Mapping the feminist imagination: From redistribution to recognition to representation. *Constellations 12*(3): pp. 295–307.

Fraser, N. (2009). *Scales of Justice: Reimagining Political Space in a Globalizing World.* New York: Columbia University Press.

Friedman, M., and Friedman, R. (1980). *Free to Choose: A Personal Statement*. New York: Houghton Mifflin Harcourt.

Grossberg, L. (1986). On postmodernism and articulation: An interview with Stuart Hall. *Journal of Communication Inquiry 10*(2): pp. 45–60.

Guan, Q., and Meng, W. (2007). China's new national curriculum reform: Innovation, challenges and strategies. *Frontiers of Education in China 2*(4): pp. 579–604.

Hall, S. (1980). Race, articulation and societies structured in dominance. In *Sociological Theories: Race and Colonialism*. United Nations Educational Scientific and Cultural Organisation (Eds.). pp. 305–345. Paris: UNESCO.

Hall, S. (1985). Signification, representation, ideology: Althusser and the post-structuralist debates. *Critical Studies in Media Communication 2*(2): pp. 91–114.

Hannum, E., An, X., and Cherng, H. Y. S. (2011). Examinations and educational opportunity in China: Mobility and bottlenecks for the rural poor. *Oxford Review of Education 37*(2): pp. 267–305.

Harvey, D. (2005). *A Brief History of Neoliberalism*. Oxford, UK: Oxford University Press.

Henig, J. R. (1994). *Rethinking School Choice: Limits of the Market Metaphor*. Princeton, NJ: Princeton University Press.

Khan, S. R. (2012). The sociology of elites. *Annual Review of Sociology 38*: pp. 361–377.

Lauder, H., and Hughes, D. (1999). *Trading in Futures: Why Markets in Education Don't Work*. Philadelphia, PA: Open University Press.

Leng, S. L., and Leng, C. Z. (2004). An analysis of high school fees and costs in Jiangxi Province. *Finance and Economy 6*: pp. 31–34.

Li, F. (2008). Analysis of the current situation of educational investment in general senior high schools in China [in Chinese]. *Research in Educational Development 11*: pp. 55–59.

Liu, S. (2015). "International Access Project": A network analysis of an emerging international curriculum program in China. In *Mapping Corporate Education Reform: Power and Policy Networks in the Neoliberal State*. W. Au and J. J. Ferrare (Eds.). pp. 86–105. New York: Routledge.

Liu, S. (2016). *Becoming International: High School Choices and Educational Experiences of Chinese Students Who Choose to Go to U.S. Colleges* (Doctoral dissertation, University of Wisconsin–Madison).

Liu, Y., and Dunne, M. (2009). Educational reform in China: Tensions in national policy and local practice. *Comparative Education 45*(4): pp. 461–476.

Liu, J., Tang, T., and Wu, J. (2012). The impact of educational funds investment and expenditure on the development of ordinary high schools – Based on the analysis of Hunan Province [in Chinese]. *Journal of the Chinese Society of Education 12*: pp. 15–19.

Maxwell, C. (2015). Elite: Some questions for a new research agenda. In *World Yearbook of Education 2015: Elites, Privilege and Excellence: The National and Global Redefinition of Educational Advantage*. A. van Zanten, S. Ball, and B. Darchy-Koechlin (Eds.). pp. 15–28. New York: Routledge.

Ministry of Education of the People's Republic of China (MOE). (2003). Regulations of the People's Republic of China on Chinese-foreign Cooperation in Running Schools. Available at: www.moe.edu.cn/publicfiles/business/htmlfiles/moe/moe_861/200506/8646.html. Accessed 18/08/14.

Ministry of Education of the People's Republic of China (MOE). (2004). Implementation Measures for the Regulations of the People's Republic of China on Chinese-foreign Cooperation in Running Schools [in Chinese]. Available at: http://www.crs.jsj.edu.cn/index.php/default/news/index/6. Accessed 18/03/2014.

Ministry of Education. (2006). *Ministry of Education and Other Six Departments' Implementation Guideline on the Work of Curbing Arbitrary Fee Collection* [in Chinese]. Available at: www.moe.edu.cn/publicfiles/business/htmlfiles/moe/s3144/201001/81023.html.   Accessed 04/02/17.

Ministry of Education. (2012). *Ministry of Education and Other Six Departments' Implementation Guideline on the Work of Curbing Arbitrary Fee Collection in 2012* [in Chinese]. Available at: www.moe.edu.cn/publicfiles/business/htmlfiles/moe/s7503/201407/171881.html. Accessed 04/02/17.

Ministry of Education. (2014). *Implementation Guideline on Standardizing Education Charges and Governing the Work of Curbing Arbitrary Fee Collection in 2014* [in Chinese]. Available at: www.mof.gov.cn/zhengwuxinxi/zhengcefabu/201405/t20140505_1074921.htm. Accessed 04/02/17.

Ministry of Education. (2016). *Letter on Reply of Proposal No. 0140 (Education No. 029) of the Fourth Session of the 12th National Committee of the Chinese People's Political Consultative Conference* [in Chinese]. Available at: www.moe.gov.cn/jyb_xxgk/xxgk_jyta/jyta_zgs/201610/t20161019_285559.html. Accessed 04/02/17.

Ministry of Education of the People's Republic of China (MOE). (2010). National Guidelines for Medium- and Long-term Educational Reform and Development (2010–2020) [in Chinese]. Available at: www.moe.gov.cn/publicfiles/business/htmlfiles/moe/moe_838/201008/93704.html. Accessed 05/06/14.

Mok, K. H. (1997). Privatization or marketization: Educational development in post-Mao China. *International Review of Education* 43(5): pp. 547–567.

Mok, J. H. (2001). From state control to governance: Decentralization and higher education in Guangdong, China. *International Review of Education* 47(1): pp. 123–149.

Mok, K. H., Wong, Y. C., and Zhang, X. (2009). When marketisation and privatisation clash with socialist ideals: Educational inequality in Urban China. *International Journal of Educational Development*. 29(5): pp. 505–512.

National People's Congress of the People's Republic of China. (1986). *Compulsory Education Law of the People's Republic of China* [in Chinese]. Available at: http://www.lawinfochina.com/display.aspx?id=1166&lib=law. Accessed 11/10/17.

National People's Congress of the People's Republic of China. (2006). *Compulsory Education Law of the People's Republic of China (amended)*. Available at: www.npc.gov.cn/englishnpc/Law/2007-12/12/content_1383936.htm. Accessed 03/09/15.

NetEase Education. (2015). *Educational experts said that the international classes created by public high schools should not be across the board. Ministry of Education will announce guidelines.* Available at: http://edu.163.com/15/0311/13/AKEA301N00294MBF_all.html. Accessed 03/21/17.

Ngok, K. (2007). Chinese education policy in the context of decentralization and marketization: Evolution and implications. *Asia Pacific Education Review*. 8(1): pp. 142–157.

Niu, W. (2007). Western influences on Chinese educational testing. *Comparative Education* 43(1): pp. 71–91.

Olssen, M., Codd, J. A., and O'Neill, A. M. (2004). *Education Policy: Globalization, Citizenship and Democracy*. Thousand Oaks, CA: SAGE.

Plank, D. N., and Sykes, G. (Eds.). (2003). *Choosing Choice: School Choice in International Perspective*. New York: Teachers College Press.

Power, S., & Whitty, G. (2006). Education and the middle class: A complex but crucial case for the sociology of education. In *Education, globalization, and social change*. H. Lauder, P. Brown, J. A. Dillabough, and A. Halsey (Eds.). pp. 446–453. Oxford, UK: Oxford University Press.

Qin, H. (2008). School choice in China. *Frontiers of Education in China 3*(3): pp. 331–345.

Robertson, S. (2003). WTO/GATS and the global education services industry. *Globalisation, Societies and Education 1*(3): pp. 259–266.

Rollock, N., Gillborn, D., Vincent, C., and Ball, S. (2014). *The Color of Class: The Educational Strategies of the Black Middle Classes*. London: Routledge.

Shao, Z., and Zhang, L. (2013). Why is it so difficult to solve the problem of school choice [in Chinese]. *Educational Research 9:* pp. 4–11.

Shen, B. (2006). Analysis of the regional differences of tuition in Chinese general senior high school in China [in Chinese]. *Forum on Contemporary Education 5:* pp. 24–27.

Slack, J. D. (1996). The theory and method of articulation in cultural studies. In *Stuart Hall: Critical Dialogues in Cultural Studies*. D. Morley and K. Chen (Eds.). pp. 113–129. London: Routledge.

Swartz, D. (1997). *Culture and Power: The Sociology of Pierre Bourdieu*. Chicago, IL: University of Chicago Press.

The State Council Rectification Office of the People's Republic of China. (2001). *Opinions of the State Council Rectification Office and the Ministry of Education on Further Curbing Arbitrary Fee Collection* [in Chinese]. Available at: www.moe.edu.cn/moe_879/moe_165/moe_0/moe_7/moe_16/tnull_166.html. Accessed 02/15/17.

Tsang, M. C. (1996). Financial reform of basic education in China. *Economics of Education Review 15*(4): pp. 423–444.

Tsang, M. C. (2003). School choice in the People's Republic of China. In *Choosing Choice: School Choice in International Perspective*. D. N. Plank and G. Sykes (Eds.). pp. 164–195. New York: Teachers College Press.

Wang, H. (2011). Access to higher education in China: Differences in opportunity. *Frontiers of Education in China 6*(2): pp. 227–247.

Waters, J. L. (2006). Emergent geographies of international education and social exclusion. *Antipode 38*(5): pp. 1046–1068.

Whitty, G. (1997). Creating quasi-markets in education: A review of recent research on parental choice and school autonomy in three countries. *Review of Research in Education 22:* pp. 3–47.

Whitty, G., Power, S., and Halpin, D. (1998). *Devolution and Choice in Education: The School, the State and the Market*. Philadelphia, PA: Open University Press.

Williams, R. (2014). *Keywords: A Vocabulary of Culture and Society*. New York: Oxford University Press.

Wu, Xiaogang. (2010). Economic transition, school expansion and educational inequality in China, 1990–2000. *Research in Social Stratification and Mobility 28*(1): pp. 91–108.

Wu, Xiaogang and Zhang, Z. (2010). Changes in educational inequality in China, 1990–2005: Evidence from the population census data. In *Globalization, changing demographics, and educational challenges in East Asia*. H. Emily, H. Park, and Y. Butler (Eds.) pp. 123–152. Bingley, UK: Emerald Group Publishing Limited.

Wu, Xiaoxin. (2008). The power of positional competition and market mechanism: A case study of recent parental choice development in China. *Journal of Education Policy 23*: pp. 595–614.

Wu, Xiaoxin. (2011). The power of positional competition and market mechanism: An empirical study of parental choice of junior middle school in Nanning, PR China. *Research Papers in Education 26*(1): pp. 79–104.

Wu, Xiaoxin. (2012). School choice with Chinese characteristics. *Comparative Education 48*(3): pp. 347–366.

Wu, Xiaoxin. (2014). *School Choice in China: A Different Tale?* New York: Routledge.

Wu, Y. (2013). The Keypoint School System, Tracking, and Educational Stratification in China, 1978–2008 [in Chinese]. *Sociological Studies 4*: pp. 179–202.

Wu, Z. and Shen, J. (2006). School choice and education equity—Change in school choice policies and new direction in public school reform in China. *Tsinghua Journal of Education 6:* pp. 111–118.

Xie, Y., Zhang, X., Li, J., Yu, X., & Ren, Q. (Eds.). (2013). *Wellbeing Development Report of China 2013* [in Chinese]. Beijing: Peking University Press.

Xue, H. and Tang, Y. (2016). Educational funds investment in general senior high school in China: Current situation, problems and suggestions [in Chinese]. *Journal of Educational Studies 12*(4): pp. 89–101.

Yan, G., & Chang, Y. (2009). The circumstances and the possibilities of critical educational studies in China. In *The Routledge International Handbook of Critical Education*. M. W. Apple, W. Au, and L. A. Gandin (Eds.) pp. 368–386). New York: Routledge.

Yang, D. (2005). A research into the senior high school students' social class stratification and education acquisition. *Tsinghua Journal of Education 26*(3): pp. 53–59.

Yang, D. (2006). *The ideal and reality of educational equity in China* [In Chinese]. Beijing: Peking University Press.

Yang, P. (2009). Three-restriction policy and public high school choice [in Chinese]. *Research in Educational Development 19:* pp. 36–40

Ye, H. (2015). Key-point schools and entry into tertiary education in China. *Chinese Sociological Review 47*(2): pp. 128–153.

Ye, X. (2012). "Use power for school choice": Parents' political capital and children's school choice [in Chinese]. *World Economic Papers. 4*: pp. 52–73.

You, Y. (2007). A deep reflection on the "key school system" in basic education in China. *Frontiers of Education in China 2*(2): pp. 229–239.

Yu, M. (2016). *The politics, practices, and possibilities of migrant worker schools in contemporary China.* New York: Palgrave Macmillan.

Yuan, Z. G. (1999). *On changes of Chinese educational policy: A case study on the relationship between equality and benefit in key middle schools* [in Chinese]. Guangzhou, China: Guangdong Education Publisher.

Zhang, L. (2010). *In Search of Paradise: Middle-class Living in a Chinese Metropolis.* Ithaca, NY: Cornell University Press.

Zhong, Q. (2006). Curriculum reform in China: Challenges and reflections. *Frontiers of Education in China 1*(3): pp. 370–382.

5

CAN CRITICAL DEMOCRACY LAST?

PORTO ALEGRE AND THE STRUGGLE OVER "THICK" DEMOCRACY IN EDUCATION

Luis Armando Gandin and Michael W. Apple

Introduction

Creating a path to what have been called "real utopias" (Wright 2010) is not easy. But doing so is absolutely crucial if we are to reconstruct our economic, political, and cultural institutions so that they become sites of serious critically democratic transformation. For those who have labored for years to connect movements in and around education with larger social movements for equality (see, e.g., Apple 2013, 2006; Anyon 2005; Lipman 2011; Apple 2010), understanding the limits and possibilities of these connections has been a central focus.

A fundamental question lies at the heart of the issues surrounding the connections between educational projects and larger socially critical movements and projects. What would a democratic education *system* look like? The word "system" is the key here. In a previous chapter, we examined a specific school that, even with its contradictions over race and class, took the issue of democracy seriously. But what of an entire school system? Can this be done?

One place immediately comes to mind, a locale where this question was answered through real transformations: the municipal educational system of Porto Alegre, the capital of the state of Rio Grande do Sul in Brazil (Gandin 2010, 2009; Gandin and Apple 2002). This chapter examines the structural changes that were put in place in Porto Alegre's municipal system, and especially the development of the critically democratic practices of "Participatory Budgeting" and then the Citizen School, during the 16-year tenure of the Popular Administration (a coalition of left-wing parties, led by the Workers Party that governed the city from 1989 to 2004) and offers an evaluation of the conditions that allowed the experience of the Citizen School project to take place. We also focus on some of the lessons we can learn about building democratic educational systems. Among the questions we address are: How did these changes come about? What were the conditions that allowed this experience to be constructed? What were the components of the Porto Alegre experience? What did it achieve? What is its legacy? What does this tell us about the prospects for democratic critical reforms?

To answer these questions, we first situate Porto Alegre in its context of struggles over larger issues of injustice both historically and currently, especially the growth of new social movements from below. We then examine why Porto Alegre's educational system deserves to be studied and what it achieved. We also present some challenges that the experience is currently facing and finally we revisit the Porto Alegre school system six years after the Workers Party left office and address both some of what has lasted and what has changed.

Mapping the Conditions of Democracy: New Social Movements, New Unionism, and the Workers' Party

Understanding how a transformation like the Citizen School project was possible requires studying the context in which democracy can flourish. "Thick" democratic experiences require participation; and participation is not something that can occur from one moment to the other. It requires practice. In the following section, we trace the history of the construction of democracy and participation—in the most adverse conditions—that led to the possibility of the Citizen School project.

In 1964, Brazil experienced a military coup against a democratically elected president. The military *junta* took power to avoid the supposed menace of communism in the country, even though the government at the time was a center-left populist administration. The military started a dictatorship that would last until 1985, when a civilian was elected president (through an indirect vote in Congress—the first direct election after the dictatorship would not be held until 1989). In the beginning of the junta's reign, the government banned all political parties and closed the House of Representatives and the Senate. Traditional spaces for mobilization like unions and oppositional political parties were made illegal, and all opposition was fiercely persecuted. The stories of assassinations, torture, and forced exile, performed by many military personnel trained in the United States Army School of the Americas,[1] are innumerable and very well documented.[2] Gradually, the military government started to reopen Congress, and due to political pressure, created two parties: one defending the interests of the government and of the coalition that supported the coup, and another one that would represent the opposition. In the early 1970s, Congress had no real power, and the majority of the population did not support the opposition party, preferring to "annul" their vote. (Voting is compulsory in Brazil.)

With no institutional spaces to organize in, the oppositional movements had to go underground. The absence of institutional spaces for mobilization created the conditions for the appearance of what are called "new social movements."[3]

These are movements which are not associated directly with parties or unions (thus the adjective "new") that started to appear in poor neighborhoods all over Brazil. During this period, urban conditions were deteriorating and salaries were stagnating, thereby also generating counter-hegemonic mobilizations. These new social movements were created to struggle against a range of conditions such as poor transportation, the increasing cost of living, and the lack of childcare, among others.

There is a consensus among researchers in Brazil that the progressive leadership inside the Catholic Church, which was developing Liberation Theology[4] at that point, was crucial in providing spaces for mobilizations and organizations, starting in the worst period of political repression, the late 1960s. This organization occurred in the local parishes, in neighborhoods and communities. The best example of this organization is the Ecclesiastic Base Communities (*Comunidades Eclesiais de Base* or CEBs).[5] The way these CEBs worked is described by Keck (1986): "They meet regularly to reinterpret the day to day experiences of their members in the light of Biblical teaching, and vice versa. Through a reexamination of Christian teachings, many communities, particularly in the poor areas, develop a social critique based on immediate experience" (pp. 135–136). To understand the reach of the CEBs in Brazil, one only needs to know that, at the height of its organization, there were 80,000 of them operating all over Brazil (Della Cava 1988).

Perhaps the best example of the kind of mobilization that the CEBs initiated in Brazil is the Cost of Living Movement. In 1973, commissions of mothers, all participants in the CEBs, organized strikes against the excruciating cost of living that the poor families were faced with. At the height of the movement, thousands of neighborhoods in Brazil (with many being particularly active in Porto Alegre) mobilized and had connections with several other movements, including women's movements and students' organizations. Many of them were also members of church-sponsored organizations in the educational area, like the Young Catholic Students (JEC) and the Young Catholic University Students (JUC). As Keck (1986) emphasizes, the Church had a multiple role as "arena, promoter, and protector as well" (p. 138). It is clear that this encouraging and protective environment provided a space that did not exist previously in military-ruled Brazil. It fostered social movements that would last and become crucial for future mobilizations.

The spaces that the CEBs provided were also places for establishing connections between these and other movements. Since the traditional spaces of mobilizations as parties and labor unions were being extremely repressed, the safe haven that the CEBs created helped to foster connections between groups that would not otherwise meet. In Keck's (1986) words:

> The CEBs have been extremely important in producing self-conscious activists who participate in other social movements. CEB members have

been active in neighborhood movements and in the renewal of the labor movement. There was a great deal of overlap among CEB activists in neighborhood and labor organizations; the social space provided by the Church during the seventies facilitated communication among these organizations.

(p. 136)

The CEBs were not alone. Other organizations inside the Catholic Church such as the Young Catholic Workers (JOC), with members who participated in the CEBs as well, were also crucial spaces of organizations for workers that could not meet in unions. As Telles says:

> the neighborhood mobilizations made possible the birth of many militants, something that the environment of the factories did not allow or happened in a much-reduced rate. Many workers learned about organizations in the neighborhoods [and CEBs] before they were militants in the factories.
>
> *(Telles as cited in Kowarick 2000, p. 37)*

In the late 1970s, the dictatorship was forced to ease up on its repressive policies and practices. This was largely due to the electoral gains of the oppositional party—those citizens who had been annulling their votes started voting for the oppositional party, highly influenced by the work in the neighborhoods. At the same time, popular protests, new labor unions, especially the ones in São Paulo, the industrial center of Brazil, started to become much more active. This period also witnessed growing criticism of the historically received labor unionism of the 1930s, 1940s, and 1950s, a labor unionism that was increasingly seen as bureaucratic and not sufficiently combative. The new unions that were formed in response to this were highly influenced by the democratic experiences of the neighborhood organizations and CEBs and would not accept any centralism in their structure. Consequently, the new unions distanced themselves from the traditional "vanguardist" position of the orthodox Marxist currents of the time.

In 1978, the metalworkers in São Bernardo (a city in the metropolitan region of São Paulo), highly organized in democratic shop floor committees, launched a strike and, after a fierce battle, achieved their goal of a pay increase. Luís Inácio da Silva, or as he is known in Brazil, Lula, was the leader of this union. In 1980, he would become one of the founders and leaders of the Workers' Party. The victory of the union would be more than only an economic gain. The democratic nature of the union, its high level of organization with delegates in every factory, would become an example of how to organize successful mobilizations. The years of 1978, 1979, and 1980 witnessed strikes in several sectors, ranging from banks to schools. Indeed, schools were often significant sites of action and teachers' unions in schools became even more important to the story we need to tell.

Among the mobilizations of teachers in their unions, the ones in the state of Rio Grande do Sul were certainly the most active. In 1978, the teachers' union, the CPERS (Rio Grande do Sul Teachers' Center)—at that moment technically not a union, because civil servants were prohibited by law from organizing unions, but clearly operating as one—started to change its structure and instituted a decentralized organization across the state. With 42 sub-divisions located in every region of the state, the CPERS had meetings every month with delegates from all the sub-divisions. In a historic strike for better salaries in 1979, the CPERS gathered 15,000 teachers in a meeting and decided to take action.

The power of the union can be measured by the number of teachers that belong to it. In 1991, 70% of all teachers of state schools were members of the CPERS, making it the largest teachers' union of Brazil, with 78,000 members (Bulhões and Abreu 1992, pp. 13-14). Between 1979 and 1991, the state teachers of Rio Grande do Sul organized nine strikes. The economic gains of the strikes were significant; but the economic situation of the country, one that was marked by high inflation, ended up drastically reducing many of the gains. However, there was an important gain that is not emphasized enough at times in the literature about teachers' struggles. The union's mobilizations overcame dominant corporatist policies and tendencies and were directed at the defense of public schools and democratic management inside schools. Thus, the CPERS was able to resist many of the conservative reforms that governments tried to introduce in the state schools over the years, including performance pay that gave teachers higher pay for better grades and Total Quality Management (TQM). As Hypolito (1999) says:

> All the conservative proposals initiated in Rio Grande do Sul by the last governments could not be implemented. Even the ones that had a pedagogical character did not even reach the classrooms. ... The actions of the union and teachers, sometimes with strikes, manifestations, and protests—when the measures demanded a contestation of the official policy and struggle for better work conditions—sometimes with silence—when the government was trying to impose some pedagogical orientation—were crucial to stop the consolidation of an explicit conservative educational project.
>
> *(p. 95)*

This resistance of the organized teachers' movement[6] has been crucial to public education and it has directly influenced the educational policy initiatives in Porto Alegre, particularly because all its leaders were part of the teachers' mobilizations in the CPERS. These mobilizations of teachers and the struggle for democratic management between state and schools and inside schools are a crucial component of conditions that allowed for the Citizen School project in Porto Alegre.

From what we have said, we can see that the organized movement of workers and subaltern groups grew steadily in Porto Alegre and all over Brazil. Connections were being established, and the growing organizations in the neighborhoods were not just reduced to localized practices. Yet, it is important to resist classifying the struggles in the neighborhood associations and CEBs as a mere preparation for a larger and more important activism. As Kowarick (2000) highlights, these organizations were not only important because they "fed" workers' struggles (which is true), as an orthodox Marxist interpretation would claim. These "new" social movements were crucial as well because they represented a moment where groups could reflect on the conditions of exploitation and domination that they were living in. These critical reflections generated a "consciousness of exclusion," and served to open the space for oppressed people to actively construct new practices that enabled them to change these conditions (p. 37). Again, Kowarick's (2000) description is accurate here:

> At that historic moment, in great part thanks to the Catholic Church action through CEBs, clubs of mothers, youth associations and other articulations connected with Catholic pastoral, people started to recognize themselves, to lose the fear of thinking and acting and, in an embryonic and fragmented form, started to organize a field of popular resistance and organization.
>
> *(p. 38)*

This "field of popular resistance and organization" is the exact origin of the Workers' Party, and this origin is exactly what marked its novelty. These processes of learning how to *live* participatory democracy were crucial when the Citizen School project created the spaces for participation. It was not a new practice for most communities. They had already experienced democratic practices.

The Workers' Party was born out of these mobilizations and started with radical democratization as its goal. Created in 1980, it was one of the first parties created after the political reform conducted by the military that allowed the creation of new political parties. (The objective of the government had been to weaken the opposition, concentrated in the only legal oppositional party at that moment. However, the strategy backfired, because the government lost the majority of the elections in the following years.) According to Meneguello (1989), the Workers' Party was created by a coalition of forces: the new trade unionism, led by Lula; some of the left-wing members of the only legal oppositional party at that moment; leftist intellectuals; some Marxist organizations; and parts of the new social movements, coordinated by the left wing of the Catholic Church (members of the CEBs, neighborhoods associations, JOC, and so forth) (pp. 57–58).

Even though the party is currently in dire need of finding its way back to its democratic origins, at its birth the Workers' Party was highly opposed to the tradition of centralism in communist parties. The organization provided a "basis for an apprenticeship in democratic participation and decision-making and … also created an opportunity for new leaders to emerge from the ranks" (Keck 1986, pp. 299–300). The creation of the Workers' Party represented a radical change in politics in Brazil. In a country where politics were always something to be left to the elite,[7] the creation of the Workers' Party was the materialization of the first political party (apart from the Communist Party that was illegal for the majority of its history in Brazil) created to defend and promote the interests of the Brazilian working class (Pinheiro 1989). As Keck explains in a long but crucial quote:

> The very organization of the Workers' Party challenged important ele-
> ments of the dominant conception of politics in Brazil. The notion that
> workers should represent themselves on the political stage was 'non-sen-
> sical' in several respects. First, workers did not possess political knowl-
> edge to represent themselves; they lacked not only education, but also the
> exposure to public concerns which members of the political elite must
> have. Secondly, ... workers clearly did not possess the network of relations
> which would render them effective actors in the public arena. For most
> Brazilians, these observations were no more than 'common sense'. ... The
> Workers' Party, on the other hand proposed a new 'common sense' for
> workers, one ... that argued that 'if you want to get something done you
> have to do it yourself.'
>
> *(p. 490)*

This is an essential change of perspective. Since the elites and the dominant groups in Brazil would not do it for them, workers and subaltern classes would have to propose new forms of governing themselves. As Gramsci (1997) reminds us, interrupting dominant common-sense understandings of the world and creating a new more liberating one are both crucial to a more democratic society. The task of creating a new common sense was something that would be an important part of the agenda of the Workers' Party. And, as we will soon see, it is something that would be a core part of the Citizen School project.

Since its beginning, the Workers' Party insisted that it was important for the unions and the social movements in general to stay independent. It also empha-sized the need to consider struggles *other than* economic ones. In his discourse in the first convention of the party in 1981, Lula, the leader of the party, already insisted that:

> in the past people believed that only political parties were capable to cen-
> tralize the organization of the popular movement. Today we recognize that
> the best fruits are the ones obtained by movements that, just like our party,
> have their roots in the organizations of the rural areas, neighborhoods, *fave-*
> *las*, work and study places, and specific issues like the black and women
> struggles.
>
> *(Lula as cited in Gadotti and Pereira 1989, p. 67)*

This position increasingly became a key to its emerging electoral strategy. The Workers' Party was not able to convert popular mobilization into votes in the first election it participated in 1982. Because of this, the discourse of a party that had a project specific to the working class changed quite a bit in the subsequent elections. The Workers' Party learned very quickly that it could not be elected if it did not have a project for all of society.

Perhaps the best example of this recognition by the Workers' Party of the importance of a wider focus, and what it meant for the building of "thick" democracy in education and in other spheres, is the city of Porto Alegre and its Popular Administration. In the next section, we describe the goals of the Popular Administration and the primary mechanisms it created to involve the population in the governance of the city, the policy of "Participatory Budgeting."

The Popular Administration and Participatory Budgeting

From 1989 to 2004, the city of Porto Alegre was governed by a coalition of left-ist parties, under the strong leadership of the Workers' Party, called the Popular Administration. Each mayoral term has four years in Brazil. The Workers' Party was re-elected three times in Porto Alegre. It governed the city for four terms—1989–1992, 1993–1996, 1997–2000, 2001–2004.

According to one of the former mayors of Porto Alegre (a nationally respected member of the Workers' Party), the purpose of the Popular Administration is to

> recuperate the utopian energies, … [to] create a movement which contains, as a real social process, the origins of a new way of life, constructing a 'new moral life' (Gramsci) and a new articulation between state and society … that could lead social activity and citizenship consciousness to a new order.
>
> *(Genro 1999, p. 9)*

The Popular Administration brought significant material improvements to the most impoverished citizens of the city. To give just one example, as Santos points out, "as regards basic sanitation (water and sewage), in 1989, only 49% of the population was covered. By the end of 1996, 98% of the households had water and 85% were served by the sewage system" (Santos 1998, p. 485). In terms of education, the number of schools has more than doubled since the Popular Administration took office.

One particularly important measure adopted by the Popular Administration—"Participatory Budgeting" (Orçamento Participativo or OP)—is credited with the re-allocation of resources to the impoverished neighborhoods. The OP[8] is a mechanism that guarantees active popular participation and deliberation in the decision-making process for the allocation of resources for investment in the city. In Santos' words,

> The participatory budget promoted by the Prefeitura of Porto Alegre is a form of public government that tries to break away from the authoritarian and patrimonialist tradition of public policies, resorting to the direct par-ticipation of the population in the different phases of budget preparation

and implementation, with special concern for the definition of priorities for the distribution of investment resources.

(Santos 1998, p. 467)

In fact, the politics in Brazil has historically been characterized by patrimonialism and clientelism.[9] In order to have investments in their communities, the neighborhood associations would have to look for an alderperson that could propose the investment in that area to the municipal government. There are all sorts of "clientelistic" arrangements which exchange support for the cause of the communities for votes. The state tradition in Brazil has also been one highly suspicious of popular input. This tradition prevents ordinary people, especially poor people, from having any valid input in state matters. This stands in stark contrast from the commitment of the Workers' Party to put popular sectors at the center of policy discussion.

The government of the Popular Administration was able to break with the dominant elitist tradition, and active popular participation in the construction of policy and allocation of resources has been part of its success. The OP is the core of the project which was aimed at transforming the city of Porto Alegre and incorporating a historically excluded impoverished population into the processes of decision-making. The history of urban social movements examined above, in which the members of the Workers' Party were directly involved, was certainly a source of inspiration for the Popular Administration that now had the chance of institutionalizing the spaces for popular participation and direct forms of democracy. A new relationship between the state and civil society could help to reduce the historic urban despoliation in Brazil. That is exactly what the OP has been doing in Porto Alegre, reinstituting the role of the state as the provider of public goods that guarantee the material conditions for real citizenship.

It is important to say, though, that according to those in charge of the Popular Administration, and also to several researchers of the experiment in Porto Alegre (Baiocchi 1999; Santos 1998; Abers 1998; Avritzer 1999), providing the impoverished population with access to previously non-existent public goods is not the only change that was significant. In addition, the OP has generated an *educative* process that has forged new organizations and associations in the neighborhoods. The citizenry of the city has been empowered by a process of political learning in the construction of the organization for the participation in the OP. Therefore, the educational aspect of the municipal administration's actions is extremely visible. In fact, the OP can be considered what Wright and Fung call a "school of democracy" (Wright and Fung 2003) because the learning acquired within the OP is transferred to other spheres of social life (Baiocchi 1999). Theorists of deliberative democracy[10] claim that although the "deliberative settings take place in unequal social contexts where domination structures most social relations, the expectation is that deliberation itself can foster parity within the participatory setting (Baiocchi 2001, p. 397). The main mechanism is the process of learning that occurs when citizens, individually and collectively, appropriate the necessary skills to struggle for their needs in solidarity with others.[11] The state in Porto Alegre acts proactively to create channels where this parity is possible and does not have a voluntarist perspective of waiting for participation to occur magically.

But there is another very interesting educational aspect in the OP. The state agencies themselves had to be "re-educated." Participatory budgeting entails the transition from "technobureaucracy" to "technodemocracy" (Santos 1998). This constitutes an alternative form of governance, one that is different from the market and the pure bureaucratic state. It involves active participation of the citizenry in the process of planning and monitoring, allowing for efficiency and public control at the same time. The state agencies' technical personnel have had to learn how to communicate with the lay population, to enable people's real participation and efficient deliberation and monitoring.

Santos offers a compact description of how the OP works:

> In a brief summary, the OP centers on the regional and thematic plenary assemblies, the Fora of Delegates, and the Council of the OP (COP). There are two rounds of plenary assemblies in each of the sixteen regions and on each of the five thematic areas. Between the two rounds there are preparatory meetings in the microregions and on the thematic areas. The assemblies and the meetings have a triple goal: to define and rank regional or thematic demands and priorities, to elect the delegates to the Fora of Delegates and the councillors of the COP, and to evaluate the executive's performance. The delegates function as intermediaries between the COP and the citizens, individually, or as participants in community or thematic organizations. They also supervise the implementation of the budget. The councillors define the general criteria that preside over the ranking of demands and the allocation of funds and vote on the Investment Plan proposal presented by the executive.
>
> *(Santos 1998, p. 469)*

Through this sophisticated structure of governance, the OP has been able to involve the most impoverished communities in the process of mobilizations that, as we stressed before, have consequences that are not only economic.

In the late 1980s, municipalities in Brazil were granted higher levels of autonomy, including fiscal autonomy, which was highly beneficial, and the Popular Administration was very fast in exploring this opportunity. It was able, for example, to gather more resources due to the fiscal reforms it implemented. Guided by a strong commitment to the ethics of social distribution and justice, high value properties started to pay more property tax, while citizens in poor neighborhoods had their tax reduced. The process of decentralization being implemented in Brazil at that moment (highly influenced by neoliberal principles of devolution, but with contradictions that the Popular Administration was able to explore and use for more thickly democratic purposes) also created more resources directly for municipal administrations, resources that had been highly concentrated in the federal government before.

Working in tandem with the OP, the educational project for the city, the Citizen School, was implemented by the Municipal Secretariat of Education (Secretaria Municipal de Educação or SMED). The Citizen School project pushed in the same direction and aimed at initiating a "thick" version of education for citizenship very early in the formal education process through the creation of democratic institutional mechanisms.

This context we have described is crucial to understand if we are to grasp significant parts of what made the Citizen School possible. In the following section, we go on to describe in more detail the transformations that took place in the municipal school system of Porto Alegre.

The Democratization in the School System

From the moment the Popular Administration was first elected, the leaders of the Citizen School project knew that they would have to change the way decisions were made in the educational system and in schools. If thick democracy was to be lived in the schools of Porto Alegre, then the decisions had to be made democratically. The basic goals of the project—democratization of access to school, democratization of knowledge, and democratization of governance—were created collectively through the Constituent Assembly, a participatory structure especially created for conceiving these goals.

In order to construct the principles that would guide the actions of the Citizen School, a democratic, deliberative, and participatory forum was created in the form of a Constituent Assembly. This project was constituted through a long process of mobilization of the school communities, one that used the invaluable lessons learned in the mobilization for the Participatory Budgeting and in the history of community organization. It had the goal of generating the principles that would guide the policy for the municipal schools in Porto Alegre. The whole process started in March of 1994, lasted 18 months, and involved thematic meetings in the schools, regional meetings, the Assembly itself, and the elaboration of the schools' internal regulations. The themes that guided the discussion were school governance, curriculum, principles for living together, and evaluation.

The Citizen School project was created under the principle of not separating the determination of the goals from the creation of the mechanisms to implement these goals. Rather, the process of generating the practical goals should represent in itself an innovative mechanism that would be able to produce transformations in the relationships between the schools and the community. The normative goals that guide the practice in the schools were to be collectively created through a participatory process. The idea was to foster a government that creates channels for real development of collectively-constructed normative goals and that replaces the traditional relationship of distant government officials managing schools that they know little about.

The Constituent Assembly—with elected delegates, including teachers, parents, students, and staff—selected the radical democratization of the education in the municipal schools as the main normative goal of the Citizen School project. This radical democratization would have to occur in the three dimensions we noted above: democratization of access to school, democratization of knowledge, and democratization of governance. These three principles would be the ones guiding every action in the municipal system of Porto Alegre. These principles changed the structure of the schools and the relationship between schools and the Secretariat of Education (SMED). We now turn to describing and examining these changes.

Democratization of Access to Schools

The municipal schools are situated in the most impoverished neighborhoods of Porto Alegre. If the schools were to have an impact on the lives of the children living there, the issues surrounding initial access to schools had to be a priority. For the Popular Administration, guaranteeing this access was, therefore, the first step to promote social justice to communities historically excluded from social goods.

Granting access to all children at school age is not as easy as it might sound. Historically, Brazil has had an enormous number of children who did not attend school. National statistics show that this has been changing rapidly. But in 1991, when the Popular Administration was just starting, and even in 1994, when the Citizen School project had only been in existence for one year, the situation was grave in terms of initial access to schooling. Almost 17% of the Brazilian children at school age were not being formally educated in 1991. In 1994, although this number had dropped to almost 13%, it was still clearly a crisis.

This was a central preoccupation for the Popular Administration and the SMED. The fact that the goal of democratization of access to schooling was one of the central priorities is proof of it. The SMED invested in building more schools and increasing the number of teachers prepared to work on these schools.

When the Workers' Party was elected in 1988, the city of Porto Alegre had only 19 K–8 schools ("fundamental education," as it is called in Brazil), with 14,838 students and 1,698 teachers, curriculum coordinators, and educational supervisors. Under the Popular Administration the number of students grew at a remarkable rate. Between 1988 and 2000, the number of students in fundamental education increased by 232%. This number shows how profound the impact of the actions of the SMED has been in Porto Alegre and, although the comparison is not between equal circumstances, it is worth pointing out that between 1991 and 1998 the number of school-age children in Brazil increased by only 22.3% (INEP 2000, p. 53).

The number of fundamental education schools increased by 126% under the Popular Administration government. And if we consider all the schools under the municipal government—including the schools geared towards early childhood, adolescents and young adults, and special education—the increase rate is actually 210%. It is important to point out that these schools were all constructed in very impoverished areas of the city and that the majority of new schools were actually built inside or around *favelas*. This means that the schools are not only bringing back students who drop out of state schools, but they are also creating a space for many children who never attended school and possibly never would have were it not for the new municipal schools.

But guaranteeing initial access to schooling does not guarantee that these children will benefit from school. In order to really democratize the access to schools, in 1995 the SMED proposed a new organization for the municipal schools. Instead of keeping the traditional structure of grades with the duration of one year (first to eighth in the fundamental education), the idea was to adopt a new structure called Cycles of Formation. It is important to note that the idea of reorganizing the curriculum and the space-time of the schools in cycles instead of grades does not originate from Porto Alegre. What the Citizen School was implementing was not new *per se*, but a new configuration that, according to the SMED, would offer a substantially better opportunity for dealing with the need for democratization of access and knowledge.

The administrators at the Secretariat were convinced that the issue of access to schools could be dealt with in a much better way using cycles. According to the SMED, "the cycle structure offers a better way of dealing seriously with student failure, because its educational perspective respects, understands, and investigates the socio-cognitive processes that the students go through" (SMED 1999a, p. 11). The idea is that by using a different conception of the equation learning/time, the Citizen School would not punish students for allegedly being "slow" in their process of learning. In this new configuration, the traditional deadline—the end of each academic year—when the students had to "prove" that they had "learned," was eliminated in favor of a different time organization. The establishment of the cycles was a conscious attempt to eliminate the mechanisms in schools that perpetuate exclusion, failure, and dropouts, as well as the blaming of the victim that accompanies these.

In the cycles, students of the same age were grouped in each of the years of the three cycles. This aimed at changing the reality in the majority of public schools that cater to popular classes in Brazil. When the Popular Administration started to govern the city, the SMED was faced with a very significant problem. There were large numbers of students with multiple failures inside classrooms intended for much younger children. To deal with this, the SMED's solution was having students of the same age in the same year of the cycle. In this way, the SMED claimed that students who had failed multiple times would be re-motivated.

In the schools using these cycles, students would progress from one year to another within one cycle. Thus, the notion of "failure" is eliminated. This constituted a major gain in the relationship between schools and impoverished students.

Despite this victory, the SMED also understood that the elimination of mechanisms of exclusion was not enough to achieve the goal of democratization of knowledge. Because of this, the Citizen School created several mechanisms that aim at guaranteeing the inclusion of students. It established Progression Groups for the students that have discrepancies between their age and what they have learned. The idea is to provide these students who have experienced multiple failures in the past with a stimulating and challenging environment where they can learn at their own pace and fill in the gaps in their academic formation that exist because of the multiple failures they experienced. Furthermore, the Progression Groups are also a space for the students who come from other school systems (from other city or state schools, for example), and who have experienced multiple failures, to be given more close attention so that they are ultimately integrated into the cycles according to their age. The idea was that the school had to change its structure to adapt to the students, and not the reverse, which has been historically the case (Souza et al. 1999, p. 24–25).

This idea of constructing a new structure to better respond to students' needs led to the creation of another mechanism: the Learning Laboratory. This was a space where students with more serious learning problems get individual attention, but also a place where teachers conduct research in order to improve the quality of the regular classes. For the students with special needs, there are Integration and Resources Rooms, which "are specially designed spaces to investigate and assist students who have special needs and require complementary and specific pedagogic work for their integration and for overcoming their learning difficulties" (SMED 1999a, p. 50).

With all these mechanisms, the Citizen School project not only radically improved initial access, but also guaranteed that the educational space occupied by the subaltern children was a space that treated them with the dignity and respect, and of the quality necessary to keep them in the school and educate them to be real participating citizens.

Democratization of Knowledge

As we noted, curriculum transformation was a crucial part of Porto Alegre's project to build active citizenship. It is important to say that this dimension is not limited to access to traditional knowledge. What was constructed was a new epistemological understanding about what counts as knowledge as well. It was not based on a mere incorporation of new knowledge within the margins of an intact "core of humankind's wisdom," but a radical transformation. The Citizen School project goes beyond the mere episodic mentioning of cultural manifestations or class, racial, sexual and gender-based oppression. It includes these themes as an essential part of the process of construction of knowledge (Apple 2000).

In the Citizen School project, the notion of "core" and "periphery" in knowledge was made problematic. The starting point for the construction of curricular knowledge was the culture(s) of the communities themselves, not only in terms of content, but in terms of perspective as well. The whole educational process was aimed at inverting previous priorities and instead was being rebuilt so that it better served the historically oppressed and excluded groups. The starting point for this new process of knowledge construction was the idea of "thematic complexes." This organization of the curriculum is a way of having the whole school working on a central generative theme, from which the disciplines and areas of knowledge, in an interdisciplinary effort, will structure the focus of their content.

Through research (a process performed by teachers in the communities where the schools are situated), the themes that interest and/or concern the community are gathered. After this process of gathering the statements of the members of the community, the most significant statements will be selected by the collective of teachers participating in discussions specifically allocated for this and which will guide the construction of the thematic complex. This thematic complex provides the whole school with a central focus that guides the curriculum of that school for a period of time, one that can be one semester or an entire academic year.

After having determined the principles, the task is the development of both the larger contribution of each knowledge area for the discussion of the thematic complex, and the building of a conceptual matrix that included a web of concepts from the knowledge area. Care was taken to ensure that this was not simply a list of isolated facts or information. Rather it was grounded in the teachers' understanding of the forms and content of the knowledge that are essential to use when dealing with the thematic complex. In engaging in these tasks, the teachers have meetings organized by their knowledge areas and by each year in the cycles, to elaborate and plan the curriculum. Teachers have to "study" their own knowledge areas and select the concepts that would help to problematize the thematic complex. They also have to work collectively with teachers of other areas in order to assemble a curriculum that is integrated and dense enough to simultaneously address the issues listed in the thematic complex. Collective critical democracy at the level of the teachers is then constantly being built at the same time.

According to one of the "creators" of this conceptualization, in the context of the Citizen School project, "the thematic complex brings about the perception and comprehension of the reality and makes explicit the worldview that all the ones involved in the process have" (Rocha as cited in SMED 1999a, p. 21). Because the thematic complex is closely related to social problems, the process makes teachers search for the relation of their discipline to social reality as a whole. Finally, because the starting point for the thematic complex is popular knowledge or common sense, teachers are also forced to think about the relation between official knowledge and this common sense. Therefore, this approach deals simultaneously with three major problems of traditional education: the fragmentation of knowledge, the "apparent" neutrality of school content, and the absolute supremacy that traditional schools grant to "scientific/erudite" knowledge over local knowledge of the communities, especially very impoverished ones—as is the case in Porto Alegre.

The Citizen School project conceives the organization of the curriculum around a thematic complex not only as a form of generating alternative knowledge inside the curriculum, but also as a form of political intervention.

> To teach using thematic complexes not only generates the possibility of selecting knowledge that is significant to students but also presents us with the perspective of having a tool for analysis that can help students to organize the world they live in, so that they can understand it and act upon it through a critical, conscious, and collective social practice.
>
> *(Goroditch and Souza 1999, p. 78)*

The traditional rigid disciplinary structure is broken and general interdisciplinary areas are created. These areas of study are given the names of social expression, biological, chemical and physical sciences, socio-historic, and logic-mathematical.

To give a concrete example of how this works, let us describe how organizing the curriculum in the socio-historic knowledge area proceeded in one school of Porto Alegre. After the phase of carrying out research in the community, the school elected "the quality of life in the *favela*" as its thematic complex. The socio-historic knowledge area had to construct the principle of that area, i.e., the contribution of this area to deal with the elected thematic complex. This area expressed its possible contribution as "the individual and collective transformation of the citizen, in his/her time and space, recuperating his/her origins, aiming at improving the quality of life, taking into account the ideas of the community where this individual is situated."

From the major thematic complex—the quality of life—three sub-themes were listed by the teachers in the socio-historic area: rural exodus, social organization, and property. In the rural exodus sub-theme, the issues reflected the origin of the community—living now in a *favela*, but originally from the rural areas. This is a common story in the *favelas* where people who had nothing in the rural areas came to the cities only to find more exclusion. In this sub-theme, the issues discussed were migration movements, overpopulation of the cities, "disqualification" of the working force, and marginalization. In the sub-theme social organization, the issues were distributed in terms of temporal, political, spatial, and socio-cultural relations. The issues, again, represent important questions in the organization of the community: the excessive and uncritical pragmatism of some in the neighborhood associations, and cultural issues such as religiosity, body expression, African origins, dance groups, and samba schools. In the third sub-theme—property—the issues were directly linked to the situation of the families in the *favela*, living in illegal lots with no title, having to cope with the lack of running water, basic sanitation and other infrastructure problems, the history of this situation and of the struggles for lots legalization, and their rights (of having basic public goods in the neighborhood) and duties as citizens (of understanding the importance and the social function of taxation).

This example shows the real transformation that occurred in the curriculum of the schools in Porto Alegre. The students were not studying history or social and cultural studies through books that never address the real problems and interests they have. Through the organization in thematic complexes, the students learned history by beginning with the historical experience of their families. They studied important social and cultural content by focusing on and valorizing their own cultural manifestations. It is important to note that these students will ultimately still learn the history of Brazil and the world, including "high" culture, but these will be seen through different lenses. Their culture will not be forgotten in order for them to learn "high status" culture. Rather, by understanding their situation and their culture and valuing it, these students will be able to simultaneously learn *and* will have the chance to transform their situation of exclusion. By studying the problems (rural exodus, living in illegal lots, etc.) and not stopping there, but studying the strengths of self-organization (in neighborhood associations and in cultural activities and groups), the Citizen School helps to construct alternatives for the communities living in terrible conditions.

This shift of what is considered the core or the center of knowledge affects not only the pedagogical conception that guides the daily life in the classrooms; it also transforms how the school itself functions as a whole. This conception of knowledge spread throughout the entire school system. The project not only served the "excluded" by generating a different formal education for students, but also served them by creating an innovative structure that made it possible for the community of those who have historically been excluded to regain their dignity (both material and symbolic).

Democratization of Governance

We now come to the third principle that had been identified—governance. As we saw, one of the most important mechanisms that guaranteed the democratization of governance was the Constituent Assembly. It not only provided a space to decide on the administration of the project, but also allowed for real participation on the definition of the goals of the Citizen School.

But there were other mechanisms that were central to the democratization process. The School Council was a central element, since the SMED recognized that the goal of democratization had to also take seriously the need to establish thick forms of democracy not only in establishing the principles that would guide schools, but just as crucially *within* the schools themselves. The school council's role was to promote the democratization of the decision-making process and governance in education at a very local level in Porto Alegre. A product of the political will of the Popular Administration and the demands of social movements involved in education in the city, the school councils, which were established by a municipal law in December of 1992 and implemented in 1993, are the most important institutions inside the schools. They are formed by elected teachers, school staff, parents, students, and by one member of the administration, and they have consultative, deliberative, and monitoring functions.

The school council reserves 50% of its seats for teachers and staff and 50% for parents and students. One seat is guaranteed to the administration of the school, usually the principal, who is elected by all members of the school.

The task of the school council is to deliberate about the global projects for the school, the basic principles of administration, to allocate economic resources, and to monitor the implementation of the decisions. The principal and her/his team are responsible for the implementation of the policies defined by the school council.

In terms of resources, it is important to say that, before the Popular Administration took office, there was a common practice throughout Brazil of a very centralized budget. Every expense (even the daily ones) had to be sent to the central administration before it was approved, and then the money was sent to the school, or a central agency would purchase the product or the service necessary. In such a system, the school council would have "their hands tied," with no autonomy at all. The SMED changed this structure and established a new policy to make the amount of money available to each school every three months. According to the SMED, this was the measure that instituted the financial autonomy of the schools, which allowed the schools to manage their expenditures according to the goals and priorities established by the school council. At the same time that it creates autonomy, this measure gives parents, students, teachers, and staff who are present in the council a notion of social responsibility in administering public money, and it teaches them to hierarchize the investments with solidarity in mind (SMED 1999b).

The school council also has the power to monitor the implementation, through the principal and her/his team, of its decisions (SMED 1993, p. 3). In fact, the school council is an empowered structure in the schools. It is the main governance mechanism inside the schools, and its limitations are only the legislation and the policy for education collectively constructed in democratic fora. Decisions about the curriculum can be part of the deliberation, and the inclusion of parents, students, and staff (or even teachers, if we consider the traditional school) in this process is a great innovation of the model.

The school council does not stand as the lone mechanism of thicker democratization. Along with the school council, another structure guaranteed democratic spaces in the Citizen School. In the municipal schools of Porto Alegre, the whole school community elects the principal by direct vote. Thus, the one responsible for the implementation of the decisions of the school council, i.e., the principal, is her/himself elected. In the process, she or he has to propose and defend a particular project of administration for the school. There is a legitimacy that comes from this fact. The principal then is not simply someone who necessarily represents the interests of the central administration inside the school councils, but someone with a majority of supporters inside that particular educational community. Principals have a great degree of embeddedness and, because of this, the SMED feels that it is possible to avoid the potential problem of having someone responsible for the concretization of the deliberations occurring in the school councils who is not connected with the project. But the responsibility of the community does not stop there. Through the school council, the school community has a way of monitoring the activities of the principal and holding her/him responsible for implementing its democratic decisions.

The direct election of the one responsible to implement the directives created by the school council, also elected directly by the school community, represents a mechanism that aims at generating the principle of democratic management at the local level of the school.

These processes of democratization of access to school, democratization of knowledge, and democratization of governance that are lived in the Citizen School project offer important lessons for all of those who struggle for democracy in education. In what follows, we examine the reasons that made the Citizen School project an example of thick democracy in education worth studying.

Some Challenges

The previous sections of this article focused on the ambitious policies and practices that were instituted in Porto Alegre. But we need to ask about the current situation of the Porto Alegre educational system, especially since the Workers' Party has been replaced by more "centrist" and at times much more neoliberal and conservative governing parties. One of us has closely followed the situation and has encountered many encouraging signs that a large number of the principles of the transformation started during the Popular Administration's tenure have not been lost. The opening up of the schools to the communities and the ethic of care for the children and their many social problems are still strong in the schools. The schools' role as a reference for the communities and as a space that they consider their own are both alive and visible. Nevertheless, there are serious challenges to the policies and practices that were implemented, challenges that threaten the quality of the experience as a socially just educational system. We briefly examine two of the main problems in the municipal schools today.

The first issue is related to the school councils. In the schools (four schools in different parts of the city) currently being researched by one of us, the situation of the school councils is not very encouraging. In some schools there are not enough students or parents participating in the meetings. In the schools that have councils in which all members are elected, they rarely meet. And when they meet, most of them seem to ratify decisions taken by the school administration or even to simply sign off on the budgets of the administration's financial reports. In these four schools, it is hard to see important decisions being taken up by the council, or an active and participatory school council itself. This is serious, since the school councils are the official gateway for the interests of parents and students in schools. In none of the four schools researched does the school council have active participation of more than a few parents and students. There are cases of involved parents, but this is the exception in the visited schools. It will be important to continue to monitor whether the feeling of not having anything to contribute ("What do I know?" was a sentence from a mother) that many mothers participating in school councils expressed to Moira Wilkinson (2007) in her continuing research will spread. Wilkinson showed not an empowerment but an increased discrimination against mother's knowledge in the school councils she studied. This is cause for worry and represents the opposite of the schools councils' mandate.

The second problem is related to the curriculum. From the moment the cycles of formation were established by the Popular Administration, opposition forces claimed that it offered a less rigorous education for the poorest people, especially due to its no-failing policy. There is strong evidence showing that this was not the case during the Popular Administration's tenure (Gandin 2002). Rigorous evaluation coupled with mechanisms like the Learning Laboratories meant that the curriculum that was built and that took the communities' knowledge and concerns into consideration was guaranteeing that all students would learn—albeit at different paces—what was taught. In a series of recent visits to these four schools, it is possible to feel a different tone. One school in particular, a school that has a strong majority of teachers identified with the Popular Administration's policies, offers an example of what has become a serious problem. There have been substantive difficulties in transforming the school into a place where children are challenged intellectually *and* where children are cared for and feel protected. The curriculum coordinator of that school explicitly said in an interview that:

> We have given up on many teachers and do not believe they will change and seriously commit to the students. We now direct all our energy directly towards the kids, because they need the concreteness of someone believing in them. We make them feel welcome and many students still come to the school even when they have graduated.

This is something that is not unimportant, especially in those communities in which drug trafficking, vigilante actions, and police raids steal the lives of a significant number of children and adolescents. But it certainly represents a challenge in terms of offering students serious academic work that also connects knowledge to their lives.

However, we need to be careful with this critique, because the choices that the principals and curriculum coordinators face are extremely difficult. As the quote from an interview shows, many of them have been devoting all of their energy to creating an environment where children feel welcomed and are treated as valuable human beings, something that is not the case in other locales in their lives. One of us has documented the dilemma (although without the more political connotation present in this example) that women teachers face between professionalism and caring (Apple 1988; see also Lynch et al. 2012), showing the risks both for teachers' work and for students. This is an even more difficult situation in Porto Alegre for, paradoxically, even when it is not always an overt choice on their part, by concentrating on "caring," these principals and curriculum coordinators in Porto Alegre do not simultaneously reinforce the academic message that all children can learn.

In visits to these schools, there was the clear sense that teachers were not demanding much from the students academically or even sending clear messages that they were coming from an environment that condemns them to stay where they are. As one example, one teacher said that she did not assign homework and that the notebooks were locked in the school and not sent to children's homes, because teachers believed that these notebooks would not come back, or come back dirty or damaged, due to the living conditions of the children and the lack of care of their parents. By combating traditional content-pushing and by not enforcing a more Freirian approach of being rigorous with the construction of knowledge process, there is the danger of recreating a situation where, in Freire's terms, poor students are "ghettoized in their language." Freire goes on:

> In overromanticizing students' language so as to discourage them from acquiring multiple discourses, including the 'standard' discourse of the dominant society in which they live, teachers run the risk of becoming entrapped in a 'feel good' pedagogy that passes as progressive. If they do this, teachers are not engaging with their students in a mutual process of liberation.
>
> *(Freire 1997, 305–306)*

This danger is exactly what the Popular Administration and the SMED expressly fought against with their curricular policies. However, the current centrist administration started a process of trying to centrally establish a minimum curriculum for each cycle year. This obviously stands in direct opposition to the position of the Popular Administration in favor of a localized curriculum. Keeping a close watch on the developments surrounding this proposed change will be crucial to understand the direction that the administration will take toward the schools. Also crucial will be the reactions toward this proposal by the schools themselves and by the educators, communities, and students that have been transformed by the more critically democratic policies and practices that were institutionalized by the Popular Administration.

The problems mentioned above are not small obstacles. Clearly, it will be important to keep following these schools to see what happens with these and other problems of continuity in the Porto Alegre experience.

Current Politics and the Importance of Recognizing Gains

In January 1, 2005, a new centrist political coalition took office, ending the 16-year tenure of the Workers Party and the Popular Administration in Porto Alegre's City Hall. During the campaign one could not help but notice that the soon to be victorious candidate, José Fogaça, constantly said that he would "maintain what was good and change what was not." He promised that he would not touch the Participatory Budget which he labeled "an achievement of the city."

During the campaign, there were attacks on the way the municipal schools organized the times for learning. The opposition to the Workers' Party claimed that education in Porto Alegre was not as strong as it was in the past, because of the no-failing policy in the schools. In his educational platform, Fogaça included the idea of "revising the school cycles policy." However, soon after the election, a survey was conducted with the teachers of the municipal schools and the vast majority of them said that they wanted the cycles to stay. In interviews by one of the teachers who worked in the secretariat at the time, such strong support for the cycles was a surprise to the new administration and they decided to maintain the cycles policy.

The new administration took a hands-off approach, leaving the schools open to decide on their curricular organization. It did not enforce, as the Worker's Party administrations did, both the thematic complexes and the research in the communities as the centerpieces of curriculum design. For many teachers identified with the Popular Administration, there was a clear political meaning to the government's policy. It was seen as a strategy of destroying the Workers' Party policy without openly confronting it. By not conveying any clear policy to the schools, the current administration would end up emptying out the previous proposal's meanings. In fact, the vast majority of the schools started organizing the curriculum without resorting to the thematic complex.

Nevertheless, and this is more than a little significant, this same group of schools did *not* go back to the content-centered tradition prevalent before the Workers' Party governments were in power. Many schools have been using Freirean "generative themes" (Freire 1993) actively researched by students through projects (see Hernandez and Ventura 1998). On the one hand, one could say that the projects involving such generative themes are not the same as the thematic complex that was made such a priority by the Popular Administration. For the Popular Administration, the complex was the ideal way of dealing with the difficulties of reading the word and the world simultaneously. But on the other hand, it is equally plausible to see this as compelling evidence that the schools of Porto Alegre learned the lesson of the need to build the curriculum locally and democratically in a profound way. While they are not necessarily repeating and/or reinventing what the Popular Administration conceived, they are indeed keeping many of the principles intact.

This is just one indication that, despite some opposition from groups of schools and teachers during the Popular Administration's tenure, after the Workers' Party government was gone the majority of the schools maintained the basic structure of the proposal. Teachers say openly in interviews that they miss having an administration with a clear vision for education, even if they did not necessarily agree with all the principles that were put forward.

There are reasons for this positive assessment. Part of it is based on a sense that such a positive vision is crucial in a world where people care deeply about what is happening—and not happening—in their daily lives. But even with the concerns about some of the elements of the Workers' Party agenda, part of it is also based on a recognition of the accomplishments of the changes brought about by Participatory Budgeting and the Citizen School. These accomplishments remind us why this whole-system transformation remains so significant. Some of these accomplishments—involving respect for the community, students, and teachers—are worth noting again.

In the *vilas* (or *favelas*), where the majority of dwellings have plywood, cardboard, or zinc walls, the school building is the most well-constructed in the neighborhood. The school can become, therefore, a place for the community to meet, engage in sports, and participate in cultural activities. Whereas in other school systems (Brazil has both municipal and state public school systems) the school is usually completely separate from the community, in the Porto Alegre experience the education secretariat constantly found ways to expand and create new channels for the relationship between the school and the community. In this way, the schools actually served not only the students, but also the communities in which they are situated. As the leader of a neighborhood association told one of us in an interview taped during the Popular Administration's tenure:

> We are very proud of this school. We fought really hard, through the Participatory Budgeting assemblies, to have this school built. The school was built because we were organized and demanded it. ... We have a very good relationship with teachers and administration, and the whole community uses the school for meetings, for practicing sports, and for all kinds of cultural activities. We take a good care of it, because we consider it ours.

As the neighborhood association leader pointed out, another illustration of democratizing access not only to students but to all the community is the concept of the school as a cultural center, which brings to the building performances and activities that otherwise would not have a space to be enacted.

The "care" that the communities dedicate to the schools is readily apparent as well. While state schools are constantly damaged, robbed, and vandalized, the municipal schools are almost never targeted in this manner. The majority of the school buildings do not have any significant problems, and even the older ones are in very good condition. This is not something to be taken for granted. All over the country, and even in the state schools in Porto Alegre, there are complaints from teachers, students, and parents about the material conditions.

In interviews conducted by one of us, students confirmed the remarkable difference in conditions between the municipal and state schools. When asked how they felt in this school, one of the students declared, and the others strongly agreed with him:

> This school is much more organized than the one I attended last year. The food is very good; we did not have lunch at the other school, only a snack. … This school is also really clean; the bathrooms are very clean and always have toilet paper and paper for you to dry your hands. We did not have any of that in the other school.

The above list of items may seem banal, but the students clearly understand that these material conditions say a good deal about how the school views and treats students. In this school, students feel welcomed. But they had more to say:

> I think that other schools should be like this as well; a school where you have a good relationship with the administration, teachers, cleaning personnel, cooks. We feel that they all care about us. … This is just like a private school.

These students openly express that they understand that this school is different from the others. This is a school that "cares about them." They mention private schools because in the prevalent cultural model in Brazil, private schools are the best schools that one can attend. They have the best material conditions, what are thought to be the most dedicated teachers, and the most extracurricular activities. By using this comparison, these students show clearly that they understand that theirs is a good school and that they are proud to attend it.

This is crucial. But the way teachers are treated also tells a great deal about the seriousness of a socially-just educational reform. In order to prepare for the participation of the teachers in the project, the Popular Administration and the education secretariat also implemented a process of "formation" (ongoing teacher development and education) on the job and, just as critically, a policy of better salaries.

In terms of formation, every year the education secretariat promoted two seminars dealing with themes closely linked to the challenges faced by schools. During these seminars, all classes were suspended, and the teachers were stimulated to participate. One of the seminars occurred in March, and was used to bring Brazilian researchers to the event. The other occurred in July and had an international character. The idea was to bring the best progressive researchers in education to have discussions with the teachers. The International Seminar was considered one of the best (if not the best) of the Brazilian seminars in the field of education, attracting not only teachers from the municipal schools, but also teachers from the private and state systems, professors, and researchers from various regions of the country. These seminars allowed municipal teachers to have contact with national and international "state-of-the-art" progressive educational research, something that was not common at all in Brazil at that time. Continuous education of the teachers in terms of educational theory was part of the policy in Porto Alegre.

Besides the seminars, the education secretariat promoted "formation" (ongoing collective teacher education) meetings, ten per year, in every school, so teachers had a space to learn from their mistakes and successes and to discuss pedagogical issues connected to the reality of the school. The teachers' contracts were also changed to allocate five hours per week to planning and studying.

Another aspect that helped to guarantee the thoughtful and committed performance of teachers was the salary policy. Teachers in public schools in Brazil had suffered tremendous salary reductions. Salaries in state schools were extremely low, leading people to characterize teachers as "the new poor." The Popular Administration knew that this was a crucial point. If teachers are literally struggling to survive, how could they become involved in a process of participation and transformation that demands more from them as professionals and promotes discussions of injustice in their classrooms if their own economic situation is not discussed? The salary of municipal school teachers became much higher than state school teachers during the Popular Administration's tenure. This salary was two to three times higher during that period. Indeed, the difference is even higher today, because of the absence of increases in state school teachers' salaries. A teacher with 18 years of experience in a municipal school, working 40 hours a week (and the Popular Administration encouraged teachers to work 40 hours during their tenure) earned (and still does) as much as or even more than a university professor. This clearly shows how comparatively well-paid teachers were (and still are) in the municipal schools.

By valuing teachers, changing the whole environment of the schools, involving the community with the school as a public institution, and insisting that every student counts, the Porto Alegre system attained its goal of democratizing access to school. In doing so, it made possible a level of access to public benefits that were not previously available to its students and the community. And all of this was done in addition to a fundamental change in the way in which the state itself is democratized.

Conclusion

The current administration of Porto Alegre (one that espouses managerial proposals), that started its tenure in January of 2017, has been showing signs that it will try to concretely change some of the structures of the Citizen School project, particularly the ones that guaranteed extra teachers and time for all teachers to work together in their planning. In this case, the structures created during the Popular Administration years and weakened in the last three administrations, will be put to a real test. But even with these issues of defending and maintaining the core of a thick and truly participatory form of critical educational democracy, there are lessons to be learned. What are some of these lessons that made Porto Alegre so important to the creation of thicker forms of democracy in education? Let us highlight some of the most significant elements.

1. Unlike most reforms, Porto Alegre's experience was not only participatory in the implementation of the policy, but also in the creation of the policy and its goals as well.
2. Porto Alegre problematized concretely the prevailing common-sense views of poor students from *favelas* and their communities. The Popular Administration understood that the material state of the buildings and teachers' working conditions and professional development were an essential part of the changes that were necessary in the way the state acts in these neighborhoods.
3. In the Porto Alegre experience, there was a combination of mobilization from civil society and changes in the state agencies in order to incorporate the communities' needs. It is a classic case where the state itself is "educated," an ongoing education that was caused both by the development of the policy it implemented and by community organizations and movements.
4. The experience in Porto Alegre was centrally interested in students' inclusion and academic success. But, unlike many other reforms, it understood very well that these goals could not be achieved without a radical discussion of and change in what counts as knowledge, whose knowledge is part of the formal and informal school experience, and how to create a new relationship between popular knowledge and academic knowledge.

An intense dedication to these ideals and to their embodiment in real critically reflective practices with real administrators, real teachers, real students, and real communities made the above lessons workable. It was not and is not ever "easy." But Porto Alegre shows that it can be realized.

In the documentary *Žižek!*, during a lecture in Argentina, Slavoj Žižek says the following about utopia:

> True utopia emerges when there are no ways to resolve the situation within the coordinates of the possible and, out of the pure urge to survive, you have to invent a new space. Utopia is not a free imagination; utopia is a matter of innermost urgency; you are forced to imagine something else as the only way out.

This conception of utopia seems to apply perfectly to the case of Porto Alegre and its social and educational transformations. Out of the real struggles in authoritarian times, out of the impossibility of constructing socially-just relations in the city within the prevailing patterns of the state/community relationship and the dominant institutional framework, the Popular Administration was forced to imagine and to act in utopian terms. They had to ask—and then to act upon—some of the most crucial questions that can be raised in a time of neoliberal and neoconservative agendas. What if "thick" democracy was truly implemented? What if the poorest citizens of the city could decide on where public money would be invested? What if the poorest neighborhoods would receive brand new schools and the best paid teachers in the state? What if the pedagogical notion that everyone can learn in school was implemented? What if what counts as knowledge was critically revisited and school organization was reconstructed based on this notion?

Perhaps one of the most important lessons from Porto Alegre is that the state was absolutely necessary to institutionalize the changes and protect the schools from an international and federal neoliberal agenda, something that is absolutely crucial to remember in a time of neoliberal attacks on the entire public sphere. But this lesson could not exist without another equally significant one. Real transformation comes when the state is no longer the primary origin of the transformations. It is when teachers in schools start living the premise of democracy, when they build the curriculum with the students and communities, that real transformation happens (see also Apple and Beane 2007).

The educational system of Porto Alegre offered a real alternative to the apparent consensus of educational reform around market-based managerialism through economic accountability, competition, and choice. But it was not and is not a utopia that comes from "free imagination," it emerges from the concrete struggle to create a socially-just educational system (see also Wright 2010). It certainly had many flaws and contradictions in its implementation, but what it has to offer is the radical idea that it is possible to break away from that forged (and at times forced) consensus, thus opening up the space for a new social and educational imagination. It shows that new educational structures are truly possible within the existing educational systems—if social movements and political alliances are built that both challenge an accepted common sense and begin to create a new one (see also Apple 2010, 2013).

There is another implication that needs to be stated here, this one for research on educational policy and practice. Too often research on policy and practice—even research that is critically oriented—is based on relatively short time periods. Yet lasting transformations take time to accomplish. And their effects, especially those that are aimed expressly at substantial transformations in the relationship between the state and civil society, in the ways in which social movements and school realities interact, in the politics of knowledge, and in the fundamental place of education in social change, take years to show their long-term effects. Not only do we need more instances of "real utopias" such as that found in Porto Alegre, but we need many more studies of the "long revolution" (Williams 1961) that such examples may exemplify and in which they participate. This chapter is but one attempt to do this. We need many more.

Notes

1 This is a school maintained by the US Army, and its official goal is to train the armed forces of Latin America, promote military professionalism, and foster cooperation among multinational military forces. Its involvement with training military personnel that performed torture and assassinations in Latin America is well known and very well documented. The school still exists, despite attempts of activists to close it down. It is now called Western Hemisphere Institute for Security Cooperation (WHISC) and it is situated in the state of Georgia. According to the group called School of the Americas Watch, "In September 1996, under intense pressure from religious and grassroots groups, the Pentagon released seven Spanish-language training manuals used at the SOA until 1991. The New York Times reported, 'Americans can now read for themselves some of the noxious lessons the United States Army taught thousands of Latin Americans... [The SOA manuals] recommended interrogation techniques like torture, execution, blackmail and arresting the relatives of those being questioned'" (School of the Americas Watch 2002). For more on the School of Americas history see Nelson-Pallmeyer (1997).

2 A book documenting the torture performed by military governments in Brazil during the dictatorship published by the Catholic Archdiocese of São Paulo, Brazil was published in 1985, the year the dictatorship ended. For the English translation of the book see Archdiocese of São Paulo, Brazil (1998).

3 For a comprehensive analysis of the "new social movements" in Brazil, see Schrer-Warren and Krischke (1987).

4 Liberation Theology is a movement that started in the Latin American Catholic Church, which connected progressive (and in some cases, revolutionary) social and political activism to religion and incorporated Marxism and class analysis to its analysis and practice in the social reality. For an academic account of this movement see Löwy (1996).

5 For more on the CEBs, see Azevedo (1987). For more on the CEBs and the involvement of the Catholic Church in progressive politics in Brazil, see Mainwaring (1986).

6 For more on the history of teachers' mobilization in the state of Rio Grande do Sul, see Bulhões and Abreu (1992). For an example of how the CPERS was able to rearticulate symbols to support its cause, see Gandin and Hypolito (2000).

7 For more on this see Kowarick (1979); Keck (1986).

8 Here we offer a brief description of the Participatory Budgeting structure. For more on this renowned experience, see Santos (1998); Baiocchi (2001); Fedozzi (1997).

9 Patrimonialism can be defined as the *pretense* of independence of the bureaucratic structure of the state from the social conflicts. In this conception, the independent bureaucratic structure of the state is the best space for decisions that are always "technical." As many researchers show, in Brazil this tradition ended up representing a privatization of the state by the interests of the technical personnel acting in favor of dominant groups in Brazil. For more on this, see Faoro (1958); Schwartzman (1988). Clientelism is the practice of exchanging electoral and political support for economic and social benefits. For more on this, see Santos, F. G. M. (1995); Schmidt (1977).

10 For a closer examination of the dilemmas of democracy and participation, something we do not have the space to do in this chapter, see Cohen and Rogers (1995); Wright and Fung (2003).

11 Baiocchi's doctoral dissertation is dedicated to examining this process, and his findings support this affirmation. For this see Baiocchi (2001). See also Abers (1998).

References

Abers, R. (1998). From clientelism to cooperation: Local government, participatory policy and civic organizing in Porto Alegre, Brazil. *Politics & Society 26*(4): pp. 511–537.

Anyon, J. (2005). *Radical Possibilities: Public Policy, Urban Education, and a New Social Movement.* New York: Routledge.

Apple, M. W. (1988). *Teachers and Texts.* New York: Routledge.

Apple, M. W. (2000). *Official Knowledge* (2nd ed.). New York: Routledge.

Apple, M. W. (2006). *Educating the "Right" Way: Markets, Standards, God, and Inequality* (2nd ed.) New York: Routledge.

Apple, M. W. (Ed.). (2010). *Global Crises, Social Justice, and Education.* New York: Routledge.

Apple, M. W. (2013). *Can Education Change Society?* New York: Routledge.

Apple, M. W. and Beane, J. A. (Eds.). (2007). *Democratic Schools: Lessons in Powerful Education* (2nd ed.). Portsmouth, NH: Heinemann.

Apple, M. W., Au, W. and Gandin, L. A. (Eds.). (2009). *The Routledge International Handbook of Critical Education.* New York: Routledge.

Archdiocese of São Paulo, Brazil (1998). *Torture in Brazil: A Shocking Report on the Pervasive Use of Torture by Brazilian Military Governments, 1964-1979.* Austin, TX: University of Texas Press.

Avritzer, L. (1999). *Public Deliberation at the Local Level: Participatory Budgeting in Brazil.* Unpublished manuscript.

Azevedo, M. C. (1987). *Basic Ecclesial Communities in Brazil: The Challenge of a New Way of Being Church.* Washington, DC: Georgetown University Press.

Baiocchi, G. (1999). *Participation, Activism, and Politics: The Porto Alegre Experiment and Deliberative Democratic Theory.* Unpublished manuscript.

Baiocchi, G. (2001). *From Militance to Citizenship: The Workers' Party, Civil Society, and the Politics of Participatory Governance in Porto Alegre, Brazil.* Unpublished doctoral dissertation. University of Wisconsin-Madison.

Bulhões, M. G. and Abreu, M. (1992). *A Luta dos Professores Gaúchos de 1979 a 1991: A Difícil Aprendizado da Democracia.* Porto Alegre, Brazil: L&PM.

Cohen, J. & Rogers, J. (Eds.). (1995). *Associations and Democracy.* London: Verso.

Della Cava, R. (1988). *The Church and the Abertura in Brazil – 1974–1985.* Working Paper Series. Working Paper 114. Notre Dame, IN: The Kellogg Institute for International Studies, University of Notre Dame.

Faoro, R. (1958). *Os Donos do Poder.* Porto Alegre, Brazil: Globo.

Fedozzi, L. (1997). *Orçamento Participativo: Reflexões sobre a experiência de Porto Alegre.* Porto Alegre, Brazil: Tomo Editorial.

Freire, P. (1993). *Pedagogy of the Oppressed.* New York: Continuum.

Freire, P. (1997). A response. In *Mentoring the Mentor: A Critical Dialogue with Paulo Freire.* P. Freire (Ed.) pp. 303–329. New York: Peter Lang.

Gadotti, M. and Pereira, O. (1989). *Pra que PT: Origem, Projeto e Consolidação do Partido dos Trabalhadores.* São Paulo, Brazil: Cortez.

Gandin, L. A. (2002). *Democratizing Access, Governance, and Knowledge: The Struggle for Educational Alternatives in Porto Alegre, Brazil.* Doctoral Dissertation. University of Wisconsin–Madison.

Gandin, L. A. (2009). The citizen school project: Implementing and recreating critical education in Porto Alegre, Brazil. In *The Routledge International Handbook of Critical Education.* M. W. Apple, W. Au, and L. A. Gandin (Eds.) pp. 341–353. New York: Routledge.

Gandin, L. A. (2010). The democratization of governance in the Citizen School Project: Building a new notion of accountability in education. In *The Routledge International Handbook of the Sociology of Education*. M. W. Apple, S. J. Ball, and L. A. Gandin (Eds.) pp. 349–357. London: Routledge.

Gandin, L. A. and Hypolito, A. L. M. (2000). Reestruturação educacional como construção social contraditória. In *Educação em Tempos de Incertezas*. A. L. M. Hypolito and Gandin, L. A. (Eds.) pp. 59–92. Belo Horizonte, Brazil: Autêntica.

Gandin, L. A. and Apple, M. W. (2002). Challenging neo-liberalism, building democracy: Creating the Citizen School in Porto Alegre, Brazil. *Journal of Education Policy* 17(2): pp. 259–279.

Genro, T. (1999). Cidadania, emancipação e cidade. In *Escola Cidadã: Teoria e Prática*. L. H. Silva (Ed.). pp. 7–11. Petrópolis, Brazil: Vozes.

Goroditch, C. and Souza, M. C. (1999). Complexo temático. In *Escola Cidadã: Teoria e Prática*. L. H. Silva (Ed.) pp. 76–84. Petrópolis, Brazil: Vozes.

Gramsci, A. (1997). *Selections from the Prison Notebooks* [Ed. Hoare, Q. & Smith, G. N.] (Reprint, 1st ed. 1971). New York: International Publishers.

Hernandez, F. and Ventura, M. (1998). *A Organização do Currículo por Projetos de Trabalho*. Porto Alegre: ArtMed.

Hypolito, A. L. M. (1999). Trabalho docente e profissionalização: Sonho prometido ou sonho negado? In *Desmistificando a Profissionalização do Magistério*. I. P. A. Veiga and M. I. Cunha (Eds.) pp. 81–100. Campinas, Brazil: Papirus.

INEP (2000). *Education for All: Evaluation of the Year 2000*. Brasília, Brazil: INEP.

Keck, M. E. (1986). *From Movement to Politics: The Formation of the Workers' Party in Brazil*. Doctoral Dissertation. New York: Columbia University.

Kowarick, L. (1979). *A Espoliação Urbana*. Rio de Janeiro, Brazil: Paz e Terra.

Kowarick, L. (2000). *Escritos Urbanos*. São Paulo, Brazil: Editora 34.

Lipman, P. (2011). *The New Political Economy of Urban Education: Neoliberalism, Race, and the Right to the City*. New York: Routledge.

Löwy, M. (1996). *The War of Gods: Religion and Politics in Latin America*. New York: Verso.

Lynch, K., Grummell, B. and Devine, D. (2012). *New Managerialism in Education: Commercialization, Carelessness and Gender*. New York: Palgrave Macmillan.

Mainwaring, S. (1986). *The Catholic Church and Politics in Brazil, 1916-1985*. Stanford, CA: Stanford University Press.

Meneguello, R. (1989). *PT – A Formação de um Partido – 1979-1982*. Rio de Janeiro, Brazil: Paz e Terra.

Nelson-Pallmeyer, J. (1997). *School of Assassins: The Case for Closing the School of the Americas and for Fundamentally Changing U.S. Foreign Policy*. Maryknoll, NY: Orbis.

Pinheiro, P. S. (1989). Prefácio. In *PT – A Formação de um Partido – 1979–1982*. Meneguello, R. (pp. 9–13). Rio de Janeiro, Brazil: Paz e Terra.

Santos, F. G. M. (1995). Microfundamentos do Clientelismo Político no Brasil: 1959–1963. *Dados* 38(3): pp. 459–496.

Santos, B. S. (1998). Participatory budgeting in Porto Alegre: Toward a distributive democracy. *Politics and Society* 26 (4): pp. 461–510.

Schmidt, S. W. (Ed.). (1977). *Friends, Followers, and Factions: A Reader in Political Clientelism*. Berkeley, CA: University of California Press.

Schrer-Warren, I. and Krischke, P. J. (Eds.). (1987). *Uma Revolução no Cotidiano? Os Novos Movimentos Sociais na América Latina*. São Paulo, Brazil: Brasiliense.

Schwartzman, S. (1988). *As Bases Autoritárias do Estado Brasileiro.* Rio de Janeiro, Brazil: Campus.

SMED. (1993). *Projeto Gestão Democrática - Lei Complementar no. 292.* Unpublished text.

SMED. (1999a). Ciclos de formação – Proposta político-pedagógica da Escola Cidadã. *Cadernos Pedagogicos 9*(1): pp. 1–111.

SMED. (1999b). *Official Homepage of the SMED.* www.portoalegre.rs.gov.br/smed. Accessed 12/15/99.

Souza, D.H., Mogetti, E.A., Villani, M., Panichi, M.T.C., Rossetto, R.P., and Huerga, S.M.R. (1999). Turma de progressão e seu significado na escola. In *Turma de Progressão: A Inversão da Lógica da Exclusão.* S. Rocha and B. D. Nery (Eds) pp. 22–29. Porto Alegre, Brazil: SMED.

Wilkinson, M. N. (2007). *Learning to Participate: Poor Women's Experiences in Building Democracy in Porto Alegre, Brazil.* Doctoral Dissertation. Columbia University.

Williams, R. (1961). *The Long Revolution.* London: Chatto & Windus.

Wright, E. O. (2010). *Envisioning Real Utopias.* New York: Verso.

Wright, E. O. and Fung, A. (2003). *Deepening Democracy: Institutional Innovations in Empowered Participatory Governance.* London: Verso.

Žižek! (2005). Documentary. Zeitgeist Films.

6

THE STRUGGLE CONTINUES

Lessons Learned and What Can Be Done

Michael W. Apple

Facing Complexity

The previous four chapters of *The Struggle for Democracy in Education* have documented the gains, losses, and tensions associated with ongoing attempts to institute both "thicker" and "thinner" democratic policies and practices in education, or to defend existing critically democratic gains that have been made over the years. It should be clear by now that democracy is a sliding signifier. It has no essential meaning, but is defined by its use (Wittgenstein 1963). Neoliberals and neoconservatives employ the word constantly to convince people to come under their leadership. For them "democracy" is largely guaranteed through marketization, individual choice, and the defense of "traditional" cultures, identities, and structures (Apple 2006; 2014). For progressives, democracy is also a "key word" (Williams 1985), one that participates in a different emotional economy. It signifies commitments to thick, fully participatory visions connected to structural equalities and an emancipatory politics.

In this final chapter, I want to focus both on some general and more specific lessons we can learn from the stories we have told. I also want to note a number of cautions that should guide us in these understandings. In addition, I will detail what all of this means for many of our actions as critical educators. Finally, I will argue that honestly facing the realities of what can happen as we continue to struggle for a more robust critical democracy in education—to its possible tensions and contradictions—should not lead to paralysis or cynicism. Given the nature of our societies, there are and will always be contradictions and conflicts both in the larger society and thus in education. And there undoubtedly will always be differences in our positions on how we deal with this. But this is not like a pendulum that automatically swings from one way to the other. It takes concrete, committed, and *continuous* efforts to interrupt selfish individualism and the destructive effects of economic inequalities to argue for, and institute, more critically oriented participatory and deliberative forms of democracy.

There is of course a very long history of debate over the meaning of democracy and over the contradictions generated by a primary focus on possessive individualism and an almost religious faith in the market both in the United States and elsewhere (Foner 1998). There also is an extensive continuing history of just as robust a debate within the Left over exactly these issues and over the ways to get to a "real democracy" (Eagleton 2011; Honneth 2016; Schroyer 1973; Stedman-Jones 2016). These arguments are mirrored within education in such things as the differing positions on both democracy and how we should get there in the indoctrination debates between such figures as John Dewey and George Counts (Apple 2013) and between Dewey and the less politically inclined child-centered progressives (Dewey 1938). These arguments are also signified by the very important claims by people of color, women's mobilizations, LGBTQI groups, disability rights movements, environmental activists, and others, that any version of democracy that does not involve a substantive recognition of and participation in their (our) struggles cannot be considered truly critically democratic at all.

If these debates are to be taken seriously, one thing is certain. Understanding the social and economic context is crucial to what actually happens and who wins or loses. However, even this is too general. As we saw, we need to focus on the complex and specific power relations that exist *inside* as well as surrounding these contexts. Not paying sufficient attention to the *multiple* dynamics at work in a specific situation can lead us not only to being overly optimistic, but it can lead us to not focus on things that could be preventable if we had only thought harder about them. My example in Chapter 1 of the gendered realities of girls and young women's lives and bodies and the lack of clean toilets is a case in point.

However, while recognizing multiplicity is essential, it can carry its own dangers. It can lead us to underplay the significance of the dominant power of particular dynamics in any one situation. Thus, economic forces and class relations may be primary, such as in Kenosha. But recognizing this can also be too reductive in other contexts. Thus, many critics of capitalism and its accompanying destructive class dynamics are apt to assume that all of the serious issues we face—crucial dynamics that occur around such relations as racism, sexism, fundamentalism, homophobia, and many other oppressive conditions—are the direct results of dominant economic relations. This is more than a little reductive and should be resisted (Wright 2010, p. 38; Honneth 2017; Fraser 1997; Eagleton 2011).

Take the discussion in Chapter 2 of the ways in which class dynamics and the conversion strategies employed by even critically inclined middle-class parents intersected with the realities of the racial structuring of local political economies, neighborhoods, and school staff. An understanding of the ways these intersecting histories and relations jointly created the realities of that school could generate a very different and honest discussion of this in other schools that are trying to build a similar antiracist, two-way bilingual program. At the very least, it can serve as a warning to be quite watchful of what can happen when class relations interrupt very progressive antiracist priorities.

Curriculum Politics and Democratic Mobilizations

One of the things that set the school in Chapter 2 apart from many others was its creation of a curriculum that was expressly critical. That chapter does not stand alone. In a number of chapters in the central section of this book, it is clear that struggles over the curriculum are essential to building thick democratic education both in the content of what is taught and how it is taught, as well as who makes the decisions about these issues.

This emphasis on the actual content of schooling is a continuation of gains that have been made over many decades of dedicated work by critical educators and writers, librarians, community activists, and social movements at all levels. Indeed, one of the most significant advances that has been made in education is the transformation of the question of "What knowledge is of most worth?" into "Whose knowledge is of most worth?" This rewording is not simply a linguistic issue. While we need to be careful in not assuming that there is always a one-to-one correspondence between "legitimate" knowledge and groups in power, in changing the focus the question asks that we engage in a radical transformation of our ways of thinking about the connections between what counts as important knowledge in educational institutions and in the larger society and the existing relations of domination and subordination and struggles against these relations. This has crucial implications for what we choose to teach, how we teach it, and what values and identities underpin such choices (Apple 2014).

Just as importantly, the question also demands that one word in the final sentence be problematized—the word *we*. Who is the "we"? What group arrogates the center to themselves, thereby seeing another group as the Other? That word—"we"—often symbolizes the manner in which ideological forces and assumptions work inside and outside of education. Especially when employed by dominant groups, "we" functions as a mechanism not only of inclusion, but powerfully of exclusion as well. It is a verb that masquerades as a noun, in a manner similar to the word "minority" or "slave." No one is a "minority." Someone must *make* another a minority; someone or some group must *minoritize* another person and group, in the same way that no one can be fully known as a slave. Someone or some group must *enslave* someone else.

Ignoring this understanding cuts us off from seeing the often-ugly realities of a society and its history. Perhaps even more crucially, it also cuts us off from the immensely valuable historical and current struggles against the gendered/sexed, classed, and raced processes of dehumanization. By severing the connections between nouns and verbs, it makes invisible the actions and actors that make dominance seem normal. It creates a vacant space that is all too often filled with dominant meanings and identities. The attempt to change this situation was the key for the school on which we focused in Chapter 2.

This vacant space is legitimated by many things, but one of the most powerful forces of legitimation is the way we even think about rationality and objectivity. The stories of real people's lives, the realities of our connections to the ways in which the continuing process of, for example, racial dominance is built and maintained—all of these are hidden by the fiction of neutrality and of keeping ourselves above any substantive commitment to challenge such dominance. This is perhaps best seen in Charles Mills' (1997) exceptional analysis of the way in which the development of our belief in the rational individual that lies at the heart of our usual conceptions of the public sphere is deeply connected to the construction of an "other" who is irrational, not fully worthy—Black, Brown, Asian, Indigenous, Woman, and the list goes on. Accepted conceptions of rationality require the creation of the irrational. It is no accident that the relational aspect of this guiding principle of "being a rational person" has its roots in empire and the history of racial judgments.

These points may seem too abstract. But behind them is something that lies at the heart of being critically democratic educators. A major role they must play is to articulate both a vision and the reality of the fully engaged critical scholar and educator, someone who refuses to accept an education that doesn't simultaneously challenge the unreflective "we" and also illuminates the path to a new politics of voice and recognition in education. The task is to give embodied examples of critical pedagogies and of a more robust sense of socially informed educational action as it is actually lived out by real people, including committed educators and cultural workers in the complex politics at multiple levels of education, even when there predictably are tensions and contradictions. This was one of the primary aims of the analysis in Chapter 2 and in Chapter 5's detailed discussion of Porto Alegre.

As I noted above, this concern is not new. Teachers, social activists, and scholars in multiple disciplines have spent years challenging the boundaries of that usually unexamined space of the "we" and resisting the knowledge, perspectives, epistemological assumptions, and accepted voices that underpin them. There was no time when resistance, both overt and covert, was not present (Berrey 2015). This is especially the case in education, a field where the issues surrounding what and whose knowledge should be taught and how it should be taught are taken very seriously, especially by those people who are not included in the ways in which dominant groups define that oh-so-dangerous word of "we" (Apple 2013; Apple and Au 2014; Au et al. 2016; Warmington 2014).

There is another reason that the issues surrounding the curriculum are central here. For all of the well-deserved attention that is given to neoliberal agendas and policies, to privatization and choice plans, to audit cultures and standardization, we must continue to pay just as much attention to the actual stuff that is taught—and the "absent presences" (Macherey 2006) of what is not taught—in school, as well as to the concrete experiences of students, teachers, administrators, school counselors, cooks, janitors, school secretaries, parents, community members and volunteers, to all who live and work in those buildings called schools. Documenting and understanding these lived realities are crucial to an interruptive strategy and to making connections between these experiences and the possibilities of building and defending something so much better. The failure to do this in Kenosha was one of the reasons for the failure to build a lasting alliance. That the mobilization in Jeffco was successful shows the power of connecting multiple groups of teachers, students, parents, and community members around an issue that they shared.

As we saw in the chapter on Kenosha and Jeffco, among the most important actors were the students. Their mobilization and leadership was based not only on the larger concerns with the claims of neoliberalism. Rather the radical changes that the conservatives wanted to make in the actual subject matter also drove the students to act. Clearly, then, the curriculum itself can be and is a primary focus of educational struggles, something that can be seen as well in the struggle by African American youth involved in the Algebra Project in Baltimore who employed that project and its knowledge to build alliances and successfully stop the building of a new juvenile prison there. A form of knowledge that was usually seen as "useless" and simply the knowledge of elites was connected to the lived realities of youth in a manner that enabled them to become activists of their own lives (Apple 2013). This is of course similar to work that is being done in hip-hop pedagogies and similar forms that connect daily lives and cultural forms that affirm new identities and resistances (Emdin 2010, 2016). It is also certainly visible in the transformations in Chapter 5.

For these very reasons, it is worth stressing again that these examples of the politics of culture and identity surrounding schooling document the significance of curriculum struggles in the formation of both hegemonic and counter-hegemonic movements. The fact that there is all too often an absence of in-depth analyses of what is and is not actually taught, of the politics of "official knowledge," (Apple 2014) in so many critical discussions of the role of neoliberalism in education, is notable. Yet as we saw in Chapter 1, these have been central to recent educational policy conflicts throughout the nation—in Texas with its textbook treatment of enslavement and conservative values, in Arizona with its attacks on ethnic studies and even attempts there to prohibit teaching courses on "social justice" (Levin 2017), in the struggles over "culturally relevant" curricula, in the debates over climate change and evolution, and in the centrality of the conflicts over the common core throughout many parts of the nation. We simply cannot grasp the reasons why so many people are convinced to come under the ideological leadership of dominant groups—or act to resist such leadership—if we don't give a prime place to the struggle over meanings in the formation of identity.

Social movements—both progressive and retrogressive—often form around issues that are central to people's identities, cultures, and histories (Giugni et al.

1999; Apple, 2013; see also Binder 2002). More attention theoretically, historically, and empirically to the centrality of such struggles could provide more nuanced approaches to the reasons various aspects of conservative modernizing positions are found compelling, and just as importantly to the ways in which movements that interrupt neoliberal agendas have been and can be built (Apple 2013).

The importance of this is again clearly visible in Chapter 3. The alliance that was built in response to the conservative takeover of the school board, galvanized students, teachers, parents, and other community groups to not only overturn the very conservative curricular decisions, but also resulted in the election of a more progressive school board. Both neoliberal and neoconservative policies were challenged successfully, in spite of the fact that the conservative majority of the school board had received a large amount of financial and ideological support by the Koch brothers' backed group Americans for Prosperity. As Schirmer and I detail, there are important lessons to be learned here.

Are Alliances Possible? Democracy, Intersectionality, and Religious Movements

The issue of alliances that I highlighted above is an important one. Clearly, the relationship between the meanings and the values one attaches to the social and educational world and identity is complicated. As we documented in Chapter 2, class is crucial here. But as I noted earlier on, it often intersects with other dynamics such as gender/sexuality and race (Bhopal and Preston 2012). And these also intersect with the relatively autonomous actions surrounding religious forms and traditions. One of the things that is visible in the chapter on Porto Alegre is the role of progressive religious institutions and movements in supporting and generating counter-hegemonic mobilizations and transformations. This was especially the case in Brazil, but from personal experience I know that it is not only there. For example, when I was arrested in South Korea for speaking out against the military dictatorship in power at that time, a number of the people who were arrested with me were also deeply religious, guided by an understanding that "Jesus spent his life working for the poor and oppressed. I will commit myself to this myself no matter what the risks." This is a powerful sentiment, one I believe needs to be supported (see Apple 2013).

In saying this, I do not at all wish to ignore the growing power of ultra-conservative and repressive religious movements and ideologies in many nations. Indeed, I have written very critically about them in *Educating the "Right" Way* and elsewhere (see, e.g., Apple 2006). However, I fear that many progressive activists and scholars who are struggling to build and defend more thickly democratic institutions and social relations may be pushing away a considerable number of people who are religiously motivated. This is a very real limitation of a number of the critical positions that the Left has taken over the years. Too often advocates for radical egalitarian positions have been overly dismissive of religious motivations and understandings (see Wallis 2010; see also Stone 2017). This is more than a little unwise tactically and also forgets the history that a number of religious movements have played in the ongoing struggles for social justice in so many societies (see, for example, West 2002).

In countering this, we need to focus more of our attention on a more general issue. Rather than assuming that religious conservativism is based on a totally rightist sensibility about everything we may hold dear, it would be wiser to look at what I call the elements of "good sense" as well as bad sense in people's anger about current policies inside and outside of education and how they are convinced to follow the leadership of more neoliberal and neoconservative groups (Apple 2006; see also Hochschild 2016). This is a wise position not only theoretically, but strategically as well. People are not "puppets." They have real reasons for their worries—and it is not automatic that they move to the Right rather than toward more progressive politics. It takes hard ideological work, what I have called a vast social/pedagogic project, for people to agree with rightist "solutions." Discursive politics are crucial elements here, both in responding to religious sentiments, but also in other areas of social life.

But the fact that dominant groups have been successful in moving many people to the Right by connecting to people's partly accurate understandings of their daily lives, means that progressives must also do a much better job of making connections to the core meanings of their lives and to the real problems people experience (Hochschild 2016). A politics based on better attempts to understand the realities of people's lives has a much greater chance of having them listen more carefully to our arguments.

There is of course a danger here. People's common sense may already be articulated around racist nativist understandings, by unarticulated assumptions grounded in possessive individualism and selfishness rather than a concern for a more robust sense of the common good. Thus, while I agree that there is a definite need to listen carefully and to talk across our ideological differences, not only do *both* sides have to be willing to do this, but we must not do it in a manner that somehow legitimates things such as anti-immigrant racism and other profoundly racist positions,[1] educational visions of children as simply future workers, the attacks on women's control of their bodies, religious arrogance in assuming that "God only talks to me," and similar ethically problematic positions. This will be difficult. Obviously, we need to go into these dialogues with respect for real people's concerns and a greater knowledge of the local. But we also need to realize that respect must come from both sides and that we will have to think very carefully about what compromises are worth making in order for the dialogue to go further and lead perhaps to joint understandings and joint actions.

This is something I've given a good deal of thought to and, like many readers of this book I'm certain, have tried to embody in personal and professional actions. For example, in *Educating the "Right" Way* (Apple 2006), I call for "hybrid alliances" between what are usually very different ideological and religious allegiances. A prime example in education in the United States is the case of Channel One, a for-profit television station that is broadcast in a very large number of public and private schools. Channel One provides 10 minutes of "news" accompanied by two minutes of well-designed commercials (see Apple 2014). Many schools agree to have Channel One in their schools not only because it is slickly marketed as a "solution" to real school problems about making our students "more knowledgeable about current affairs," but also because it gives the school equipment such as a satellite dish, TV monitors, and other things that can add up to many tens of thousands of dollars. The catch is that, as a captive audience, students are required to watch the commercials. This connects to the growing concern about the increased uses of schools as sites of profit (see also Ball 2009; Ball 2012; Burch 2009; Gunter et al. 2017).

In response to this, I and others have formed an alliance with conservative religious groups to remove Channel One from schools. For the conservative evangelicals, "children are created in God's image" and it is "ungodly" for them to be bought and sold as commodities for profit in schools. For me and other progressives, we may not agree with the specific theological position taken by the conservative religious advocates, but we too are deeply concerned about commodifying children as a captive audience for corporate profits. Thus, these two usually diametrically opposed ideological positions are unified around a specific educational project, stopping the selling of children for profit. This has enabled the removal of Channel One from a number of school districts. But it has also led to the reduction of stereotypes on both sides and to keeping open a space for further dialogue.

This was partly the case in the analysis of Porto Alegre that Gandin and I discussed in Chapter 5. Religiously inspired movements played a very large role in the growth of progressive mobilizations there—and of keeping them together. Of course, the United States is not Brazil. But if too many progressives in the United States tend to automatically mistrust groups who find meaning in religious understandings, in the process the traditional Left may risk marginalizing religious motivations and traditions that could underpin alliances over crucial elements of agreement. These alliances are visible in such growing grassroots populist movements surrounding the "Moral Monday" actions that have been stimulated by important religious leaders such as the Reverend Dr. Benjamin Barber and others. They are visible as well in the pro-immigrant sanctuary commitments advanced by multiple churches, mosques, synagogues, and other formal and informal religious institutions and meeting grounds found among multiple populations here. They are also visible in the growing pro-environmental worries among a number of evangelical movements. It is well worth considering whether "hybrid" alliances across our differences that advance specific progressive projects can be built.

But, and it is an important but, in even considering this let us recognize that the continuing growth of "authoritarian populist" conservative religious movements who are actively defending existing and even more radical thin democratic policies may still make this difficult in education and other areas (see Apple 1996). These movements are among the fastest growing advocates for particular kinds of educational reform throughout the nation. Take as one example the growth of home schooling, one in which millions of children are engaged (see, e.g., Apple 2006). In some ways, the home schooling phenomenon is partly a reaction to the attention being given to the ways in which the "crisis in public schools" is portrayed in the media. Yet it is also part of a larger reaction to the perceived dominance of secular values in schools, to the feelings that conservative religious knowledge and ways of understanding the world are not given equal weight in the curriculum, and in all too many cases to the creation of ideological "gated communities" in which the culture and body of the "Other" are seen as forms of pollution that must be avoided at all costs (Apple 2006; see also Kintz 1997). Struggles over culture, over identities, and over Whiteness and the feeling that one is part of the "new oppressed" are core parts of the emerging politics of education on the Right and within the religious Right in particular.

In many parts of this movement, issues of biblical authority intersect with long histories of racial fear, of the loss of "our" God-given roles as men and women, and of a government that actively takes away "liberty" (Apple 2006; Apple 1996; MacLean 2017). It will be more than a little difficult to find dialogic space when faced with these kinds of positions.[2] Thus, there will be dangers as well as possibilities and any attempts to engage cooperatively with such groups should be approached with honesty and the maintenance of a deep commitment to justifiably held antiracist, anti-homophobic, and social justice values about this. These are not things that should be sacrificed as we try to build a broader "we."

Given this, although I continue to believe that the lessons of Porto Alegre are important and that we should look for more ways to work with religiously motivated groups, once again I would ask us to be careful of not romanticizing such possibilities. With a very conservative evangelical Christian now serving as the Secretary of Education in the United States, the defunding of public schools and the substitution of private for public in education is now high on the national agenda (Smith 2017). While the evidence does not support arguments for this set of policies, there may actually be little support on the Right, and among the religious Right, for substantive dialogue that is other than an exercise in ideological legitimation for the Right.

Thus, there are still fundamental differences between the larger agendas of the groups involved in these debates. Dialogue across ideological boundaries and a focus on the elements of good sense among people who disagree are necessary and can engender more respect and understanding. Therefore it should be sought after. However, let us be honest about two things. As I noted above, such dialogue can give legitimacy to positions which we justifiably find homophobic, sexist, racist, and anti-immigrant. Furthermore, this activity is not a substitute for other things. A "talking cure" will not be sufficient to alter the social and ideological conditions of dominance and subordination that so clearly characterize so many societies (Teeger 2015). Thus, it must not serve as an excuse for not engaging in the time-consuming and much more long-term and difficult task of forming social mobilizations that aim at fundamentally challenging these conditions and differential relations of power. We would need to constantly reflect on whether these dialogues, possible hybrid alliances, and the policies and practices that might evolve from them, are leading in more critically democratic directions in the long term.

Local Struggles Count

The ideological issues I discussed in the previous section are tough ones. But one of the most difficult and substantive dilemmas we face is more grounded in material reality. A major area of conflict that is so visible in the four chapters at the core of this book is money. It should go without saying that battles over budgets will need to be waged continuously. We know that the fiscal crisis that we face is often caused by capital basically going on strike by refusing to pay its fair share of taxes, the decision by large corporations to off-shore their profits, the very real decline in wages and of respectful jobs with dignity and benefits like health care, a racialized political economy and a racial state, (Lipman 2011; Rothstein 2017), a deep disrespect for the labor of public employees, and by the hard work in which the Right engaged as it creates a new common sense that emphasizes that public is necessarily bad and private is necessarily good (Mayer 2016; MacLean 2017). The effects of these damaging trends have made it ever more difficult to maintain an education that is able to do all of the things that it is now expected to do.

A good deal of the focus of progressive criticism of these economic and educational realities has been on the national or the state level. This is understandable given the current national administration's economic, political, and educational policies, the appointment of an ultra-conservative Secretary of (war on) Education, and the attacks on and withdrawal of support for public schools in a large number of states. The discussion by Eleni Schirmer and me of what is happening in Wisconsin is but one example. Yet, as that chapter also indicates, it is equally crucial to direct our attention to the local level, not only to the larger arenas. This is particularly salient when we consider the recent moves by right-wing groups to pay close attention to school board races as the sites of significant victories. As we saw in Chapter 3, Americans for Prosperity and other right-wing groups have aggressively occupied the space of local influence (Mayer 2016) and have added a determined focus on important school board elections as part of their overall strategy of a war of position.

Electoral politics, especially at a local level, then has become even more crucial than before. Let us admit that this is hard in an age when the usual rules of governance have been trampled by Trump and Trumpism and its legacy and when well-funded conservative groups are able to spend huge amounts of money in quite manipulative ways on local, state-wide, and national issues. There is almost a perverse sense of enjoyment, of "Can you believe this!", in each outrageous tweet, each demeaning comment, each move toward much more destructive environmental, health, housing, and educational policies. It is too easy to shift our attention to what is a strange combination of the comical and the diabolical. Yet all of this is happening at one and the same time, so that not only are national policies in all these areas being radically transformed, but so too are our close to home institutions and relations.

This means that we also need to pay much closer attention to what stands behind these local transformations. Americans for Prosperity and ALEC (the American Legislative Exchange Council) among other groups are spearheading radical neoliberal and neoconservative agendas. They do this with large amounts of money, but also with feet on the ground. In addition, they also engage in the writing and disseminating of model conservative legislation that is sent to state legislatures and governors throughout the nation—and by coordinating political efforts to get these laws approved (see, e.g., Underwood and Meade 2012; Anderson and Montoro Donchik 2016). Just as importantly, they run educational programs and legislative "camps" that equip current and future legislators and youth with the kinds of media and legislative skills to ensure that they can shift the balance of arguments in their direction. We have much to learn from the Right in this regard (Apple 2013, 2006). Thus, our critical analyses and actions on the local level must be complemented by a rigorous analysis and action on the national and regional sources of the financial and ideological support and leadership that make such local mobilizations more powerful than they otherwise would be. Here too we can learn from the Right about how one engages in the long-term building of movements—with our own legislative training, "camps" for young activists, model legislation that is ready to go, working with youth, teachers, and community members on developing and spreading tools such as participatory action research (Winn and Suoto-Manning 2017) that can be used to interrupt the "epistemological fog" so depended upon by dominant groups, in building critical media skills and groups, and so much more. We also have much to learn from the creative and dedicated strategies of counter-hegemonic alliances, media work, and movement building developed by the participants in the Black Lives Matter campaigns and in the grassroots work of "Our Revolution" (see, for example, https://ourrevolution.com/). Many more groups could be noted here. All of these will be critical to connect the local with the regional and national. But this also requires that we actively teach each other what works and what doesn't—and that we are *willing* to be taught.

Thinking Internationally

Being willing to be taught implies rejecting the comforting illusion, one based in imperial (mis)understandings, that the United States is by its very nature "special," that it is the center of the world and that "we" have little to learn from other nations. Thus, we will need to pay close attention not only to the struggles in the United States, but to how democracy is being redefined in other nations. This makes the chapters on Brazil and China even more important. In Brazil currently, the Right is growing in power, with rightist politicians and conservative religious activists having won mayoral elections in Sao Paulo and Rio de Janeiro (Phillips 2017). Support there for rightist "free market" positions is being stimulated by a good deal of money and advice from rightist foundations in the United States. The Free Brazil Movement and Students for Liberty, for example, represent key aspects of these trends. They are bolstered by external rightist groups such as the Atlas Network, made up of U.S. based conservative evangelical movements, and a number of the organizations affiliated with the Koch brothers. The implications of this for Porto Alegre are worrisome. We need to look carefully at the ways in which conservative economic and religious movements work in establishing and maintaining hegemonic identities that support neoliberal and neoconservative agendas throughout the world, even among very poor communities. Once again, their success can teach us something about connecting to the daily lives of people and about how to organize a successful social/pedagogic project that interrupts rightist common sense.

We don't need to only learn from the Right about these things. The continuing struggles to ensure that the egalitarian forms of Participatory Budgeting and the Citizen School are robust in Porto Alegre are now even more crucial both in Brazil and elsewhere. They allow us to point to a powerful example that can serve as a model for a critical education and a set of state/community relations that exemplifies the principles of thick democracy.

Certain specific questions come to the fore in this regard. What did the educators, community activists, youth, and the progressive state workers in Porto Alegre do to defend the gains that had been made? How are these groups acting to defend these gains given the even more current situation of rightist resurgence? What specific strategies were employed? What compromises had to be made? All of the questions that have served as the underpinnings of *The Struggle for Democracy in Education* need to be asked. Answering them could provide crucial lessons for all of us. Thus, ongoing long-term politically engaged educational research is more important than ever.

In addition to Brazil, engaging in thoughtful analyses of other influential nations is essential for the thick democratic project as well. While China is very different than Brazil in many ways, China's combination of a very strong state with an increasingly corporatized economy is an example that many nations may model themselves after, especially given China's increasing economic influence throughout the world. Such a "hybrid" system can have a strong effect on the ways in which neoliberal versions of democracy are practiced. Mechanisms that allow affluent parents a system (be it formal or informal) of "democracy as choice" in conjunction with stronger ideological control of what is taught can at least temporarily appear to governments as a wise way to solve the question of state legitimation in many cases. This is a model that may justifiably make many progressives quite uncomfortable, but that does not mean that its possible influence can be ignored.

There are other reasons that those of us in the United States, United Kingdom, and elsewhere need to pay close attention to the struggles over democracy in education in nations such as China. Our own decisions on education have real effects on other nations. Thus, our chapter on the ways in which Chinese policies have evolved and now function is quite important to the arguments we have made in this book. The idea that democracy involves individuated consumer choice on a market that is growing more influential here in the United States has spread exponentially internationally. When it is recontextualized in a different nation, one with a strong state tradition, it will be mediated and employed in complicated ways (see Wong 2002; Lim and Apple 2016). It can be used to give legitimacy to governmental agencies. It can lessen pressure on the state from newly emergent class fractions. It can help create new inequalities, even when a government rightly doesn't want this to happen. It can assist in maintaining an epistemological fog by keeping these inequalities officially invisible. At one and the same time, it can create economic linkages over curriculum between Chinese schools and U.S. companies. And all of this is going on simultaneously. These hidden effects need to be uncovered and subjected to scrutiny.

The issue of unanticipated consequences and hidden negative effects cuts across a number of our analyses. The chapters on the antiracist school and Chinese policies may seem dissimilar. But they speak to something that brings them together. Both describe situations in which middle-class and affluent parents employ their accumulated economic, social, and cultural capital as part of a conversion strategy to ensure that their children are advantaged in the competition for advancement. This is a reminder to us of the crucial importance of two things. First, even with a necessary focus on intersectionality, class is an essential dynamic to a substantive critical understanding of the politics of education and of the role of the local, regional, and national state. Second, a two class model—"dominant/ruling class versus working class"—is insufficient to fully comprehend the ways in which education functions in class and race stratification. The relatively autonomous actions of the new middle class can act as an interruptive strategy that makes it even harder for very real progressive gains in education to survive and flourish in the United States (Posey-Maddox 2014; see also Weis et al. 2014; Bernstein 1977).[3] In China, the upwardly mobile middle and upper-middle classes find spaces within the contradictory politics of the state there to defend and expand their own gains.

It is worth asking some partly heretical questions about this. Does this always have to be a source of expanded inequalities? The history of struggles for "person rights" over "property rights" in the United States both led to "safe" reforms that did not challenge overall hegemonic power *and* to much more substantive transformations in politics and the economy when the discourse of person rights got taken up by more committed women's and antiracist groups (Apple 2014). Does this have implications for nations with strong states? Are there unexplored potentials in the movement for "choice" that could open spaces for expanded funding? Can the idea of consumer power open spaces for collective action? Will this increase pressure on the state for increased equality and for increased voice in the curriculum? Given the very real complexity of China and other nations in that region, it is difficult to predict what can happen. Answering these questions and exploring the possibilities and dangers there will certainly require that we develop more subtle and nuanced ways of understanding that are sensitive to the specificities and multiplicities of China and of the larger Asian sphere (Lim and Apple 2016).

No matter which countries we focus upon, in the end this makes one more analytic and political issue even more critical. Nuanced and substantive ways of judging the potential of the emerging alternatives to neoliberal, neoconservative, authoritarian populist, and new managerial policies and practices are crucial in every nation. Are we going in the right (not the Right) direction? Who is the "we"? Are we building a more inclusive "we" that combines the politics of redistribution, recognition, and representation? There will be—and must be—disagreements on this. Such debates are the engine of further democratization. Yet, thoughtful criteria to judge the potential and effects of more radical plans in education, in the state, in the economy, and in civil society have been articulated. As I have said elsewhere (Apple 2016), perhaps one of the best places to start is in Erik Olin Wright's very detailed treatment of such criteria in his book *Envisioning Real Utopias* (Wright 2010). While Wright's analysis is not as powerful on issues of race and gender than it might be, it is still a major contribution to the development of a more responsive set of critically democratic alternatives. His discussion of how to judge the value, processes, and effects of more substantive and radical economic, political, and cultural projects and assemblages is a welcome addition to the debates about whether our answers to the question of "what is to be done" do indeed provide lasting interruptions of dominant forms.

Difficult Does Not Mean Impossible

Making such judgments is a collective process, one that when done well embodies a participatory and deliberative commitment to radical egalitarian democracy. In doing these kinds of analyses and raising these kinds of questions, it is important to constantly remember that there is *systematic* oppression. It requires fundamental transformations both of the national, regional, and local institutional structures and practices of a racist and racializing state (see, for example, Joseph 2016; see also Rothstein 2017), of the gendered and sexed nature of state policy (Fraser 2013), and of an economy and its paid and unpaid labor system that continues to create lasting inequalities.

Recognizing and being honest about this larger system of domination can, however, make it all too easy to throw up our hands in despair and to neglect the role of schooling in supporting these structures—and very importantly to minimize the significance of the dedication all of those who are working so hard in contributing to a better understanding and interruption of these structures and processes. There are things that can and should be done in education. This is clear in our analysis in Chapters 2 and 5 of the counter-hegemonic curriculum, pedagogy, relationships with the community, and staffing patterns of schools that are overtly committed to a thick and socially/culturally critical democratic set of values.

If you will forgive the military metaphors, what we are advocating is a term I mentioned earlier, what Antonio Gramsci (1971) called "a war of position." This is a set of counter-hegemonic actions in which *everything* counts. Critically democratic action in education, in health care, in community lives, in paid and unpaid workplaces, in the family—all of these count. Action against dominant relations involving gender and sexuality, race, class, ability, age, environmental degradation all count. The task is to then work hard to *connect* these actions to each other and to build alliances across our differences so that the "we" is broader and more mutually supportive. Thus, the local counts, not only the regional and national. As noted above, in Nancy Fraser's words, the politics of recognition and of representation count as well as a politics of redistribution (Fraser 1997, 2013).

This is not new. In fact, it is exactly what the Right has been doing for decades. It is what makes our discussion of local electoral politics in Kenosha and Jeffco in Chapter 3 so important. The Right clearly recognizes the importance of winning at multiple levels and then connecting those victories to each other. The battles were over multiple issues—shrinking the state, reducing taxes on the affluent, destroying the power of unions, attacking progressive curricula, privatization, moving schools toward a goal of making them sources of profit, and much more.

At the same time, in both of these school systems, not only were multiple issues brought together, but the Right knew that the struggles had to be fought in multiple sites, using multiple strategies—in public meetings, in door to door campaigns, in getting its proponents on the ballot, and, profoundly, in the media. It was also extremely creative in its linguistic politics, thereby providing a pathway for people to enter into their alliance even when they didn't agree with all of the Right's positions.

What Jeffco provided was a counter-example in which youth took important leadership roles and where the mobilizations against the Right and in support of teachers and a richer curriculum was more varied. Pathways to join that alliance were created that reached into people's sense of fairness, of support for articulate students who visibly cared about their education and about what they learned, and also won major victories in how the message was presented by the media. Thus, it wasn't "just" about teachers, the rights of labor, and "taxpayers'" rights. These *are* important of course. But tactically, Jeffco demonstrates the need for a richer sense of political dynamics and strategies.

What we need then is a politics that is both vertical and horizontal. Vertically, each level has significant actions that need to be engaged in, with the aim of ultimately connecting these levels to each other as part of a larger movement to build and defend critically deliberative forms. Horizontally, at each level there are multiple dynamics of power that need to be considered, with substantive actions to support movements and to search for and build intersecting alliances around the politics of redistribution, recognition, and representation. Class, gender, sexuality, race, ability, age, environmental degradation, and other forms of "difference" are then seen not as divisive, as impediments, but as resources that can be jointly mobilized through hard work whenever possible.

Thinking Long-Term

There are other important lessons to be learned from many of the chapters in the central section of this book. But one of them that stands out is that victories can be temporary. Cementing them in place requires that the long-term mobilizations and hard practical work that brought them about must not stop. Rightist attacks, fiscal crises, managerial initiatives, privatizing and marketizing pressures, class conversion strategies—all of these will not cease on the day that we declare "we won" in this school, in this curriculum conflict, in this electoral campaign, in this fiscal battle, in this policy arena. Exactly the opposite is usually the case. The Right *learns* from each of its campaigns. It widens its discourse to take account of what did and did not succeed and so that more groups find "answers" under its umbrella of leadership. They are always in it for the long term (See Hall 2016).

The story of Porto Alegre is instructive in this regard. Decades of social and educational activism from below led to changes in the state and its political, economic, cultural, and educational policies and practices. This led to truly fundamental transformations in the daily life of schools and in the relationship of the school to its community. The development of the Citizen School and participatory budgeting provided a model of thick democratic educational and social reforms not only on Brazil but throughout the world.

But conservative forces in Brazil have not rested. They have constantly attempted to limit the sphere of these reforms, to make them more rhetorical than embodied in real schools and communities, and to make them "safer." Yet these thick democratic policies and practices have still lasted in many spaces because of the continuing hard work of teachers, community members, and social movements. This is an ongoing dynamic, one that never ceases.

Similar things need to be said about Jeffco. The coalition that was built among students, teachers, and community activists was crucial in restoring a necessary curriculum and in changing the school board. But the Right has taken the lessons learned from this defeat and is applying them to similar races all over the nation. The victory in Jeffco will be a temporary one if we do not observe what the Right is now doing there and elsewhere, and develop tactics to counter it before it is brought back to Jeffco and other places. Of course, we need to celebrate the gains that we make. Joy is an emotion that needs to be cherished. But at the same time, we cannot rest.

Take the case of the two-way bilingual school in Chapter 2. It remains one of our very favorite schools in its curriculum and pedagogic practices and in its ongoing attempts to embody antiracist and critically democratic policies. Here, it was not the Right that posed the only threat, although the fiscal crisis caused by capital flight and the ensuing neoliberalization of educational policies were and are clearly major pressures affecting the school, just as these forces had such a powerful effect in Kenosha. It was a different kind of class dynamics that emerged, one that demonstrates the complexity of class and race politics that exist in the life of a critically-oriented school. It would be surprising if these dilemmas did *not* occur. And it would be equally surprising if the Right did not seek to exploit these tensions. We need to think carefully about these dynamics in every school that attempts to build such thick forms of democracy and develop participatory and deliberative strategies for honestly dealing with them.

In saying these things and pointing to these lessons, our aim is decidedly *not* to increase cynicism. Nor is it to make us doubt the importance of the critically democratic "thick" values and the policies and practices that stem from them. Rather, we are asking educators and communities to be honest about what can and does happen—to face the complex realities and power relations in the real world. This means that we think simultaneously about both the past and the future. What has happened in the past when such thick democratic policies and practices have been pushed forward? And what must be done in the long term to defend these policies and practices if upwardly mobile middle class groups occupy the space of reform for their own purposes, and just as importantly when the Right as embodied in groups such as Americans for Prosperity and others respond, as they most surely will (Mayer 2016; McLean 2017).

Expanding Our Responsibilities

Throughout this chapter, and overtly in the final paragraph of the previous section, I raise the issue of "what must be done." In Chapter 1, I pointed to three of the tasks of the educator who is deeply committed to building and defending thicker forms of critical democracy. But the number of responsibilities does not end there. Because of this, in this section of the final chapter, I want to ask if critical educators at colleges and universities are part of "we," what are our responsibilities? Drawing upon what I say in *Can Education Change Society?* (Apple 2013), I want to argue for an even more activist role on the part of educators like myself and many others who may be reading this book. Let me enumerate a wider range of tasks in which critically democratic educators should engage as "public intellectuals" in supporting and participating in these transformative movements.

In the process, I argue for a policy of what I call *decentered unity*—a substantive and much more inclusive expansion of the "we"—and for an expansion of the groups who can act as our teachers about the tactics of interruption (see, e.g., Fraser 1997 and Honneth 2016). Such expansion is even more crucial today if we are to more fully participate in building answers to the question of "What is to be done?"

This expanded range of tasks draws upon what Michael Burawoy has called "organic public sociology," arguing that this model provides key elements of how we might think about ways of dealing with a politics of interruption. In his words, but partly echoing Gramsci as well, in this view the critical sociologist (and in my mind, the critical educator, what I call the *critical scholar/activist*):

> ... works in close connection with a visible, thick, active, local, and often counter-public. [She or he works] with a labor movement, neighborhood association, communities of faith, immigrant rights groups, human rights organizations. Between the public sociologist and a public is a dialogue, a process of mutual education ... The project of such [organic] public sociologies is to make visible the invisible, to make the private public, to validate these organic connections as part of our sociological life.
>
> *(Burawoy 2005, p. 265)*

In general, there are nine tasks in which critical analysis (and the critical analyst) in education must engage in creating and defending these organic connections.

1. It must "bear witness to negativity." That is, one of its primary functions is to illuminate the ways in which educational policy and practice are connected to the relations of exploitation and domination—and to struggles against such relations—in the larger society.
2. In engaging in such critical analyses, it also must point to contradictions and to *spaces of possible action*. Thus, its aim is to critically examine current realities with a conceptual/political framework that emphasizes the spaces in which more progressive and counter-hegemonic actions can, or do, go on. This is an absolutely crucial step, since otherwise our research can simply lead to cynicism or despair.
3. At times, this also requires a broadening of what counts as "research." Here I mean acting as critical "secretaries" to those groups of people and social movements who are now engaged in challenging existing relations of unequal power (Apple 2012; see also Apple and Beane 2007; Apple et al. 2009). Some examples of this kind of work are worth noting. The first is "Community of Research on Excellence for All" (CREA), an interdisciplinary research center at the University of Barcelona. It is a model of how to build a research agenda and then create policies and programs that empower those who are economically and culturally marginalized in our societies (see Soler 2011). The second is the deeply committed work carried out by Kathleen Lynch and her colleagues and students at the School of Social Policy, Social Work and

Social Justice at University College, Dublin. Although some of its counter-hegemonic programs have recently been under attack, it too has been at the center of research and action that stresses not only poverty and inequality, but movements towards equality (see *Lynch* et al. *2009; Lynch* et al. 2012). There are of course many other programs that can give us hope. For example, in the process of illuminating the role of the arts in promoting community and social justice in Finland, the ArtsEqual research project, and a number of the researchers affiliated with it have documented important examples of on-the-ground counter-hegemonic successes, while extensively broadening our understanding of who "we" are (see, e.g., Kallio 2015; Laes 2017).

Yet again, documenting these gains still requires that we continue to be unromantic, to be fully cognizant that we are not the only actors on this terrain and that it is not necessarily the case that "thick" visions of democracy will prevail. Indeed, this is one of the reasons we wrote this book. Thus, as I argued in Chapter 1, we need to better understand what actually happens when these distinctly different ideas about democracy confront each other in schools and communities. Thus, it is important to again take very seriously that this is a time when rightist ideological visions, assumptions, and commitments are powerfully present, are well funded, and increasingly have become core parts of the prevailing common sense in so many nations of the world. In a social context such as this, rhetorical responses are simply not sufficient. Certain questions become even more essential. When victories are indeed won, can these thicker forms of critically democratic education remain true to their values and principles? Can they last? What does the reality of this "democracy" look like? What forces are at work to challenge it? What compromises have been made? And what can we learn from these conflicts and compromises? These questions are complicated, but documenting answers to them is of great significance right now, something I and my colleagues are continuing to do in this book and elsewhere (see also Lim and Apple 2016; Gunter et al. 2017).

4. When Gramsci (1971) argued that one of the tasks of a truly counter-hegemonic education was not to throw out "elite knowledge" but to reconstruct its form and content so that it served genuinely progressive social needs, he provided a key to another role "organic" and "public" intellectuals might play. Thus, we should not be engaged in a process of what might be called "intellectual suicide." That is, there are serious intellectual (and pedagogic) skills in dealing with the histories and debates surrounding the epistemological, political, and educational issues involved in justifying what counts as important knowledge and what counts as an effective and socially just education. These are not simple and inconsequential issues and the practical and intellectual/political skills of dealing with them have been well developed. However, they can atrophy if they are not used. We can give back these skills by employing them to assist communities in thinking about this, learning from them, and

engaging in the mutually pedagogic dialogues that enable decisions to be made in terms of both the short-term and long-term interests of the dispossessed.

5. In the process, critical work has the task of keeping traditions (plural) of radical and progressive work alive. In the face of organized attacks on the "collective memories" of difference and critical social movements, attacks that make it increasingly difficult to retain academic and social legitimacy for multiple critical approaches that have proven so valuable in countering dominant narratives and relations, it is absolutely crucial that these traditions be kept alive, renewed, and when necessary criticized for their conceptual, empirical, historical, and political silences or limitations. This includes not only keeping theoretical, empirical, historical, and political traditions alive but, very importantly, extending and (supportively) criticizing them. And it also involves keeping alive the dreams, utopian visions, and "non-reformist reforms" that are so much a part of these radical traditions (Apple et al. 2009; Apple et al. 2010).

6. Keeping such traditions alive and also supportively criticizing them when they are not adequate to deal with current realities cannot be done unless we ask, "For whom are we keeping them alive?" and "How and in what form are they to be made available?" All of the things I have mentioned above in this taxonomy of tasks require the relearning or development and use of varied or new skills of working at many levels with multiple groups. Thus, journalistic and media skills, academic and popular skills, and the ability to speak to very different audiences are increasingly crucial (Apple 2006; Boler 2008; Del Gandio 2008; Del Gandio and Nocella II 2014). This requires us to learn how to speak in different registers and to say important things in ways that do not require that the audience or reader do all of the work.

7. Critical educators need also to *act* in concert with the progressive social movements their work supports or in movements against the rightist assumptions and policies they critically analyze. This is another reason that scholarship in critical education implies becoming an "organic" or "public" intellectual. One must participate in and give one's expertise to movements to transform both a politics of redistribution and a politics of recognition and representation. It also implies learning from these social movements (Anyon 2014. See also Bourdieu 2003; Eagleton 2011).

8. Building on the points made in the previous paragraph, the critical scholar/ activist has another role to play. She or he needs to act as a deeply committed mentor, as someone who demonstrates through her or his life what it means to be *both* an excellent researcher and a committed member of a society that is scarred by persistent inequalities. She or he needs to show how one can blend these two roles together in ways that may be tense, but still embody the dual commitments to exceptional and socially committed research and participating in movements whose aim is interrupting dominance (see Winn and Souto-Manning 2017). It also requires that we constantly seek to put ourselves

in a position to be taught how to do this by others. It should be obvious that this must be fully integrated into one's teaching as well.

9. Finally, for those of us who are lucky enough to have paid positions, participation also means using the privilege one has as a scholar/activist. That is, each of us needs to make use of one's privilege to open the spaces at colleges and universities and elsewhere for those who are not there, for those who do not now have a voice in that space and in the "professional" sites to which, being in a privileged position, you have access. This can be seen, for example, in the history of the "activist-in-residence" program at the University of Wisconsin Havens Center for Social Justice, where committed activists in various areas (the environment, indigenous rights, housing, labor, racial disparities, education, the arts, and so on) were brought in to teach and to connect our academic work with organized action against dominant relations. Or it can be seen in a number of Women's Studies programs and Indigenous, Aboriginal, and First Nation Studies programs that historically have involved activists in these communities as active participants in the governance and educational programs of these areas at universities.

This list of course is only a beginning and needs to be constantly expanded. And none of the activities will be easy. All will involve personal and academic risks as the "we" gets larger and more inclusive and as the struggles for alternative forms of sociality and the building of the institutional conditions that support them continue and the spaces of interruption widen.

Hope as a Resource

Raymond Williams reminds us that creating and defending a fully participatory democracy requires providing the conditions that make it possible for all people to actually fully participate (Williams 1989). It is exactly this more "full" participation, and what that actually means in all its contradictions, that is one of the main bases for the stories that we have told in *The Struggle for Democracy in Education*. Yet looking around us, it is more than a little visible that these conditions are increasingly difficult to build and sustain. The economic conditions experienced by so many people, the racist rates of incarceration, the defunding of absolutely necessary health centers for poor women and women of color, the destruction of communities, the loss of safety nets, the attacks on paid and unpaid labor, the defunding of education at all levels—and the list goes on and on—all of this is real and truly damaging. This can only be described as a national disgrace.

Thus, there is much to do and many places where it needs to be done. There is growing recognition that truly radical changes in our structures, policies, and common sense are essential. The task seems so big. This can be disheartening, and even paralyzing. But we must start somewhere. We need to resist the all too widespread assumption that education is epiphenomenal, that it can only change after "society" is transformed. Educational institutions and the people who work in them are key parts of society. Struggles there are essential parts of the war of position (Apple 2013). Chantal Mouffe makes a key point when she states that "now we first need to restore democracy, so we can then radicalize it" (quoted in Judas 2016, no pages). The act of restoring democracy is where we can start in education.

As I said earlier, this will not be easy, and not just in the examples we focus upon such as the United States and Brazil. The case of China, for example, gives us an even more complex instance where "democracy" in education is sought. But even when the government is overtly concerned with equalizing access and funding, specific groups of parents turn to spaces within the contradictions of government policies to enable democracy as consumer choice to be practiced. As Chapter 4 so clearly documents, the hidden effects of these actions privilege particular class fractions and also creates a new international role for certain schools that ties them to global neoliberal agendas.

Despite what we know about this and about the tensions and contradictions that are visible throughout the cases we explore in the central section of this book, we continue the struggle for thick democracy inside and outside of the institutions of education that seem so very important to the project of social empowerment to us and to so many millions of people in the world. One of the best statements of the importance of such continued work and commitment is made by Erik Olin Wright when he says that:

> The best we can do, then, is treat the struggle to move forward on the pathways of social empowerment as an experimental process in which we test and retest the limits of possibility and try, as best we can, to create new institutions which will expand these limits themselves. In doing so we not only envision real utopias, but contribute to making utopias real.
>
> *(2010, p. 373)*

In his detailed arguments for what he calls "real utopias," Wright reminds us that "Social institutions can be designed in ways that eliminate forms of oppression that thwart human aspirations towards living fulfilling and meaningful lives. The central task of emancipatory politics is to create such social institutions" (2010, p. 6).

My own position and that of the other co-authors of this book, can perhaps be characterized as optimism with no illusions whatsoever. Thus, we can be and frequently are disappointed in the results of the labors of building an emancipatory politics in and through education. But we refuse to be disillusioned. Raymond Williams again provides wise words. As he says, "We must speak for hope, as long as it doesn't mean suppressing the danger" (Williams 1989, p. 322). As he goes on to say,

> It is only in a shared belief and insistence that there are practical alternatives that the balance of forces and chances begins to alter. Once the inevitabilities are challenged, we can begin gathering our resources for a journey of

hope. If there are no easy answers there are still available discoverable hard answers, and it is these that we can now learn to make and share. This has been, from the beginning, the sense and impulse of the long revolution.

(Williams 1983, pp. 268–269)

The struggle for democracy in education is a key part of challenging the inevitabilities. Let us continue.

Notes

1   There is a complex historical connection between conservative religious forms in the United States and racist understandings and positions. See for example Heyrman (1997), Kintz (1997), Noll (2002), and Gloege (2015).
2   There is a growing population of Black home-schoolers, however. This is a group with whom I have a good deal of sympathy. The lamentable conditions within which large numbers of minoritized students have to somehow survive in all too many schools are too painful to recount once again.
3   The structure of class dynamics is also crucial within communities of color and other oppressed communities. See Rollock, Gillborn, Vincent, and Ball (2015).

References

Anderson, G. and Montoro Donchik, L. (2016). Privatizing schooling and policy making: The American Legislative Exchange Council and new political and discursive strategies of education governance. *Educational Policy 30*(2): pp. 322–364.

Anyon, J. (2014). *Radical Possibilities*. New York: Routledge.

Apple, M. W. (1996). *Cultural Politics and Education*. New York: Teachers College Press.

Apple, M. W. (2006). *Educating the "Right" Way: Markets, Standards, God, and Inequality* (2nd ed.). New York: Routledge.

Apple, M. W. (2012). *Education and Power* (Revised Routledge Classic ed.). New York: Routledge.

Apple, M. W. (2013). *Can Education Change Society?* New York: Routledge.

Apple, M. W. (2014). *Official Knowledge* (3rd ed.). New York: Routledge.

Apple, M. W. (2016). Piketty, social criticism, and critical education. *British Journal of Sociology of Education 37*(6): pp. 879–883.

Apple, M. W. and Beane, J. A. (2007). *Democratic Schools: Lessons in Powerful Education* (2nd ed.). Portsmouth, NH: Heinemann.

Apple, M. W. and Au, W. (Eds.). (2014). *Critical Education Volumes I–IV*. New York: Routledge Major Works.

Apple, M. W., Au, W., and Gandin, L. A. (Eds.). (2009). *The Routledge International Handbook of Critical Education*. New York: Routledge.

Apple, M. W., Ball, S., and Gandin, L. A. (Eds.). (2010). *The Routledge International Handbook of the Sociology of Education*. New York: Routledge.

Au, W., Brown, A., and Calderon, D. (2016). *Reclaiming the Multicultural Roots of U.S. Curriculum: Communities of Color and Official Knowledge in Education*. New York: Teachers College Press.

Ball, S. (2007). *Education plc*. New York: Routledge.

Ball, S. (2012). *Global Education Inc*. New York: Routledge.

Bernstein, B. (1977). *Class, Codes, and Control Volume III* (2nd ed.). London: Routledge and Kegan Paul.

Berrey, S. (2015). *The Jim Crow Routine*. Chapel Hill, NC: University of North Carolina Press.

Binder, A. (2002). *Contentious Curricula*. Princeton, NJ: Princeton University Press.

Bhopal, K. and Preston, J. (Eds.). (2012). *Intersectionality and "Race" in Education*. New York: Routledge.

Boler, M. (Ed.). (2008). *Digital Media and Democracy*. Cambridge, MA: MIT Press.

Bourdieu, P. (2003). *Firing Back: Against the Tyranny of the Market 2*. New York: Verso.

Burawoy, M. (2005). For public sociology. *British Journal of Sociology. 56(2)*: pp. 259–294.

Burch, P. (2009). *Hidden Markets*. New York: Routledge.

Del Gandio, J. (2008). *Rhetoric for Radicals*. Gabriola Island, BC: New Society Publishers.

Del Gandio, J. and Nocella II, A. (Eds.). (2014). *Educating for Action*. Gabriola Island, BC: New Society Publishers.

Dewey, J. (1938). *Experience and Education*. New York: Kappa Delta Pi.

Eagleton, T. (2011). *Why Marx Was Right*. New Haven: Yale University Press.

Emdin, C. (2010). *Urban Science Education for the Hip-Hop Generation*. New York: Sense Publishers.

Emdin, C. (2016). *For White Folks Who Teach in the Hood—And the Rest of Ya-all Too*. Boston: Beacon Press.

Foner, E. (1997). *The Story of American Freedom*. New York: Norton.

Fraser, N. (1997). *Justice Interruptus*. New York: Routledge.

Fraser, N. (2013). *Fortunes of Feminism*. New York: Verso.

Giugni, M., McAdam, D., and Tilly, C. (Eds.). (1999). *How Social Movements Matter*. Minneapolis: University of Minneapolis Press.

Gloege, T. (2015). *Guaranteed Pure*. Chapel Hill, NC: University of North Carolina Press.

Gramsci, A. (1971). *Selections from the Prison Notebooks*. New York: International Publishers.

Gunter, H., Hall, D., and Apple, M. W. (Eds.). (2017). *Corporate Elites and the Reform of Public Education*. Bristol: Policy Press.

Hall, S. (2016). Lecture 7: Domination and hegemony. In *Cultural Studies 1983: A Theoretical History*. J. D. Slack & L. Grossberg (Eds.) pp. 155–179. Durham, NC: Duke University Press.

Honnith, A. (2017). *The Idea of Socialism*. Cambridge, UK: Polity Press.

Heyrman, C. L. (1997). *Southern Cross*. New York: Knopf.

Hochschild, A. R. (2016). *Strangers in Their Own Land: Anger and Mourning on the American Right*. New York: The New Press.

Honneth, A. (2016). *The Idea of Socialism: Towards a Renewal*. Cambridge, UK: Polity Press.

Joseph, P. (2016). The Radical Democracy of the Movement for Black Lives. *Black Perspectives* (September 18). Available at: www.aaihs.org/joseph-the-radical-democracy-of-the-movement-for-black-lives/. Accessed 07/20/17.

Judas, J. (2016). Rethinking populism. *Dissent* (June). Available at: www.dissentmagazine.org/article/rethinking-populism-laclau-mouffe-podemos. Accessed 06/06/17.

Kallio, A. (2015). *Navigating (Un)popular Music in the Classroom*. Helsinki: The Sibelius Academy, University of the Arts.

Kintz, L. (1997). *Between Jesus and the Market*. Durham, NC: Duke University Press.

Laes, T. (2017). *The (Im)possibility of Inclusion*. Helsinki: The Sibelius Academy, University of the Arts.

Levin, S. (2017). Arizona Republicans move to ban social justice courses and events at school. *The Guardian* (January 13). Available at: www.theguardian.com/us-news/2017/jan/13/arizona-schools-social-justice-courses-ban-bill. Accessed 01/20/17.

Lim, L. and Apple, M. W. (Eds.). (2016). *The Strong State and Curriculum Reform*. New York: Routledge.

Lipman, P. (2011). *The New Political Economy of Urban Education*. New York: Routledge.

Lynch, K., Baker, J., and Lyons, M. (2009). *Affective Equality*. New York: Palgrave Macmillan.

Lynch, K., Grummell, B., and Devine, D. (2012). *New Managerialism in Education*. New York: Palgrave Macmillan.

Macherey, P. (2006). *A Theory of Literary Production*. New York: Routledge Classics.

MacLean, N. (2017). *Democracy in Chains*. New York: Viking.

Mills, C. (1997). *The Racial Contract*. Ithaca, NY; Cornell University Press.

Mayer, J. (2016). *Dark Money*. New York: Doubleday.

Noll, M. (2002). *America's God*. New York: Oxford University Press.

Phillips, D. (2017). Brazil's right on the rise as anger grows over scandal and corruption. *The Guardian* (July 26). Available at: www.theguardian.com/world/2017/jul/26/brazil-rightwing-dilma-rousseff-lula. Accessed 7/26/17.

Posey-Maddox, L. (2014). *When Middle-Class Parents Choose Urban Schools: Class, Race, and the Challenge of Equity in Public Schools*. Chicago: University of Chicago Press.

Rollock, N., Gillborn, D., Vincent, C., and Ball, S. (2015). *The Colour of Class: The Educational Strategies of the Black Middle Classes*. New York: Routledge.

Rothstein, R. (2017). *The Color of Law*. New York: Liveright.

Schroyer, T. (1973). *The Critique of Domination*. New York: George Braziller.

Smith, D. (2017). Betsy DeVos: Trump's illiberal ally seen as most dangerous education chief ever. *The Guardian* (July 26). Available at: www.theguardian.com/us-news/2017/jul/26/betsy-devos-education-secretary-trump. Accessed 7/26/17.

Soler, M. (Ed.). (2011). Education for Social Exclusion. Special issue of *International Studies in Sociology of Education 21*: pp. 1–90.

Stedman-Jones, G. (2016). *Karl Marx: Greatness and Illusion*. Cambridge, MA: Harvard University Press.

Stone, L. (2017). "Mainline" churches are emptying. The political effects could be huge. *Vox* (July 14). Available at: www.vox.com/the-big-idea/2017/7/14/15959682/evangelical-mainline-voting-patterns-trump. Accessed 07/17/17.

Teeger, C. (2015). "Both sides of the story": History education in post-apartheid South Africa. *American Sociological Review 80*(6): pp. 1175–1200.

Underwood, J.K., and Mead, J.F. (2012). A smart ALEC threatens public education. *Phi Delta Kappan 93*(6): pp. 51–55.

Wallis, J. (2010). *Living God's Politics*. New York: Harper-Collins.

Warmington, P. (2014). *Black British Intellectuals and Education: Multiculturalism's Hidden History*. New York: Routledge.

Weis, L., Cipollone, K., and Jenkins, H. (2014). *Class Warfare: Class, Race, and College Admissions in Top-Tier Secondary Schools*. Chicago: University of Chicago Press.

West, C. (2002). *Prophecy Deliverance*. Louisville, KY: Westminster John Knox Press.

Williams, R. (1983). *The Year 2000*. New York: Pantheon.

Williams, R. (1985). *Keywords*. New York: Oxford University Press.

Williams, R. (1989). *Resources of Hope*. New York: Verso.

Winn, M. and Souto-Manning, M. (Eds.). (2017). Disrupting Inequality through Education Research. *Review of Research in Education. 41.* Washington, DC and

Thousand Oaks, CA: American Educational Research Association and Sage Publishing.

Wittgenstein, L. (1963). *Philosophical Investigations*. Oxford: Blackwell.

Wong, T-K. (2002). *Hegemonies Compared*. New York: Routledge.

Wright, E. O. (2010). *Envisioning Real Utopias*. New York: Verso.

AUTHORS

Michael W. Apple is John Bascom Professor of Curriculum and Instruction and Educational Policy Studies at the University of Wisconsin, Madison. He has written extensively on the relationship between culture and power in education and on the limits and possibilities of a socially transformative education. He has been named one of the 50 most significant writers in education in the twentieth century.

Luis Armando Gandin is Professor of Sociology of Education at the Federal University of Rio Grande do Sul in Porto Alegre, Brazil. He is well known internationally for his analyses of the politics of education and of the ways in which education has been employed for social transformation in Latin America and elsewhere.

Shuning Liu is Assistant Professor of Curriculum Studies at Ball State University. Her research is focused on the role of international education in the formation of social elites and on the politics of curricula and larger educational policies in China.

Assaf Meshulam is Assistant Professor of Education at Ben Gurion University. He has engaged in substantive research on critical multicultural schools and classrooms in the United States and other nations, and on the political tensions and dynamics involved in their policies and practices over time.

Eleni Schirmer is a researcher and union activist at the University of Wisconsin, Madison. She has analyzed the role of conservative movements in educational policy and the effects of these movements on teachers, students, and curricula. She is currently working on the history and reality of social justice teacher unions.

INDEX